"This book is an absolute godsend for anyone wanting to take the step into freelance journalism. It's not only fantastic as a go-to text for students but for industry professionals wanting to take the plunge. As well as de-mystifying the commissioning process, it provides a comprehensive toolkit that I wish I had when I first went freelance. Journalism courses across the country should have this as a core text".

Lisa Bradley, *Director for Learning and Teaching for Journalism, The University of Sheffield, UK*

"A comprehensive, practical, and, most importantly, honest account of how to make it work as a freelance. A lack of transparency and information is the biggest problem facing any new freelance – and this book is the perfect antidote. I wish I'd had a copy when I was first starting out".

Jem Collins, *Director and Editor, Journo Resources*

GW00660333

Freelancing for Journalists

Freelancing for Journalists offers an authoritative, practical and engaging guide for current and aspiring journalism freelances, exploring key aspects of the role including pitching a story, networking, branding and navigating freelance laws and rights.

Featuring case studies from experienced freelance journalists working in the UK, US, Asia and Australia, the book addresses the evolving media landscape and provides valuable tips on how to become established as a successful journalist across a variety of platforms. The authors also explore practical aspects of the trade including tips for setting up a business, managing tax and legal issues, getting paid and earning additional income in related sectors.

This book is an invaluable resource for both students and professionals who are interested in taking the next step into freelance journalism work.

Lily Canter is a freelance money, health and lifestyle journalist working for a range of international newspapers, magazines and websites including *The Guardian*, *South China Morning Post*, *The Sun*, Moneywise and *Metro*. She is also Senior Lecturer in Journalism at Sheffield Hallam University, UK.

Emma Wilkinson is a freelance journalist writing about health, medicine and biosciences. After several staff jobs including at The Lancet and BBC News Online, she now works for a variety of specialist websites, magazines and journals including Pulse, Chemist + Druggist, The Pharmaceutical Journal and the BMJ. She is also an Associate Lecturer at Sheffield Hallam University, UK.

Media Skills

Edited by Richard Keeble, Lincoln University

The *Media Skills* series provides a concise and thorough introduction to a rapidly changing media landscape. Each book is written by media and journalism lecturers or experienced professionals and is a key resource for a particular industry. Offering helpful advice and information and using practical examples from print, broadcast and digital media, as well as discussing ethical and regulatory issues, *Media Skills* books are essential guides for students and media professionals.

English for Journalists
Twentieth Anniversary Edition
Wynford Hicks

Researching for the Media
2nd edition
Adèle Emm

Subediting and Production for Journalists
2nd edition
Tim Holmes

Writing for Journalists
3rd edition
Wynford Hicks with Sally Adams, Harriett Gilbert, Tim Holmes and Jane Bentley

Magazine Production
2nd edition
Jason Whittaker

Interviewing for Journalists
3rd edition
Sally Adams and Emma Lee-Potter

Designing for Newspapers and Magazines
2nd edition
Chris Frost

Sports Journalism
Tom Bradshaw and Daragh Minogue

Freelancing for Journalists
Lily Canter and Emma Wilkinson

For more information about this series, please visit: www.routledge.com/Media-Skills/book-series/SE0372

Freelancing for Journalists

Lily Canter and Emma Wilkinson

Routledge
Taylor & Francis Group

LONDON AND NEW YORK

First published 2021
by Routledge
2 Park Square, Milton Park, Abingdon, Oxon OX14 4RN

and by Routledge
52 Vanderbilt Avenue, New York, NY 10017

Routledge is an imprint of the Taylor & Francis Group, an informa business

British Library Cataloguing-in-Publication Data
A catalogue record for this book is available from the British Library

Library of Congress Cataloging-in-Publication Data
Names: Canter, Lily, author. | Wilkinson, Emma, author.
Title: Freelancing for journalists / Lily Canter, Emma Wilkinson.
Description: London; New York: Routledge, 2020. |
Series: Media skills | Includes bibliographical references and index.
Identifiers: LCCN 2020008990 | ISBN 9780367135546 (hardback) |
ISBN 9780367135553 (paperback) | ISBN 9780429027178 (ebook)
Subjects: LCSH: Freelance journalism—Vocational guidance.
Classification: LCC PN4784.F76 C36 2020 | DDC 808.06/607—dc23
LC record available at https://lccn.loc.gov/2020008990

ISBN: 978-0-367-13554-6 (hbk)
ISBN: 978-0-367-13555-3 (pbk)
ISBN: 978-0-429-02717-8 (ebk)

Typeset in Goudy
by codeMantra

MIX
Paper from
responsible sources
FSC   FSC® C013985
www.fsc.org

Printed in the United Kingdom
by Henry Ling Limited

Contents

Boxes

Acknowledgements

This book owes a great debt to all the freelance journalists out there, grafting away day in, day out. They have inspired, motivated and encouraged us to write this book, lending their pearls of wisdom and amusing anecdotes. In particular we would like to say a huge thank you to the lively members of A Few Good Hacks who never once complained when we regularly mined the community for information. Our thanks also go to all of our case studies, freelance commentator Anna Codrea-Rado and Routledge colleague Margaret Farrelly for setting us on this literary journey.

Thanks to my husband Mark Dayman for his continued support and to our inquisitive sons Byron and Ivor who never fail to make me laugh or look at the world with a fresh perspective.

Lily Canter

Thanks to my partner Mark Hoyle for everything and to Lucy, Sam and Henry for their endless patience while Mummy disappears downstairs into her office to meet yet another deadline.

Emma Wilkinson

1
Introduction

OBJECTIVES

In this chapter you will learn:

- What is a freelance journalist
- About the authors as freelances
- Whether you really want to work for yourself
- The training and experience that is required
- How the internet has disrupted the media marketplace

More and more journalists – through necessity or choice – are working as freelances. This is a trend seen across the world. A 2019 report from the International Labour Organization found that digitalisation and new working practices have increased the number of media and culture workers who are freelance or self-employed.[1] While pointing out that consistent, reliable data is hard to come by, the report also found that for journalism, figures from some countries show freelancing, although once rare, has become a common way of working.

Similarly, the European Federation of Journalists (EFJ) found dramatic increases in the use of freelance work in journalism, with around 20% or more of journalists on freelance contracts.[2] The EFJ also point out that in some countries the majority of journalists are freelance. Of course, this depends on your definition. They use the term 'fake freelance' to describe journalists who may work full-time for a single employer but are hired on a freelance basis to circumvent labour or welfare rules. But on the other side of the coin, freelancing can be a very natural fit for journalists who want the 'freedom, variety and flexibility of independent employment'.[3]

In the UK, the 2018 Labour Force Survey showed that 36% of journalists are self-employed, more than double the 15% rate seen across all sectors.[4] In line with national trends, the proportion of those working in journalism who are self-employed has risen from 28% in 2012. A report on freelance journalism from the National Council for the Training of Journalists (NCTJ) in 2016 found that between 2000 and 2015, the numbers of freelance journalists increased from 15,000 to 25,000 – a 67% rise.[5]

Statistics in the US are harder to come by, but anecdotal evidence from the Society of Professional Journalists Freelance Community suggests that there has been a significant rise in freelances in the US in recent years. And staff jobs continue to be precarious. According to the Pew Research Center, a quarter of large US newspapers laid off staff in 2018 as well as 14% of the bigger digital-native news sites.[6] While not as bad as previous years, it shows that journalists continue to lose their jobs and may need to be more flexible if they want to stay in the profession.

Certainly across all jobs in the US, freelancing is becoming more common, with one study estimating that 36% of the US workforce is now freelance.[7] The report, commissioned by Upwork and the Freelancers Union, surveyed 6,000 adults and found the changes were being driven by younger people with almost half of the millennials who responded working as freelance. And again, the main driver for those freelancing full-time was freedom and flexibility. The report also found that freelances increasingly believe that having a portfolio of clients was more secure than relying on one employer.

For journalism, where the employment market has changed almost beyond recognition in the past decade or two, it is easy to see why people would want to avoid putting all their eggs in one basket. In Australia, researchers looking into what had happened to journalists made redundant during a particularly difficult period of job losses found that many were still working in journalism but not in the same way.[8] The job losses affecting hundreds of experienced staffers were largely a result of industry changes including the advent of digital-first journalism. Only one in ten of more than 200 journalists followed over a five-year period ended up in a full-time journalism role compared with 77% before the redundancies hit. Around 14% said they were freelance by 2017 but, in addition, 20% described working in multiple jobs, with some clearly changing their role frequently.

There has been much debate about what is driving more journalists to adopt freelance working, and undoubtedly some of that is dependent on the specific media environment they are in. Redundancy, a lack of job opportunities, or opportunities in the right place at the right time, coupled with desire for more control and flexibility over working patterns are all likely to play a part. The NCTJ, in its 2016 report on freelancing, found that it is more common for journalists to be pulled into self-employment for aspirational reasons rather than to be pushed into turning freelance.[5] As discussed in Chapter 2, the pace of change has been rapid and is tied to the extent to which the internet has disrupted the media market. This has created new online opportunities for journalists whilst having a detrimental effect on traditional media organisations. What is clear is that for many, freelancing is an active choice that allows them to dictate their own path.

As such, journalism students and recent graduates are now far more likely than earlier generations to experience freelance working from the very start of their careers. Data from the Journalists at Work surveys carried out periodically by the NCTJ found that since 2002 the proportion of journalists whose first job was a freelance has roughly doubled from a starting point of 5%.[9] All journalism departments will have students who are doing freelance work while learning their trade and many others will take that step when they graduate. When, before writing this book, we asked journalism students about this topic, 90% of respondents said they wanted to be taught more about freelance working as part of their studies.[10]

Yet our research also clearly shows that universities have not caught up to this changing work pattern and freelance skills are not being taught, or at least only on an ad hoc basis as part of magazine or feature writing modules. Our survey of undergraduate and postgraduate journalism students in the UK who had graduated in the past five years found that two-thirds had received no training on freelancing, a finding that was reiterated when we asked journalism lecturers the same question.[11] Yet they all said their students were doing some sort of freelance work, some of which was paid. Our results also showed that what the students wanted most was practical advice.

Journalism trainees, graduates or staffers thinking about going freelance know how to write news or features or produce a radio or video package. Their training and experience have taken them that far. But for the uninitiated, taking the leap into working as a freelance is a daunting one and comes with a vast array of questions around how to get commissioned, where to get work and how to develop ideas and build contacts. In addition, the mechanics of setting up a business, getting paid and all the legal, ethical and financial aspects that go along with it are not something routinely taught to trainees. These are issues that the authors – as experienced freelances and lecturers – are asked questions about frequently. In this book, they share their wealth of experience, as well as advice from a host of journalists and commissioning editors.

What is a freelance journalist?

To be freelance just means you are self-employed. There is no official club to sign up to or hurdle to overcome before you are allowed to define yourself as such and freelance journalists are a diverse bunch. For some the definition will be a clear cut one – a journalist is someone who writes, produces, edits, records, photographs or broadcasts 'news'. Of course, this may be too narrow a definition for those who write features, blogs, books, editorials or record podcasts, etc. Let us just say that freelance journalism work takes many forms. At one end of the spectrum is the journalist with a regular gig or single employer who is on a freelance contract. This would include the role of a stringer, a freelance journalist who regularly writes, reports or provides audio/video for an outlet with which they have a strong relationship but who is not in a salaried position. At the other end of the spectrum is the freelance who works solely from home writing, reporting or editing for a number of different outlets, wherever they can get a commission. Many, including the authors, will find a happy medium somewhere in between.

As outlined in Chapter 2, the role of the journalist has undergone rapid changes in the past decade or so. But there are some basic principles which would likely still hold true for anyone considering themselves to work as a journalist. The job is about asking questions; the classic Who? What? Where? When? Why? How? that all journalism students are taught on day 1. It is about informing members of society about issues they would otherwise not know about. It is about telling stories. It is about providing facts, verification and bearing witness to events of the day. And it is about doing that in a way that is entertaining, eye-catching, accessible and interesting. A key part of the job is having an eye for a good tale; that story that will hook the reader in and make them want to share it with someone else.

In recent years, defining the term 'journalist' has in itself become more difficult. Anyone can now take a picture or video of an event, write about an experience or host a blog, yet many would argue that that does not in of itself make them a professional journalist. In reality, the only hurdle a freelance journalist has to overcome to get paid work is to convince an editor that you have a good idea and can deliver on that promise. If you have some training or a qualification (see below on training and expertise) this hurdle will most likely be lower. Once you have a portfolio of work to show an editor and get some good contacts the bar is lowered further still.

Some freelance journalists have found themselves in that position because they were made redundant and had no choice. Others have quit staff jobs or started working for themselves immediately upon graduation because they wanted the freedom and flexibility to pick and choose projects, work in different locations or build up a more diverse portfolio. Some start to do freelance work as a way out of a job they do not like. Others as a way to tell stories that are not routinely covered by their usual outlet. Or as a form of activism, a way to use their skills to draw attention to an issue they feel strongly about or feel is under-represented.

As a freelance journalist you may be paid by the word, minute, image, hour, shift, project or a combination of those, but you do deserve to get paid and to get paid on time (see Chapter 7). Working as a freelance is not, and should not be, synonymous with working for free, although there are plenty of examples of self-employed journalists being asked or expected to do work for no pay or 'exposure'. There is debate about whether this holds true for those at the start of their careers – some argue that it can be necessary to work for free in order to build a portfolio when you are starting out. And that in turn may lead to further work down the line. On a case-by-case basis that may, indeed, be a fruitful approach, but the downside is you risk undervaluing your work and that of journalists in general.

The authors' freelance experiences

Lily Canter and Emma Wilkinson first met while doing an MA in Journalism at the University of Sheffield. Their career paths took them in fairly different directions, but more than 15 years later, they are both working as freelance journalists while also teaching journalism students at Sheffield Hallam University.

Lily specialises in money, health and lifestyle journalism. Following university, she qualified as an NCTJ reporter whilst cutting her teeth in local newspapers. She spent two years at the Newsquest weekly newspaper the *Wiltshire Gazette & Herald* covering everything from cheque presentations to bodies buried in building sites. From there she moved to Johnston Press daily newspaper the *Northampton Chronicle & Echo*, where she worked as a health reporter before taking on the role of features editor. During her time at the *Chron* she developed a passion for consumer news and personal finance whilst also building up contacts with local arts and cultural venues. Highlights of her newspaper career included travelling to Bosnia with the British army and meeting her Hollywood crush Christian Bale.

After seven years in newspapers Lily left the industry to study for a PhD in Journalism Studies examining the pioneering world of online journalism and social media within the regional press. Her ongoing research is published in a variety of academic journals, including *Digital Journalism*, *Convergence* and *Journalism*, and she is co-author of *Digital Journalism Studies: The Key Concepts* with Professor Bob Franklin. Her experience as a hybrid journalist-academic became the springboard for her university career which saw Lily climb the ladder from guest lecturer to Subject Group Leader for Journalism and Public Relations at Sheffield Hallam University, in four years. However, the pull of journalism never left her, and in 2018 she stepped down from her management role to develop a freelance career. She continues to work part-time as a senior lecturer but spends the majority of her week writing for national news-papers, websites and magazines, including the *South China Morning Post*, *Metro*, Moneywise, loveMONEY, The Sun Online, *The Daily Telegraph*, Mail Online, *The Guardian*, *The Times*, Pulse Today and The Overtake.

Emma specialises in health and science journalism, having university degrees in both. Her biomedical science undergraduate degree taught her she was more interested in learning and writing about the topic than working in a lab. A whistle-stop year-long immersion in journalism during her MA led to staff jobs at The Lancet Oncology medical journal, then Pulse, an award-winning business-to-business magazine for GPs, where she regularly worked on exclusive stories and investigations that were picked up by the national media. Emma took the leap into freelance life to allow her to move outside London where most specialist titles in the UK are based. For a few years she juggled a part-time position as a health reporter for BBC News Online, travelling to London for long shifts, with freelance writing from her home in Sheffield. After the birth of her first child in 2010 (she now has three), she chose to concentrate solely on freelance work.

After initially being asked to teach journalism and communication skills to scientists and medics, Emma now also works part-time as an associate lecturer at Sheffield Hallam University focusing on news writing and digi-tal journalism. Since shifting to freelance work, Emma has worked for the BMJ, Chemist + Druggist, Circulation, European Heart Journal, Hospital Doctor, The Lancet, The Lancet Infectious Diseases, The Lancet Oncology, The Lancet Neurology, Mother and Baby magazine, Nursing Times, Over the Counter, Pulse, Practical Commissioning, Practice Nurse, Practitioner, Pregnancy and Birth, The Limbic and The Pharmaceutical Journal. She regularly writes news and features and undertakes in-depth investigations on all things medical and NHS. Emma makes use of the training she had at The Lancet to offer writing and editing services for scientists wanting to improve their journal articles and reports.

Where does the freelance journalist work?

Pretty much all media outlets, whether local, national or international, broad-cast, online or print will use freelance journalists to some extent. Some will rely almost solely on freelance workers, while others will use them sparingly. For example, the budget for freelance copy at many local newspapers in the UK has fallen to essentially nothing, but there may be shifts to pick up here and there. By contrast some magazines may have more content from freelance writers than from staff writers.

The traditional newspaper, even with its now expanded online reach, is just a very small part of where a freelance journalist can get work (see Chapter 2). Magazines and online media outlets are also vital sources of commissions for a freelance (and can have bigger budgets). Specialist titles aimed at the general public or business-to-business magazines and websites will make use of free-lance writers. And with this in mind, it can be helpful for a journalist to have a specialism, be it sport, mental health or business, as a way of building up con-tacts and a reputation within a particular field. Freelance journalists will also work on radio packages, podcasts and documentaries; write columns; or work as 'pundits' advising on certain topics.

Despite the doom and gloom that often appears whenever seasoned journalists talk about the state of the industry and shrinking of traditional media jobs, newspapers and magazines still need to find good original content, but they are also now competing for that content with online outlets and newer media start-ups. Add in the increasing demand for social content and video and it becomes clear that for the savvy freelance there is plenty of potential work.

We discuss in Chapter 11 about supplementing your income and freelance journalists will commonly use their skills in PR, copy writing, search engine optimisation and blogging to expand the variety of work they do and ensure financial stability.

Working for yourself

Being your own boss is becoming an increasingly popular option – not just in journalism – because people want to choose where they live, avoid the commute, fit work around childcare or other family commitments, choose what work they do and have a more varied career. But not everyone is suited to life as a freelance. Working for yourself is not the same as having a staff job. You can (to a point) choose your own hours, set the amount of work you want to do, write or report about the topics you want to (as long as you can get commissioned) and do different types of work to keep things interesting. For some that freedom and flexibility is an aspect of freelance life that far outweighs any downsides they may experience, such as income uncertainty.

However, working as a freelance requires self-motivation, a knack for problem solving, the ability to take on lots of different roles and a certain amount of re-silience and independence. It can involve being your own accountant, business manager, HR expert, IT helpdesk and marketing expert. You have to be able to keep plugging away when it seems as if no one wants your ideas or think of different ways to angle a story to get new interest when something has been dismissed. In Chapters 3 and 4 we talk in detail on how to get ideas and how to get them picked up. Yet, however noble your intentions are or how hard you work, there will undoubtedly be peaks and troughs. Experienced freelances will all have tales of feast or famine, the time when they thought they may never work again then a week later suddenly being overwhelmed by commissions and wondering how on earth they will fit it all in (see Chapter 6).

While some freelance journalists will work shifts for a publication or broadcast outlet, which means they are required in the office with all the equipment and facilities provided for them, others will be working alone from home. Depending on your personality, this may be a dream option where you can busily and efficiently churn out thousands of words while sat in your pyjamas free from the distractions of the modern open-plan office. Or it could be a recipe for disaster where you pine for human company while achieving nothing under your now structureless day.

There is plenty of advice on working from home in Chapter 10, including what other options, such as co-working spaces, may be available for those who prefer an office environment. The key is to consider how you work best. There is no one size fits all, and it can very much depend on the type of work you are doing and how much human interaction you get (or want) on a day-to-day basis. And while working on the sofa on a laptop may feel like a dream scenario, after a day or two when the backache kicks in and you cannot find that key bit of paper you need, a dedicated desk of some sort is likely to become far more desirable.

There can also be a lot of rejection. Pitches sent out are commonly ignored or if you do get a response it is 'not a good fit' right now. Even worse, you pitch an idea and the outlet steals it and passes it off as their own. This is far from good practice, but it does happen. We talk about how to manage the pitching process in Chapter 4, but it can take a certain level of resilience. Often it is not personal – they might not be looking for ideas at the moment, they might have done something too similar recently – but it can feel personal when you are on your own at home trying to get someone to pick up your idea. And there may be no guidance as to why an idea has not been picked up. It is important to start out knowing this will be the case and is the case for all other freelances trying to do the same as you.

Isolation can be a real problem, and forming networks with other freelances, either locally, through national organisations, or online, is a great way to keep connected to those who will be facing the same issues and we give ideas for how to do this in Chapter 5. This can be particularly important if, or more likely when, you come across a legal, ethical or financial problem (see Chapters 7 and 8) that you do not know how to solve. While a freelance is a one-man band to all intents and purposes, everyone needs advice and wisdom from those with more experience.

One of the biggest headaches for many freelance journalists is the lack of consistency around income. For anyone used to a weekly or monthly pay cheque, the thought of not knowing how much they will earn in any given period can be disconcerting and anxiety provoking. Even when you have plenty of work, getting paid on time can sometimes be an uphill battle. This was highlighted in 2019 by the closure of online magazine The Pool leaving an unpaid bill of tens of thousands of pounds to freelance journalists who had written for them, some who had regular columns.[12] A crowdfunding campaign was started to try to secure income for writers who were struggling to pay their bills.

Some try to mitigate this financial rollercoaster by having at least one regular contract, perhaps copy-writing or PR work, that enables them more flexibility in getting commissioned for news or features. But knowing your rights and being able to negotiate is also key. Chapter 7 outlines what every freelance needs to know about how much they should be earning and how quickly they should get paid. Freelances need to keep on top of the financial side of their business or could find themselves in dire straits pretty quickly.

Whatever your personality or reason for taking the plunge into freelance working, self-motivation will be an important skill. This holds true on a grand scale, that is, where you want to be a year from now, who would you most like to work for, what are your reasons for doing this and pushing yourself, but also on a more micro day-to-day scale when there is no one to check you are at your desk doing what you are supposed to be doing. There are several techniques that can be useful in boosting motivation (see Chapter 10), and all freelances will need to hit the 'reset' button at some point to increase their productivity.

Training and expertise

The role of a journalist is, for the most part, based around traditions and norms of what the job should be. There is no one accepted career progression or trajectory or even entry requirement or educational pre-requisite for the job. Training and educational requirement also differs by country. What once was a trade that was learnt on the job, more commonly (but by no means exclusively), is now entered after a degree of some kind.

Yet whatever their background there are some core skills that all journalists need. This book is aimed at graduates of journalism courses who will hopefully have already learnt how to write, including in different styles, carry out an interview or put together a package. The advice and guidance in the following chapters will take them to the next step of successfully working for themselves.

US journalists, at least those working in mainstream media, are highly likely to have at least a Bachelor's degree.[13] In the UK, whether freelance or not, a high proportion of journalists are educated to degree level. An NCTJ survey found that around half of freelances had a journalism-specific qualification or were working towards one – a lower proportion than employed journalists. This may suggest that a freelance career is more flexible in terms of the training required.[5]

What it does show is that a journalism-related qualification is certainly not a pre-requisite to working as a freelance. For those without a journalism degree there are plenty of available courses on a range of aspects of the job, including digital and social media skills, photography, business and marketing, podcasting, investigative journalism, coding, data science and much more.

Even for those with a journalism degree, the industry has undergone, and continues to undergo, huge technological change, and there may be aspects of your job you feel less confident about. As a staffer it is likely you would be offered training as part of your job, a media law refresher perhaps or how to use your smartphone to best advantage when out on location. Wherever possible, freelances should also keep their skills updated and many organisations including journalism unions and organisations, and higher education institutions offer such training. And it does not have to be expensive. Massive Open Online Courses are free for anyone to enrol. At the start of her freelance career, Emma learnt how to create her own website using XHTML at her local community college. The skills needed will be personal to the individual and may change over time depending on the work they are doing, but the key is to be aware of any limitations or weaknesses and how to overcome them.

Doing freelance work while studying should be a vital part of every journalism student's experience. There are benefits on so many levels, not least building up a portfolio of work to showcase skills to editors. It helps you develop your confidence with freelance working while still in a position to benefit from the advice and guidance of your teachers. It can provide a valuable wealth of contacts in the industry and it means should you choose to freelance after graduation, you are more likely to hit the ground running with some sense of how the process works and how to develop an idea and finesse it to target the right publication. It will allow you to hone that news sense while developing freelance knowledge that will prepare you for an ever-shifting world of work.

There may not be a job waiting immediately on completion of your under-graduate or postgraduate course, but with freelancing as an option, you can immediately jump into the world of journalism and put that training to the test. And last but definitely not least, freelancing also offers the opportunity to make some money while you are studying.

Age of the internet

Regardless of what type of journalist you are, all journalists are now essentially online journalists. In the UK, the smartphone has now become the first point of contact with the news over radio, TV or a print newspaper.[14] In the US, social media is the main gateway to news on people's phones (compared with Finland where half would use a news app as the way to find out what was happening).[14]

This 'new' media is evolving constantly and offers a very different set of oppor-tunities for the freelance journalist than was available even a decade ago. As a sense of how rapidly the media environment has changed, it is always worth remembering that the first iPhone was launched in 2007 (by which point the authors had many years of journalism experience under their belts). The digital nature of today's media means that journalists need to have the skills to provide audio, video, hyperlinks, maps, timelines and photo galleries alongside copy that reads well on a screen and a headline that is easily searchable and appears at the top of Google results as well as being easy to find on social media.

The traditional gatekeepers of news and information were disrupted once anyone could publish their own version of events instantaneously, from anywhere in the world, 24 hours a day with only a laptop or a phone. While some journalists were copying and pasting the text to their publications website as it would appear in the newspaper, others were finding new ways to connect with their audiences and start a conversation with their readers. Case in point is HuffPost, which started as a blog site and before long was recruiting full-time journalists and breaking exclusive stories.[15] It is also a site that has received much criticism in the past for not paying freelance writers. But it heralded a dawn of new digital-only media players that offered a wider variety of places for freelance journalists to pitch their wares.

We provide more detail on how the age of the internet has dramatically shifted the media landscape for the freelance journalist in Chapter 2 as well as al-lowing them to create their own opportunities where none existed before be that a self-created podcast or blog that ended in a book deal. It is perhaps not surprising that the number of freelances has been growing at the same time as the need for online content has exploded. This book will provide budding free-lance journalists with the skills to make the most of that opportunity.

Box 1.1 Case study: Gabby Willis

As a second-year journalism student, Gabby is fully aware she needs to build a portfolio of work to boost her chances of a job on graduation and was thrilled to see her first paid freelance piece – an opinion article for Metro.co.uk on a Louis Theroux documentary – published just a day after she first responded to a query from a commissioning editor.

With an interest in feminism, body positivity, mental health and a role as Women's Representative at Sheffield Hallam University Student Union, the query she came across on Twitter about views on the latest Theroux topic – rape culture – was one she felt confident to answer. The commissioning editor was most keen to hear that Theroux had recently attended a Q&A session at the university as part of an honorary degree he was given, where Gabby heard him talk about this very subject.

"They wanted to speak to someone who had experienced sexual assault and I had a lot to say on this topic but there was also a unique connection there because I had been on the front row when he spoke at the University and I had asked him a question", she explains.

Gabby was commissioned after some quick messaging online and had to provide 650 words within a few hours after viewing a preview of the documentary.

"Because I didn't really have time to worry about it and it was a topic I knew a lot about, I just did it. I had to then look up how to write an invoice and do that as I had no idea because I'd not been paid for work before".

Gabby, who has also blogged and written for local independent and online magazines, says having been published in a national newspaper, she would now be far more confident to pitch another idea, particularly to the Metro Online where she has a contact who knows she delivered what she promised.

"I do think freelance work is something we should be taught more about as you can fit it around your studies and get some really good experience but it is hard to know how to get started. You have to say yes to the opportunities when they come up as well as being on the look out", she adds.

Gabby, who is originally from Northampton, has also been a guest on the Naked Podcast and is keen to do more as her studies progress. She has joined a University Freelancers portal as well as a local freelance networking group to expand her contacts and hopefully come across more potential projects.

@GWillisJourno

Getting started

- Write a paragraph about why you would make a good freelance
- Make a list of aspects of freelancing you need to find out more about
- Find some freelance organisations in your local area you can connect with
- Plan whom you could potentially work for
- Consider what additional skills you would like to learn

Notes

1 Gruber, M. 2019 "Challenges and opportunities for decent work in the culture and media sectors" International Labour Office, Geneva www.ilo.org/wcmsp5/groups/public/---ed_dialogue/---sector/documents/publication/wcms_661953.pdf.
2 Nies, G. and Pedersini, R. 2003 *Freelance journalists in the European media industry*. Brussels: European Federation of Journalists.
3 European Federation of Journalists. "Freelance Policy" https://europeanjournalists.org/policy/freelance/.
4 Office for National Statistics. 2018 "Trends in self employment in the UK" www.ons.gov.uk/employmentandlabourmarket/peopleinwork/employmentandemployeetypes/articles/trendsinselfemploymentintheuk/2018-02-07#introduction.
5 Spilsbury, M. 2016 "Exploring freelance journalism: report for the National Council for the Training of Journalists" NCTJ www.nctj.com/downloadlibrary/EXPLORING%20FREELANCE%20JOURNALISM%20FINAL.pdf.
6 Greico, E. 2019 "About a quarter of large U.S. newspapers laid staff off in 2018" Pew Research Center www.pewresearch.org/fact-tank/2019/08/01/large-u-s-newspapers-layoffs-2018/.
7 Upwork. 2019 "Sixth annual 'freelancing in America' study finds that more people than ever see freelancing as a long-term career path" www.upwork.com/press/2019/10/03/freelancing-in-america-2019/.

8 Zion, L. et al. 2018 "New beats report: mass redundancies and career change in Australian journalism" www.newbeatsblog.com/wp-content/uploads/2013/07/New_Beats_Report.pdf.

9 Spilsbury, M. 2013 "Journalists at work: their views on training, recruitment and conditions" NCTJ www.nctj.com/downloadlibrary/jaw_final_higher_2.pdf.

10 Canter, L. and Wilkinson, E. 2019 "Risk and reward: are we preparing students for the contemporary paradoxes of freelance journalism?" Conference proceedings 5th World Journalism Education Congress. Paris, France.

11 Canter, L. and Wilkinson, E. 2018 "Why teaching freelance journalism matters" Conference proceedings AJE Summer Conference. Canterbury, UK.

12 Craik, L. 2019 "How the pool got out of its depth according to a former columnist" Evening Standard www.standard.co.uk/lifestyle/london-life/the-pool-website-closure-a4059031.html.

13 Mitchell, B. 2003 "Journalists are more likely to be college graduates" Poynter www.poynter.org/archive/2003/journalists-are-more-likely-to-be-college-graduates/.

14 Newman, N. et al. 2019 "Reuters Institute digital news report 2019" https://reutersinstitute.politics.ox.ac.uk/sites/default/files/2019-08/DNR_2019_FINAL.pdf.

15 Bradshaw P. and Rohumaa, L. (2013) The Online Journalism Handbook. London: Routledge.

2
Evolving media landscape

OBJECTIVES

In this chapter you will learn:

- How the internet has disrupted journalism
- Why we need journalists more than ever
- Where to find freelance work
- What types of work freelance journalists do
- Where to find freelance journalism grants

It is no exaggeration to say that the gatekeeping stranglehold of legacy media has been shaken to its core by the internet. Newspapers, magazines, primetime television news programmes and radio news bulletins have all been disrupted financially, technologically and socially by the explosion of digitalisation. Generation Z, born in the mid-1990s to the early 2000s, were raised by smartphones and unlikely to have ever bought a newspaper or paid for news. These digital natives now comprise 25% of the US population, making them more numerous than Baby Boomers or Millennials,[1] and they are more likely to catch the latest headlines on SnapChat than sit down to watch a scheduled television news broadcast.

During the past 15 years the media landscape has completely shifted from one where newspaper stories were copied and pasted to static websites and broadcast media largely ignored the internet, to a world where print and broadcast brands are multidisciplinary mediums with multimedia outputs on multiple social media networks, as well as on their legacy websites. All this whilst competing with the unstoppable, limitless wave of user-generated content (UGC) produced by the public on YouTube, Facebook, Twitter and many more online platforms.

It is no longer simply good enough to have a website story with text and words, but it must be smartphone friendly, hyperlinked, include an abundance of

images, contain videos and infographics, and be financially supported by affiliate marketing, pop-up adverts or native advertising. It must also be promoted
on a multitude of social media networks and encourage audiences to comment,
share and like the content. All this disruption means there are a lot more things
for the humble freelance to think about.

From legacy to digital media

In the digital realm, the definition of journalism is one which goes beyond the
independent and accurate reporting of recent events for public consumption.
Instead, journalism online has become interactive, global, personalised, live,
long-lasting and open.[2] Consumers can react to journalism, challenge the information presented to them and share news at the touch of a button to an
international audience. Local news can be accessed via global networks, and
freelances have to be on their toes to track the unauthorised reproduction of
their work across international boundaries (see Chapter 8).

There is also an increased appetite for more intimate, first-person stories, and
freelances need to market themselves as a brand to stand out amongst the com-
petition (see Chapter 9). The live, unfinished nature of digital journalism means
that stories can be updated and corrected, which adds to the workload of freelances who are usually not paid for this additional labour. But the long-lasting,
if not permanent, nature of journalism online can be a definite advantage to
freelances who can easily link to their work in email signatures, social media
profiles and via their website without the necessity of sending hard copy cuttings
or attaching or uploading large files. It also means that stories can be more readily
returned to and followed up giving freelances additional revenue.

But with this comes the caveat that digital journalism opens up journalists to
greater scrutiny, criticism and abuse. Freelances have to be thicker skinned
than ever before because they are so easily traceable online. In the past, there
was a greater line of defence for the freelance as the public may have only been
able to contact them by writing a letter or phoning the broadcaster or publisher
who commissioned them. Now the public can verbally attack freelance journalists in comment threads on social media and in a variety of online forums
with very little recourse.

Convergence

Now deemed a rather old-fashioned term, 'convergent journalism' became a
popular phrase in the early 2000s when media companies began to merge their

print, broadcast and online offerings. The convergence of production practices meant that journalists previously placed in print, broadcast or web silos found that they had to become multi-skilled and learn how to present a story in more than one medium.[3] This led to the multimedia, mobile journalism we see to-day where reporters are expected to write copy, produce audio and video, take photographs and be proficient on social media.

Freelance journalists can offer added value by being skilled in more than one area and will have access to a greater range of projects, shift work and commissions in addition to supplementary incomes (see Chapter 11) if they are able to write copy as well as produce a social media video. There is also growing demand for journalists who are adept at coding and using Application Programming Interface (API) as well as having data journalism skills such as advanced spreadsheet knowledge and digital media production skills to create infographics.

A competent understanding of web analytics, search engine optimisation and online headline writing, which avoids inane clickbait, is also attractive to editors who increasingly expect pitches to show an awareness of what will generate hits online. This includes knowledge of appropriate online word counts, how your story will be presented on a smartphone, incorporating cross heads and supplying multiple images. All of these competencies may well be the skills of the future that become essential, rather than desirable, for freelances.

It is important, however, not to get too bogged down in presenting yourself as the all-singing, all-dancing freelance and to hone in on the most important aspect – the story itself. A strong idea and evidence that you can produce it in one format (as a written story, e.g., or as a radio documentary) should be enough to secure freelance work. Everything else is added value and may enable you to apply for a variety of freelance opportunities, but it is a mistake to assume that all editors expect you to be an expert in all mediums. The exception here is imagery. Thinking about how you will source photographs or graphics for a written story and having some photography training can be invaluable, not least because it strengthens your copyright protection if you supply images taken yourself (see Chapter 8). You may also be expected to supply photos for a broadcast package as these will be used to promote the content online.

Do we need journalists?

Convergent journalism has also brought about a change in relationship between journalists and audiences. Social media, sharing platforms, websites and blogs are awash with content produced by the public which are frequently incorporated into the work of professional journalists in the form of UGC. When a major event such as a terror attack or environmental disaster happens, more often than not it is broken on social media first, usually by eyewitnesses on the ground.[4] It is possible to follow these events through the accounts of the public which usually include photos and videos rather than via the mainstream media. Rather than simply being consumers, the public are producers of content, referred to by academics as produsers.[5] Journalists are no longer the gatekeepers of information, as anyone with an internet connection can broadcast to the world. So does this mean we no longer need journalists, or that the public can do the work of freelances?

The simple answer is that journalists are needed now, more than ever before. It is professional journalists who are able to sort the wheat from the chaff, and provide quality, reliable and accurate information in an online world filled with rumour, misinformation and influencer opinion. Journalists provide the context, analysis and facts which counter the fake news and propaganda spread by individuals, governments and business conglomerates. That is not to say that journalism is perfect, or non-partisan, but it does on the whole still uphold standards of ethics and autonomy not met by citizen journalists or the wider public.

Various journalism projects with citizens across the world have also shown that they are not in reality that active, since their time is precious and they do not like working for free.[6] There are, of course, pockets of activism journalism successfully highlighting war, suffering and social injustice across the globe, but these tend to rely on mainstream media to get their message to a wider audience. The BBC has a dedicated UGC hub to verify and curate content from the public, whilst journalists have become adept at collaborating with citizens and amplifying their content, or placing it within a package of quality context and analysis. As a freelance journalist you must be aware of the wealth of UGC available to tell your story but also have the means to verify content and be mindful of copyright laws.

Similarly, artificial intelligence, automated content, newsbots and robot journalism have been forecast as a threat to professional journalism. These intelligent tools are used for a range of tasks previously conducted by staff such as tracking breaking news, correlating information and using algorithms to generate reports from raw data, for example the quarterly corporate earnings report from the Associated Press. However, there is strong evidence that the production of trusted news stories is difficult to program and humans will always be needed to create meaningful narrative. As such, a freelance journalist should be alert to the tools that will make their job easier (see Chapter 10) while always injecting humanity into their stories.

Disrupted business models

Advertising revenues have long underpinned the business model of news organisations whether on the printed page or between television and radio shows. This has been entirely disrupted by the arrival of the web and the shift to specialised property, motor, jobs and classified websites which media organisations were too slow to develop themselves. Huge losses in advertising revenues have caused circulations to collapse, the closure of thousands of print titles, reduced pagination and significant staff cuts. This has been compounded by the emergence of news aggregation websites and social media platforms which have diverted traffic away from mainstream media without financially compensating them. The rise of citizen journalists, bloggers and social influencers on WordPress, Twitter, YouTube, Instagram, Facebook and many more platforms means the journalistic field is now an uneasy mix of creators all fighting for the same audience, who have a decreasing amount of consumption time to share out.

This has impacted freelance journalism in multiple ways. Photographers have found themselves in less demand as images are lifted from the internet for free and reporters are expected to take photos together with producing words. Furthermore, each time a major title closes or makes mass redundancies the marketplace is flooded with experienced journalists turning their hand to freelancing. Freelance budgets are often the first resource to be cut, but conversely staff shortages can also lead to an increase in reliance on shift workers and contributor content, meaning there is more work available for freelances. Companies are also reluctant to raise their freelance rates and some have kept them at the same level for decades. But new opportunities are also opening up as digital native news websites are launched with diverse funding models, including subscriptions, donations, events and sponsored content.

Meanwhile surviving legacy news organisations have been clamouring to find different ways to balance the books by introducing pay walls, video advertisements, branded content and native advertisement, which blurs the line between editorial and advertorial. Freelance journalists can now often find themselves writing branded content for a newspaper website, a job previously undertaken by advertising copywriters.

Training

This disruption has also had an impact on the training of journalists. There are now more ways than ever to get into the industry and more opportunities for people to gain experience by getting their work published on a freelance basis.

Alternatively, freelances may have formal training via a college course or university degree, and in some countries, they may have followed an accredited scheme, such as the National Council for the Training of Journalists in the UK, or won a place on a graduate training scheme at a national newspaper or broadcaster.

There are also plenty of capable journalists – staffers and freelances – who have had no formal training at all and have learnt the skills of writing, research and media law on the job or whilst blogging in their bedroom. There is no right or wrong route into journalism, and as a freelance you need to decide what skills, experience and training you require in order to secure regular work. In the past, this training would have most likely been segregated into print journalism, broadcast journalism and web journalism, whereas increasingly today courses are multimedia in nature and teach a diverse range of skills and approaches to meet the demands of the digital age.

Diversification

The fragmentation of audiences online has created an environment where legacy media are not the only players in town. Independent digital native news platforms have sprung up across the world, focusing on social and political niches with the aim of giving a voice to the voiceless. These range from far-right news and opinion website Breitbart to 100% positive transsexual and transgender news source Trans News. Larger online-only news media such as BuzzFeed, HuffPost, and VICE are now jostling with legacy media in the digital marketplace and in doing so have opened up more opportunities for freelances. These alternative platforms have placed a deliberate emphasis on diversity, choosing to cover underreported stories of ethnic minorities, immigrants, disability, trans people and those with mental health difficulties. When putting calls out for pitches these organisations often ask to hear from black, Asian, minority, ethnic freelances or from those from the LGBTQ+ community.

Cutbacks in mainstream media due to collapsing sales and advertising revenue have led to the demise of investigative journalism and a democratic deficit in many parts of the press. However, not-for-profit organisations funded by the public or philanthropic organisations have given rise to investigative journalism online via sites such as The Ferret and ProPublica. These non-profit journalism websites rely on freelance contributions as do many of the growing number of slow journalism and long-form narrative journalism sites such as Delayed Gratification in the UK, De Correspondent in the Netherlands, Slow News in Italy and Longreads in the US. These alternative news platforms favour time, investigation and transparency over immediacy and clickbait and pride themselves on in-depth, quality and immersive content. This includes multimedia storytelling such as the Out of Eden Walk project which saw photojournalist Paul Salopek travel the world on foot from Ethiopia to South America tracing the pathway of human migration out of Africa in a series of articles, videos, photographs, audio files and social media posts.

Blogging has also become monetised and another revenue stream for freelance writers with expertise in a niche subject area. Hobbyist bloggers who established themselves early in the blogosphere, around the mid noughties, have gone on to quit their full-time jobs and make a lucrative career from blogging. This is still possible today but more challenging given the crowded marketplace, and freelance writers are more likely to find themselves earning money writing blog posts for established brands (see Chapter 11). Blogging is now deemed a little passé and the latest media phenomenon is podcasting. Podcast Insights statistics claim there are now over 750,000 shows and 30 million episodes in existence with Apple Podcasts alone featuring more than half a million active podcasts in more than 100 languages.[7] Many freelance journalists are turning to the growing platform to create their own shows covering niche topics such as film horror or digital disruption, finding a variety of ways to make money along the way (see Chapter 11).

Endless possibilities

It sounds like a cliché, but the diversification of journalism means there are almost limitless opportunities to earn money as a freelance. The naysayers proclaim that print is dead and journalism is no more but nothing could be further from the truth. The digital economy offers a wealth of possibilities for those willing to think beyond print or traditional broadcast platforms.

If you only focus on newspapers and magazines then the statistics are depressing. Between 2005 and 2018 there was a net loss of 245 UK local news titles according to research by Press Gazette.[8] Many daily titles have become weekly and multiple edition titles now only print one edition a day. In the UK magazine sector, 22 titles have closed since August 2014, while 15 have been launched and these reflect economic patterns across the globe.[9] Online titles have experienced casualties too with the collapse of women's online magazine The Pool and large redundancies at BuzzFeed, HuffPost, Refinery 29, and Mic.

But out of the ashes of these losses has been an explosion of new content platforms across the world. The digital age has broadened the horizons of freelances and opened up publishing opportunities for articles targeting English-speaking markets. A freelance journalist in Australia can now easily write for online publications in Hong Kong, America and the UK without ever leaving their home. If you seek freelance work not only outside mainstream media but also outside your home country, you increase the opportunity to boost your income. Worldwide Freelance Writer has a comprehensive database listing more than 2,400 publications across the globe, whilst onlinenewspapers.com is a directory enabling users to search by country.

Having a portfolio career is now part and parcel of modern life. One day you may be writing a ghost column for a chief executive of a money advice website and the next you are investigating banking scams for a trade magazine. In between these jobs you could be working shifts from home for a niche website whilst developing a workshop on financial journalism (see Chapter 11). As long as you have the wherewithal to seek diverse opportunities and turn your hand to something new, the work is out there.

Where the work is

As previously mentioned, freelance work is diverse and the key to sustaining a career is knowing where to look for opportunities and being versatile in your approach. If you only target mainstream media, with diminishing freelance budgets, you may find yourself financially impoverished. Yet turning to digital platforms, consumer titles, business-to-business publications and trade press whilst also exploring opportunities in local and regional media as well as the commercial and third sector will help you to develop a long-lasting portfolio. Having all your eggs in one basket is a risky business because you never know when a freelance budget will be pulled or a friendly editor will leave, so you should always be looking for the next potential client alongside nurturing regular contacts.

In terms of finding work there are multiple strategies and you may find yourself deploying a mixture of these:

- Previous industry contacts
- Responding to calls for pitches
- Creating your own work
- Responding to job adverts

If you have worked as a staffer in the industry, then your first port of call will be contacting all the editors you have ever worked under and letting them know you are now freelance and how they can contact you. Ask them if they would be happy to accept pitches from you or give you any freelance assignments.

Similarly, if you have done work experience or an internship at a news organisation, then get in contact with the editor or a colleague you got on particularly well with and ask about freelance opportunities. Even better, put forward some story ideas you could turn around quickly for them.

Commissioning editors are now far more proactive at making calls for pitches on particular topics via social media, newsletters and email mailing lists. Keeping track of key words on Twitter (see Chapter 4) and doing advanced searches will help you to spot when an editor is looking to commission a story in your area of expertise. Editors also use freelance newsletters to advertise topics they would like to receive pitches on or to highlight part-time work, shifts and case-study requests. There are also a number of Facebook groups that editors loiter on (see Chapter 5), and they often ask for email addresses of freelances covering certain niches to add to their story request mailing lists.

There is nothing to stop you from creating your own work. This could be by cold pitching (contacting an editor who has not asked for submissions, that you have no relationship with) or by developing workshops or offering consultation services. You can also cold pitch to public relation agencies or brands offering to write blog posts or internal newsletters. Just make sure you do your research first and send specific ideas and suggestions rather than a vague email offering your services.

You may think job adverts are just for employed work, but this is not always the case. Media organisations do advertise freelance opportunities, and sometimes there is a selection process such as a writing test or interview (see Chapter 7). More often than not, though, it is an informal process involving a few emails back and forth once you have submitted your resume and links to recent work. Sign up to job sites and LinkedIn to receive notifications for key terms such as 'freelance writer' and 'freelance journalist'.

Box 2.1 Author's experience

Having a portfolio career is what Lily loves most about her work. She is always on the lookout for new publications to write for and new ways of making money from her journalism skills. She currently writes first person experiences for finance website loveMONEY, money investigations for Moneywise magazine, and news and features for the *South China Morning Post* newspaper and website – the largest English language news publisher in Hong Kong. She also works shifts at home for GP news website Pulse Today and writes case study-led stories for The Sun website. On top of this she writes columns for money blogs, runs podcasting workshops, and creates content for baby brands. This work has come from contacting editors on spec, being recommended by colleagues and responding to editor calls on social media. A few years ago, most of her work came from mainstream media such as *The Guardian*, *Metro* and *The Daily Telegraph*, but as their freelance budgets dried up she began to widen her net and look elsewhere. Her income is spread evenly amongst different sources, meaning she is never at risk of losing a large chunk of regular money if one of them stops commissioning.

Types of freelancing

Freelance journalism comes in all shapes and sizes, and of course journalists can also turn their hand to editing, copywriting and many other transferable skills (see Chapter 11). Here are some of the ways in which you might be employed as a freelance journalist, probably juggling several of these roles at once. The list is not exhaustive but gives an indication of the variety of gigs available.

Contracted work

This is a formal arrangement usually involving a contract where a freelance works regularly for an organisation but is not a member of staff. Some examples are a weekly one-day news shift working for a trade website, covering a specified number of stories each week for a music section of a newspaper or working on a particular multimedia digital project for a set amount of time.

Pitching stories

Some freelances manage to sustain a living by continuously pitching story ideas to editors (see Chapter 4). This is an outline of a potential story including statistics, sources and, where appropriate, visuals. The pitch could be news, features or opinion, and once you have been commissioned by an editor on several occasions, they will probably expect you to keep pitching on a regular basis and will continue to commission you. In time, editors may start coming to you with topics they would like you to cover or they may eventually offer you a regular column.

Shift working

This can be done in house or remotely and involves working for a set number of hours and being assigned stories by an editor. It could be a day shift or a night shift and is usually to cover staff on leave or short-term staffing shortages. The work is usually news reporting, but some news rooms also offer subbing and feature shifts. Shifts tend to pay less than commissioned work (i.e., a story you have sold to an editor), with an average day shift in the UK being £150 compared with £200 plus for a news story that takes half a day to produce. However, shifts can be a good way of getting your foot in the door and can lead to commissioned work once you get to know the team and the editor. Finding shift work can be a little tricky as it is often through word-of-mouth, but editors are increasingly advertising them on social media and through job sites.

Box 2.2 Author's experience

When Emma started out in journalism, the publications she worked for barely had websites and if they did, any content that was uploaded was essentially a PDF of whatever had appeared in print. A few years down the line she was reporting for BBC News Online, learning all about how to write and present web stories. Now everything she does is digital first, even with outlets such as Pulse, The Pharmaceutical Journal and the British Medical Journal that also still have a physical product. As a freelance, this has opened up multiple new avenues of work. Emma regularly writes for digital-only media that did not exist when she first became freelance, including The Limbic. But it has also meant some changes in the way she works. Turnaround can often be much quicker, with breaking news stories having to be written within the hour. It has also meant that publications have more 'space' to fill and need more content as a result. Emma is also expected and encouraged by those she works for to share her articles on social media to such an extent it has now become a routine part of the job.

Case studies

Being a case study yourself can be a nice little side earner. Rather than writing about somebody else you can get paid to feature in a story. This will involve an interview and might include posing for photographs. You can earn several hundred pounds doing this, and it is a fun way to see behind the scenes of a publication and pick up contacts along the way. It is also possible to earn small amounts of money finding case studies and passing on their details to writers. Finders' fees can be around £25–100, and in some instances, you may be tasked with writing the story as well, earning you an additional fee.

Feature editors on newspapers, magazines and websites are often looking for very specific case studies hooked to topical stories or celebrity trends/photos (e.g., women over 50 with amazing abs like Jennifer Lopez or a petit man with an excessively tall wife), and you can find out what they are looking for on social media and via mailing lists and have a quick hunt around your friends, family and contacts. It is also good practice to have a case study lined up when a particular news story breaks and to act fast. If you know someone who has booked with a holiday company which suddenly goes bust overnight, have them ready to speak and provide pictures the following morning and contact relevant editors before they even ask for this type of case study.

Tip-offs

Similar to finders' fees, tip-off fees are a way of making extra cash for minimal work and can pay exceptionally well. If you have a good story but haven't got the time to produce it or are personally connected so do not want to get too involved, you can let a news organisation know about it and provide a quote, pass on a contact or sell a photo. This might be to a newspaper, news agency or magazine, and the fee will often depend on where it is placed. A front-page splash could earn you thousands, whilst a news in brief on page 14 of a tabloid newspaper could still earn you £400 plus.

Some news organisations will only pay a tip-off fee rather than outsource a story to a freelance because they want to cover it in house. Similarly, if you produce a story for one news organisation, other publishers or broadcasters may come to you wanting to follow it up with their own version and will often pay a moderate fee for passing on contact details (once you have the consent of the source). If they don't offer a fee, ask for one, as they will probably have a budget for it but will not pay unless asked.

On spec

Some freelances, particularly news reporters, upload completed stories on spec to news agencies. This means they are only paid if the story is picked up and covered by a news organisation that subscribes to the agency feed. The reporter will usually have a specialism such as a court reporter or cover a particular region of a country, perhaps overseas.

Stringers

Some freelance journalists operate as stringers for news organisations, press agencies or news wires covering stories from a specific area, usually abroad where they are currently living. This means being the person on the scene when a big news story breaks in a particular region and reporting words, photos and/or video back to publications or broadcasters in another country. The freelance will have an ongoing relationship with one or more news organisations and will either be paid a retainer (a set fee covering a period of time or number of stories) and/or a lineage (per word payment) when their story is published.

Those on a retainer with regular work are sometimes referred to as super stringers, whilst ad hoc freelances are known as stringers. They are sometimes referred to as foreign correspondents, but stringers can also cover regions of their home country for news media wanting coverage for a specific region. For example, a national newspaper in the UK, with head offices in London, might have stringer in Cardiff, Wales, and another in Manchester, north England, to report on stories and issues in those areas. Alternatively, a journalist living in Australia can operate as a stringer for tabloid newspapers in the UK, being dispatched to stories as needed because they have no staff on the ground in that country.

Collaborations

Collaborative journalism is a growing practice whereby two or more news organisations agree to work together to share resources and maximise the impact of the content produced. It is particularly popular in investigative journalism when there is a large amount of data, such as leaked government documents, to trawl through. The European Investigative Collaborations network is a collection of publications from across Europe. In 2017, more than 60 journalists in 14 countries worked together within the network to publish the largest leak in sports history investigating corruption and tax avoidance in football.[10]

The American equivalent network is the International Consortium of Investigative Journalists, an independent organisation which includes more than 200 investigative journalists and 100 media organisations from 70 countries. Many of these journalists work on a freelance basis, and being part of a collaborative team enables them to develop contacts and work on high-profile stories.

In the UK, freelance reporter Carole Cadwalladr writes regularly for *The Observer* and *The Guardian* on investigations often involving media collaborators. In 2018, she jointly won the British Journalism Award for Investigation of the Year alongside Channel 4 News for their Cambridge Analytica expose. Judges described it as 'a fantastic example of collaborative investigation'.[11] Carole also shared the story with the *New York Times* due to its potential impact in America and said the collaboration gave the story a feeling of 'strength in numbers'.[12]

Collaboration can also operate between freelances, and Hostwriter is an international network helping to facilitate this. It offers members contacts in areas and organisations they currently have no links to, and you can search the online platform to find colleagues to work with across the world who have the expertise you require. Over half of Hostwriter members also offer their couch for free to other travelling journalists.

Grants

It might come as a surprise to some that there are many grants available for journalists.

Conflict reporting, investigative journalism or long-form journalism covering social issues or diversity are the most likely to win funding bids particularly if they cover global issues. There are also schemes to help support training or to offer aid to those with financial difficulties due to becoming injured whilst working as a freelance.

To find the grants most applicable to your field of journalism there are directories on journalistscharity.org.uk, journalismfund.eu, gijn.org, walkleys.com, jninstitute.org and poynter.org.

These list a huge range of grants, bursaries and fellowships such as the Fund for Women Journalists which looks for underreported stories of global importance and offers around $10,000. The Mongabay Special Reporting Initiative is an international programme that enables professional journalists to do a series of in-depth articles published under an open Creative Commons license. The focus is on environmental issues overlooked by the media, and they offer a $15,000 honorarium and up to $5,000 expenses.

The Rory Peck Trust provides practical and financial support for freelance journalists worldwide. They have online resources and safety surgeries as well as a training fund and assistance grants. The training fund is to support freelance journalists, photographers, camera operators and filmmakers working in hostile environments so they are able to gain skills and knowledge to work in dangerous situations. Meanwhile their assistance grants can be used to pay for medical and rehabilitation costs, emergency subsistence, legal advice and relocations costs to help grantees overcome a crisis and resume work.

The European Journalism Centre (EJC) has a list of grants on its website which include Innovation in Development Reporting, which has awarded over €4 million to 140 projects involving 365 grantees and 230 media partners to date. The fund, supported by the Bill & Melinda Gates Foundation, is centred on international development issues. Other grants available via the EJC are the Global Health Journalism Grant for Germany, The New Arrivals collaborative journalism project reporting on European migration and the Engaged Journalism Accelerator fund, which supports community engagement.

If you are still at university it is also worth checking to see what bursaries and grants are available. Quite often these receive few entries because students do not know about them or think they won't have a successful application. At the authors' university there is an international project fund which supports students to work in teams with staff to report worldwide. In recent years undergraduate and postgraduate students have travelled to France, Greece and Lebanon to report on the struggles of migrants with the help of this grant.

Box 2.3 Case study: Ed Dyson

Working as a freelance showbiz journalist for national UK newspapers set Ed Dyson on the road to a burgeoning portfolio career.

Now in his early thirties, he earns a living covering showbiz events and interviewing celebrities for tabloid newspapers, websites and lifestyle magazines, alongside writing comedy for famous drag queens and comedians.

In 2018, he also released his debut women's commercial fiction novel *Friendship Never*

Ends – through Orion publishing – under the pseudonym Ella Dyson, and launched the successful podcast United Queendom and its sister programme The Ed & Charlie Show.

The podcast debuted in October 2019 to coincide with television show Drag Race UK, which has a huge global fan base, especially online.

Having previously worked in staff jobs at *The Daily Star* – where he became the youngest columnist and Showbiz Editor in the publication's history – and *The Sun*, he became acutely aware that an office nine-to-five job did not suit his personality.

"I don't like the structure and normality of being in the office, I feel suffocated in that environment. Working from home, or out at events, makes me so much happier, I don't have to deal with office politics or tell people where I am, or book holiday time".

He has taken advantage of his networks and contacts in journalism to get into the comedy writing scene now writing jokes and material for a wide variety of drag acts, and on a freelance basis for Comedy Central.

"It started when I met the drag legend Lady Bunny, and we got on really well and stayed in touch. I asked if she used writers and she said yes. I sent her some stuff and she liked it and paid for it. I have been writing for her ever since. Then I was at the airport waiting to go on a press trip and I saw the comedian Stephen K Amos. I introduced myself and asked if he used writers and he gave me his email address. I then started writing for him and I now have the same agent as him".

Drag queens also feature heavily in his podcast, which currently has interest from potential sponsors, and Ed is hoping to earn additional income from the show in the near future.

"The internet is great for publicising the show. There is a huge Reddit community around Drag Race so I post there and I use Instagram, Twitter, and have a Facebook page for UQ. My guests on the show share it with their fans and it helps to build up listeners".

And the flexibility of digital technology is enabling him to move into the next stage of his career and possibly relocate outside of London one day.

"The comedy writing is taking off now, which I can work on from anywhere, remotely, mostly over email, so I'm hoping if that all continues to build it will give me the freedom to relocate somewhere new one day".

On freelancing success, he advises: "It is about having fingers in as many pies as possible!"

uqpodcast.co.uk
@edwarddyson205

Getting started

- Make a list of 10 non-traditional media organisations you would like to work for
- Identify the two main ways you intend to find freelance work
- Create a list of five companies you could approach on spec for content writing work
- Identify three potential colleagues you could collaborate with
- Find two grants you would be eligible to apply for

Notes

1 Pew Research Center. 2018 "Projected population by generation: millennials overtake Baby Boomers as America's largest generation" https://web.archive.org/web/20180104060909/http://www.pewresearch.org/files/2015/01/FT_16_04.25_generations2050.png.
2 Malik, A. and Shapiro, I. 2017 "What's digital? What's journalism" in Franklin, B. and Eldridge II, S. (Eds) *The Routledge Companion to Digital Journalism Studies*. London: Routledge, 15–24.
3 Quinn, S. and Filak, V. F. 2005 *Convergent Journalism: An Introduction*. London: Focal Print.
4 Bruno, N. 2011 "Tweet first, verify later. How real time information is changing the coverage of worldwide crisis events" Reuters Institute for the Study of Journalism http://reutersinstitute.politics.ox.ac.uk/about/ news/item/article/tweet-first-verify-later-new-fell.html.
5 Bowman, S. and Willis, C. 2003 "We media: how audiences are shaping the future of news and information" Hypergene www.hypergene.net/wemedia/weblog.php.
6 Canter, L. 2013 "The source, the resource and the collaborator: the role of citizen journalism in local UK newspapers" *Journalism: Theory, Practice and Criticism* 14(8): 1091–1109.
7 Podcast Insights. 2019 "2019 podcast stats & facts" www.podcastinsights.com/podcast-statistics/.
8 Mayhew, F. 2019 "UK local newspaper closures: net loss of 245 titles since 2005, new Press Gazette research" pressgazette.co.uk/more-than-40-local-news-titles-closed-in-2018-with-loss-of-some-editorial-275-jobs-new-figures-show/.

9　Tobitt, C. 2019 "Net loss of seven UK print magazine titles over last five years, analysis shows" www.pressgazette.co.uk/net-loss-of-seven-uk-print-magazine-titles-over-last-five-years-analysis-shows/.

10　Football leaks. 2017 https://theblacksea.eu/stories/football-leaks/.

11　*The Guardian*. 2018 "Guardian and observer win at the 2018 British Journalism Awards" www.theguardian.com/gnm-press-office/2018/dec/11/guardian-and-observer-win-at-the-2018-british-journalism-awards.

12　Tobitt, C. 2019 "Observer's Carole Cadwalladr: data harvesting scoop was a 'hornet's nest' – but working with other news outlets gave us 'strength in numbers'" www.pressgazette.co.uk/observers-carole-cadwalladr-data-harvesting-scoop-was-a-hornets-nest-but-working-with-other-news-outlets-gave-us-strength-in-numbers/.

3
Developing ideas

OBJECTIVES

In this chapter you will learn:

- What makes a good story
- Where to find ideas
- Tricks for turning those ideas into a feature, news story or opinion piece
- The best way to capture and log the ideas you come across
- How to take one idea and use it for multiple pieces

One skill that every freelance must have is the ability to generate a constant stream of ideas to keep the work coming in. Increasingly you will come across an editor – potentially a new source of work and income – putting out a general call for pitches on a certain topic. Having a place to collect the ideas as they come to you will prevent the brain freeze that inevitably happens when you are put on the spot. Knowing where to get ideas and how to turn them into an intriguing news story, engaging feature, lively opinion piece or moving radio documentary will also help you to achieve a steady flow of work. The more ideas you have and the more you send them out into the world, the greater the chance that someone will pick one up.

What is a story?

There are some basic principles to remember about what makes a story in a first place. A good story makes you stop in your tracks because it is shocking, surprising, answers an important question or is simply interesting. It needs to elicit some kind of emotion from the reader, be it shock, anger, sadness, elation, despair or empathy. An excellent story may do all of the above. The goal is for the reader, viewer or listener, who you need to keep in mind throughout, to stick with you to the end and then want to tell someone else about it. The audience is a key factor here as you need to be clear from the start who this piece is for and what they need to know about it. Most experienced journalists would take the view that any idea can be turned into a story or opinion article if you can find the right audience.

At the most basic level you need to be able to answer those all-important five Ws: Who, What, Where, When, Why and sometimes also How. That means you need to have all the facts and a real understanding of what has happened in order to fully tell a story. Anything that is half-researched or poorly sourced will stand out a mile. If you can answer all those questions in the telling of your story, then you may well be on your way to having an interesting idea to sell.

It is important to hone that sense, that gut reaction, of when something is a story. If something has made you stop and think or caught your eye, be it a message from a friend, a throwaway comment on social media, the last line of an article in the newspaper or just something unusual you notice when walking down the street, then it is also likely to catch the eye of someone else. Your job is to develop that initial nugget of an idea into something more – to provide the reason, the detail and the background that make a fuller piece.

One thing to bear in mind is that *how* a story is told can be just as vital if not more important than what the story is about. You can have done the most thorough job of researching, fact-checking and carrying out in-depth interviews, but if you have not done a good job of hooking in the reader and making them care it will all be for naught (see Chapter 6).

It is not uncommon for the original idea or top line for a news story or feature to end up consigned to the dustbin once you have done a bit of digging. But hopefully what you will be left with is a stronger story. The authors have lost count of the number of times a small kernel of an idea has ended up going in a completely different direction based on a throwaway comment, a contact made or an unexpected bit of information that turned out to be way more interesting than whatever started you off down that road in the first place. Be open to ideas evolving. If all goes well, you can end up with many different angles or ideas from one single thought.

Human interest

More often than not, the best way to make a mediocre or complicated story into something really engaging is to make sure that human interest has a starring role. This can also be the hook that makes the story unique. It can liven up a pedestrian business or science story as well as being a way to explain the implications and consequences of something that would otherwise be fairly abstract.

For example, a large company goes bust, what does that mean for the employees or customers who had paid for services. When UK travel company Thomas Cook collapsed in 2019, in addition to the usual business pieces about financial mismanagement, there were tales of couples whose destination wedding was cancelled at the last minute or the family who had sunk their life savings into the holiday of a lifetime to be left with nothing. Set against bosses who had taken super bonuses, the stories of average holiday makers facing huge bills and uncertainty kept the story at the top of the news agenda for weeks.

Climate change is another perfect example. It will have far more impact to talk about the human cost of climate change through a story of someone who is battling environmental challenges already happening due to temperature rises or extreme weather. When a supposed 100-year flooding event becomes once a decade or even more frequent, what does that mean for the families and businesses in that area. Wildfires have dominated the headlines in recent times, and the stories that linger in the memory are those of people trying to save or forced to abandon their homes, often in life-threatening circumstances. Big abstract or technical concepts become much more interesting when there is a person with a story to tell.

By making sure human interest is front and centre, you add the emotion almost by default. When scientists carried out the first face transplants, the technical detail of the surgical procedure as reported in medical journals was only really of interest to other medics and even then scientific papers can be a real drudge to read. What puts these breakthroughs right to the top of the news agenda is the story of those involved. The recipient of the transplant undoubtedly has an interesting story about why they needed and agreed to such experimental surgery; the donor family is also likely to have a story about why they felt it was important to get involved. And do not forget the doctor who has spent years painstakingly pioneering a type of surgery straight out of the pages of a science fiction novel.

In the UK, stories about NHS pressures are an almost daily occurrence and between them the authors have written countless articles about it. It very quickly becomes a discussion of numbers, money and political mismanagement. Yet one of the most engaging articles the authors have ever seen written on the topic came from award-winning HuffPost reporter Aasma Day, who spent a week uncovering the stories of six patients passing through a single bed on an acute medical ward. Through those patients she was able to show the problems facing a health service 'bursting at the seams' but in a way that was far more engaging and emotional than usual features about the topic.[1]

In the US, new rules and policies over detention of migrants at the border with Mexico caused a great deal of debate. But it was not until the photos and stories of those detained in poor conditions after a long and dangerous journey – most notably on the plight of children – that the issue really seeped into the public consciousness. The same is true of those stuck in tents in camps at Calais, France, or risking their lives making treacherous journeys across the Mediterranean Sea. Tales of bravery, unbelievable heartache and incredible hardship will always produce much better journalism that will have a greater impact than any politician or campaigner speech and can be a much better way to explain the underlying complexity of a pressing human rights issue. It allows the reader, listener or viewer to understand and empathise in a much more real way.

Quirky

A story needs to stand out from the crowd and have something unique that sets it apart. The journalist is on the hunt for the unusual, the quirky take that no one else has thought of. It's the old adage of man bites dog. If something is unexpected and out of the ordinary (i.e., causes the reader to do a double take), then you have a story. Many online news outlets have whole sections dedicated to the weird and wonderful stories that easily go viral on social media, and if there are photos or videos involved, then so much the better.

Here the freelance should consider whether a story is likely to provoke humour or at least a certain amount of amusement. Is there some potential for a good play on words or an amazing headline that can go viral before anyone has even read the article? But quirky stories can trigger other emotions such as utter shock or surprise. Maybe there is a plot twist that will make the reader, listener or viewer cry out. And it does not have to be the kind of story seen as traditional tabloid fodder. *The Guardian* has had great success with a long-running weekly Experience feature series detailing the stories of people surviving, doing and achieving extraordinary things, which has included such gems as 'I lived in a tree for two years'[2] and 'I stopped a terrorist attack'.[3]

Timing

Timing can be key in a few different ways. The first of which is why does the reader need to know about this now? Second, if it is new information that makes it timely, you want to be the one to do that story before anyone else does. This ties in with exclusivity, and a good journalist will always want to be the first to break an important story.

Getting an idea picked up at the right time can also be about latching onto something on the calendar, such as an anniversary or event. Stories about Halloween, Christmas or summer sun would usually only work at the right time of year, and for magazines with slower turnaround times, such articles are often planned months in advance. If there is an election happening, it is likely to be the thing that everyone is interested in and you do not have to be a politics reporter to come up with fresh ideas. But you will have to produce those ideas relatively quickly depending on how long elections last in your part of the world.

As a freelance you need to be aware of what is happening in your region, specialism and in the media in general in order to get the best ideas. You need to avoid coming up with the same ideas as everyone else, so you need to know what is out there in order to provide your unique view, but also if you come to the party too late with an idea for a story, someone else will have beaten you to it, or you will have missed the boat because that topic is no longer of interest. Follow-up stories can be a fruitful source of ideas and commissions as long as you can find a way to move the story on. But a response or counterbalance to another piece that has got everyone talking or has proven controversial needs to be published quickly before everyone has forgotten it and moved on.

A few years ago, there was much excitement about a concept known as 'Hygge', a Danish word explaining a feeling of coziness. There would be little point pitching about that now, but at the time it was all the rage. It is all about having your finger on the latest zeitgeist. There may be a Royal Wedding or Presidential election or huge music festival that generates umpteen news stories, features or opinion pieces. It could just be the latest throwaway comment from a celebrity that has got everyone talking. A good freelance will make the most of the current hot topics in generating ideas. Remember, you will need to strike while the iron is hot. Once everyone has moved on, there is less chance of a story being published unless you can provide a good reason that the story can generate new interest.

One aspect you may also want to consider is whether a story is under embargo; that is, the source of a story has placed an embargo on when it can be published. This is fairly common, for example, in reporting of scientific studies where journalists may be given access to information to allow the preparation of a story in advance but are expected to hold off publication until the embargo lifts. The same may be true for the launch of a new product. There is no legal requirement to stick to an embargo, but to break one may burn some bridges with a key contact or get you kicked off a mailing list and so should not be done lightly.

Conflict and controversy

As the sheer number of column inches written about vaccine scares over the past two decades can attest, any issue where two sides can be pitted against each other is fertile ground for a good feature or news story. Beware of creating false controversy, readers can spot it a mile off. But a genuine debate or concern over the provenance of a claim, the dodgy business practices of an individual or company or a suspect comment made by a politician or celebrity is a very good starting point. This has always been a stand-out news value for most media outlets because it automatically gets people talking about and sharing the piece in question.

It may be that when you start looking into an idea that you are not aware it is potentially controversial, but if it does seem to be a topic that divides people or about which there are strong views, then you can be assured you are probably onto a winner. Or consider if there is an unusual angle you can offer on a topic that is already causing a lot of debate.

Sources of inspiration

The authors have asked many freelances for their main source of inspiration, and every single one ends up listing multiple ways in which they have got their best ideas. In essence, the freelance journalist needs to keep their story sense on high alert at all times because it can come from anywhere, including walking down the street, a conversation overheard on public transport, a flyer through the door, a post on social media or during a chat with a contact about something else entirely. Inspiration can strike at any time.

News agenda

Keeping on top of what the news media are interested in and talking about can be an essential source of ideas. Whenever a celebrity or powerful figure has said something which stoked the fires of controversy, the stage is set for an opinion piece offering an opposing or unique point of view. If a particular news event is dominating the headlines, can you think of a unique angle, get access to an expert who can answer important questions or put together a piece for a specific audience who will want to know what it means for them. Do you have a case study that can provide a human angle or engaging story on the subject? Is a certain group in the population being unfairly targeted or maligned and deserves to tell their story in their own words?

The most important thing to remember here is that you do not want to repeat what everyone else is saying but to add value or a new perspective to whatever else is out there. It is all about moving the story on.

Box 3.1 Author's experience

Over time Emma has tapped into a whole host of press release services and email alerts related to her specialism of writing about health and medical science. This also includes keeping track of what other health and science journalists are writing about both through social media and reading relevant magazines and newspaper sections. Having a handle on the current hot topics means she often finds herself writing about the same issue – most recently medicines shortages – from different angles for several outlets. She has also set up Google alerts for keywords, so even if she's distracted with other work, she doesn't miss out on any useful ideas. Part of this strategy means looking through the stuff that no one else has seen, be that research studies that have been published or hunting through official reports. And sometimes it's just being aware of the conversations that people are having online, an example of which was women frustrated at being unable to get hold of hormone replacement therapy which suggested a more widespread problem than had been previously reported.

Social media

Twitter, Facebook, Instagram, Snapchat, YouTube and LinkedIn can be a great source of ideas for the simple reason that those are the places people are having conversations and documenting what is happening in their lives. The same goes for Weibo and WeChat in China. The latest figures show Twitter has 330 million unique users.[4] In spite of several controversies around fake news, political ads and use of data, Facebook remains the largest social media platform worldwide, with 2.41 billion monthly active users.[5] Likewise Instagram continues to grow. What this offers the journalist, in addition to a platform for promoting, sharing and broadcasting their work, is a source of endless ideas. With a bit of savvy, this provides the opportunity to tap into conversations among groups of people you would not normally speak to or have access to.

It can take work to find those ideas though. Be wary of just staring at a feed from your friends and family and expecting inspiration to strike. Move outside your bubble where everyone is saying the same thing. You will need to dig deeper and go further in order to find the real gems. It can also mean wading through a lot of mundane chatter to find that one comment that will spark an idea. Here there does need to be a note of caution. Information and ideas you come across will require vetting and verification just as they would if they came from a real-life conversation. Basic steps such as checking who is behind the post that has caught your attention can avoid a lot of wasted time and potential embarrassment when your intriguing case study turns out to be a bot.

Something else to look for is the same topic coming up time and again. A problem or experience that many people seem to be having. For example, it is election time and multiple anecdotes are popping up of people being turned away from the polling booth for no good reason. Or employees of one multinational complaining they are not being paid or are being treated unfairly. Maybe discussions of a hobby or online community you had not previously heard of. Perhaps, a food or make up fad that is doing the rounds. There is plenty out there if you spend the time looking.

As a case in point, one quick glance at the author's Twitter feed shows a young woman asking if it is now usual for those applying for shelf stacking jobs in a supermarket to have to do a few hours of unpaid work before even reaching the interview stage. The responses underneath suggest this is by no means a one-off or only happening in that sector with questions raised about whether this is legal/fair/exploitation. If you have a hint of an issue, trend or problem that you suspect may be a story, make use of social media, in addition to other avenues of research, to build that idea up. Have others spotted the same thing, does anyone have any figures or know people directly affected? Who are the experts who would know more about this?

If you write or are interested in a certain specialism, be it music, art and culture, sport, technology, the environment or anything else, curate your social media to ensure you are following all the right people and do not miss out on what is being discussed by those in the know. Perhaps a politician has made a statement about something that those working in the field vehemently disagree with. Or there is a key development or problem that people have started to discuss or share information about. It can feel overwhelming to try and keep up, so be smart in making use of apps that help you filter what you need. TweetDeck, for example, enables you to create categories and lists to organise your Twitter feed. Personalised Google alerts can be a very useful way to ensure you never miss new information on a topic you are interested in.

WhatsApp groups are another great source of ideas, not least because conversations can end up going in all sorts of weird and wonderful directions and people may speak more freely about things they would not mention on other social media platforms. You may have to wade through a great deal of inane chatter before you hit that hint of an idea but hang on in there (even if you mute the group to avoid your phone blowing up with hundreds of pointless messages but check in now and then).

In addition to any private WhatsApp groups you are in, using a third-party app such as Groups for WhatsApp can help you find out what is happening in public groups. This public rather than private use of WhatsApp differs between countries. In the UK, for example, where people are less likely to join groups with people they do not know, it is relatively rare. It is also important to note that news organisations are increasingly making use of WhatsApp groups to share content or updates around specific events or topics rather than solely as a way for members of the public to contact them.

Conversations

Having conversations with people is old-fashioned but it works. Perhaps you see or hear people complaining about something and wonder if it is just a one-off or you have happened upon a wider problem. Maybe they are a unique case but their story is so striking, it's worthy of a piece anyway. Do not be so tuned into social media that you forget there are real people out there doing and experiencing interesting things – in the doctor's surgery; at the hairdressers; in the pub or bar; at the school gate; in the church, mosque or synagogue; or at the weekly market. Wherever there are people, there are stories.

Check in with your contacts. Over time you will build up a large database of people you have spoken to for stories or have proven useful. Keep in touch with them and ask questions. Follow up on previous stories you have done. What are they doing now, have they published new research, has the problem you previously reported on gone away? Are they still trying to get funding for a new project, how are they? These are all potentially fruitful questions.

Also be open to ideas when carrying out interviews for a current project. Chat to them, ask at the end of the interview if they have anything else they are working on or are concerned about at the moment. Who or what inspires them? Do not let throwaway but striking comments about something entirely unrelated to the conversation in hand disappear into the ether. Interviewees will sometimes bring up a seemingly random issue that they assume you know about. Take note as this may be a good lead.

Personal experience

For most journalists the natural instinct is to report on others while they hide invisibly in the background. Yet personal experience can be an important source of ideas. The authors between them have been the subject of features on everything from running with your other half, giving birth to a massive baby and how would your partner deal with finances if you died. If you are planning an unusual trip, are the only female invited to speak at an event on gender equality, have taken up an unusual hobby or have generally experienced something out of the ordinary, consider reporting on it, even if it is not your usual sort of piece.

Even the seemingly mundane can be made into a good piece if the idea is developed in the right way. Have you had to battle some incredibly irritating bit of bureaucracy but as a result are now an expert in how best to sort it out? Were you a witness to something happening and not sure you did the right thing? Do you know what it is like to be in debt, have to care for an ill relative, battle prejudice, overcome an injury? As long as you can work out a way for the reader to care about this story now, perhaps tapping into other stories out there or taking the opportunity of some new figures or report as a news hook, pieces based on personal stories have real potential. Not least because you are already somewhat of an expert in the topic.

Part of developing ideas around personal experience is to work out the best format. Should this be part of a wider feature with other experts quoted and research included, or does it work better as opinion piece? Do you have enough to write about based on your story or would it be better forming the starting point for something else. This will be key for pitching the idea (see Chapter 4) but also for getting the idea off the ground in the first place.

Press releases

Signing up to be included on press release lists and having friendly public relations officials in your contacts list can be very helpful. One of the first steps the authors took on going freelance was to make sure they received relevant press releases on the topics they were writing about. But the most helpful way for a freelance to view a press release is as a starting point. Unless you have been given something exclusively, a whole lot of other journalists are looking at the exact same information. What the freelance journalist really needs from a PR is information around trends, or an interesting case study, or figures. Something that can be built up into a unique offering.

The job of the freelance, on seeing a press release about, say, a product launch, survey or charity campaign, is to think how you can make that idea your own.

It may be that it has flagged up something timely or an event you were not aware of and that is now your starting point. As with any other bit of information, you need to consider the source and what agenda they may have in factoring in whether or not to use it as a basis for an article.

It may be some data that caught your eye, or an issue you agree deserves wider coverage. The trick is to turn that into a unique more fully formed idea that a commissioning editor can say yes to even if they had already seen and dismissed the original press release. Use your journalistic skills to take the original idea and make it something extra. Do not be afraid to call the PR who sent the release to find out if they have more detail if you feel you need it. The answers you get may be the thing that allows you to stand out and now you have that contact and have built up a relationship, next time they may come to you directly.

Freedom of information

Journalism is about holding those in power to account and freedom of information requests are a key way of doing just that. Many countries around the world, including the US and UK, have laws in place which enable members of the public to access data held by government bodies. Rules vary but essentially by carefully asking the right questions, the journalist is able to collect huge amounts of data that can be used as a source for a story. This can include everything from how funding for certain departments has changed over time, to buried reports, to emails. It can be a lengthy process, but for those savvy enough to know what they are asking for and what to look for in the responses that come back, it can be an excellent source of information. You will find more details on what is covered within different jurisdictions and exactly how to make a request online, for example, through the Information Commissioner's Office in the UK or at FOIA.gov in the US.

Keeping track

Ideas can turn up at any time yet are least likely to appear when you need them the most. The least efficient place to keep them is in your own head. You will forget them. The only way to ensure you make the most of any ideas you have is to keep a note of them in one easily accessible place. Ideally this should also be a place for noting on-diary stories, such as publication of reports, court cases, announcements, anniversaries, etc. It is important not to forget the things that you know are coming up and can write about in advance, or at least prepare for by getting a commission in place.

Box 3.2 Author's experience

Lily keeps all of her story ideas on a Google doc table, which she can access anywhere at any time. This means that as soon as an idea strikes her or she spots a potential story online, she inputs it into the table which has three columns: Outline Idea, Genre and Potential Publications. Most of her feature ideas are timeless or seasonal, so she works with editors to agree on the best hook. For example, when it is approaching Christmas she will reach out to commissioning editors on money websites to find out the types of stories and case studies they are looking for. She will then use niche Facebook sites to find people with relevant experiences. Many of her ideas also come from personal experience, particularly consumer issues. When Lily spent more than a year trying to rightfully claim compensation for a cancelled flight, she realised there was a problem with airline regulation and pitched an idea to Moneywise magazine to investigate the issue. She also keeps note of pending deadlines for changes in the law or consumer regulation, so she can pitch background features on these topics with case studies for added insight.

Freelances all have their own personal ways of keeping track of ideas, but they do keep track. Something as simple as a small notebook or the notes app on your smartphone can be a great way to store or log ideas as you have them, especially if you are out and about. But ultimately you will probably find it more useful to have some sort of formal document or system to transfer those notes to and make sure everything is in one place.

A Word document or Google doc can be the simplest way to do this, but if you enjoy a detailed Excel spreadsheet that would work well too. The most important aspect is that you find it easy to use and you understand it. The goal is to be able to keep track of all the information you need, whether that's in a list or table. For example, is there a key date to bear in mind? Which publications or outlets would the idea be suitable for? What other checking needs to be done? What contacts do you have? Is this a follow-up to another article? This information can be combined with a spreadsheet on current commissions/pitches if you prefer to have it all in one place.

The level of detail you include in the document is really up to you, but be aware that when you come back to an idea weeks or months down the line, you might not remember all that much of what you were thinking when you wrote it down. It should include any useful links to whatever it was that started the idea because you do not want to waste time trying to find source material again.

Having some sort of colour code on ideas that are strong or need more work can also help provide clarity on those days when you are suddenly scrabbling around for ideas. It may also be useful to note if you had pitched the idea but had zero responses. The lack of interest may have had nothing to do with how good the idea is, and as long as it is still timely or relevant or there is a new hook to attach it to, it can be worth giving it another go.

There are various planning apps, such as Evernote and Trello, which you may find easier to use than relying on a Word document. This can be handy if you have more than one document related to an idea because it can help you store everything in one place and you can add to them whether you are sat at your laptop or out and about making notes from a smartphone.

From time to time, you will need to tidy up your ideas document or folder to delete the ones that are never going to work, are no longer timely, have been commissioned or have been done elsewhere already. If someone else does beat you to an idea, it might not mean you have to give up on it entirely, though. A rethink about the intended audience or a change of angle can give the idea a new lease of life.

Box 3.3 Template: Ideas

Idea	Genre	Potential publications	Timing	Notes
Breaking up from your family	Lifestyle	*Telegraph, Daily Mail*	Link to Harry and Meghan story	
How Gen X should plan for their retirement	Finance	loveMONEY, MoneyWise	NA	Needs at least two case studies
Couch to marathon	Lifestyle/ fitness	*The Guardian,* Women's Running	Study showing marathon runners add years to lifespan	Could be done as week by week or monthly guide?

Getting the most out of a single idea

It is not only possible, but it is also very achievable to produce several pieces of work from one idea. Maybe there was an excellent case study there was no room for in a feature. Consider if this can be a separate article for someone else keeping in mind anything that makes that case study stand out or particularly unique. Think about all the different audiences who might be interested in a topic you have done a lot of research on. What would work for a national newspaper would require a different take for a specialist website and you could easily pitch both these articles. For example, the view that a consumer and business audience would take on a new venture could well be entirely different.

To not consider all the possible outputs you can deliver from one idea is a waste of the time and effort you have put into researching an issue. This is not about simply repackaging the same article over and over as an editor is unlikely to want the same story that has already been published elsewhere, and this may be breaking the terms of your commission (see Chapter 8) but looking at an idea from all its possible angles to make the most of it as well as being an efficient use of your skills. When making a note of ideas, consider the potential for multiple commissions from the beginning.

Box 3.4 Case study: Marverine Cole

Marverine Cole is a lecturer in journalism and media at Birmingham City University and an experienced broadcaster. As a freelance she worked as a producer and a newsreader and has made several radio documentaries, including Black Girls Don't Cry, a 30-minute documentary for BBC Radio 4 about black women's experience of mental illness, for which she won Journalist of the Year at the Mind Media Awards in the UK.

"When making radio documentaries or short videos, the first thing you need to know is what the marketplace looks like", she says.

This means doing your research about who does what and how.

"Commissioners will laugh you out of town if you don't know what kind of work they do", she adds.

In the UK, a big part of this is understanding how the BBC commissions including what approved independent production companies they use and when they do their commissioning rounds because that is who you need to target, she explains.

Once you get to that stage you need to make sure you have a truly unique story – which also means double checking, not just assuming, no one has done this in this way before.

"Then you need to have extraordinary access to someone, something or someplace that tells a story about something incredible", she says.

"Or you need a unique angle. And you need some surprising testimony".

"To get ideas you need to find out what people are talking about, that means being curious, being nosy, dipping into conversations online and in real life beyond your own experience. Anywhere you find interesting people you will find a story, that's where you are going to find inspiration".

The idea for her *Black Girls Don't Cry* piece came from discussions she had seen on Twitter with women being very vocal about their experiences. This prompted her to do some more research, to dig more deeply into what she suspected was a widespread problem.

"You need data, you need research. But no story will connect on any level with reader, listener or viewer unless you have strong personal testimony. At the heart of it you need someone affected by the subject matter".

Marverine likens developing an idea to making a winning cake as a contestant on the Great British Bake Off; you need to get all the right ingredients and craft it in such a way you end up with a masterpiece.

"It will need shaping, you will need to do digging and fill in all the blanks", she says.

This includes making sure you have the figures, the key bits of policy, that detail, relevant legal aspects and expert comment that supports the story you are telling.

"You need to bring all these elements together because you need to know if the idea you have had is just tittle tattle or there is really something to it. Ask yourself, is this truly interesting, do I really have a unique angle and have I got people to agree to speak about it on the record".

marverinecole.co.uk
@TVMarv

Getting started

- Organise your social media accounts to tap into potential sources of ideas
- Identify the media you need to read, listen to or watch regularly to keep up to date
- Sign up to all relevant press releases
- Make sure your contacts 'book' is up to date
- Create a spreadsheet to help you document and keep track of your ideas

Notes

1 Day, A. 2019 "The crisis engulfing the NHS – seen from one hospital bed" Huff-Post www.huffingtonpost.co.uk/entry/this-is-the-story-of-one-nhs-bed-in-2019_uk_5c8a5debe4b0fbd7662182ee.
2 Madsen, N. 2019 "I lived in a tree for two years" *The Guardian* www.theguardian.com/lifeandstyle/2019/jun/28/experience-i-lived-in-tree-for-two-years-activism-logging.
3 Clarkson, S. 2017. "I stopped a terrorist attack" *The Guardian* www.theguardian.com/lifeandstyle/2017/sep/01/i-stopped-a-terrorist-attack-experience.
4 Statista. 2020 "Number of monthly active Twitter users worldwide from 1st quarter 2010 to 1st quarter 2019" www.statista.com/statistics/282087/number-of-monthly-active-twitter-users/.
5 Statista. 2020 "Number of monthly active Facebook users worldwide as of 3rd quarter 2019" www.statista.com/statistics/264810/number-of-monthly-active-facebook-users-worldwide/.

4
Pitching

OBJECTIVES

In this chapter you will learn:

- How to target different publications
- What a commissioning editor is looking for
- How to write an eye-catching pitch
- How to sell a story or an idea multiple times
- The art of communicating with and chasing editors

There are some freelance journalists who are fortunate enough to have the work come to them. They may have worked for several news organisations for a number of years, and once they become self-employed their former employers come knocking, asking them to cover all manner of features, investigations and specialist pieces. But for the vast majority of freelances it all starts with the pitch. This is the one opportunity to grab the attention of a commissioning editor, sell an idea and hopefully secure more commissions off the back of it.

What is a pitch?

In a nutshell the pitch sells your story idea and if you are unknown to the editor, it also sells you. Consequently, a good pitch must mirror all the qualities of a good story in order to impress that all important commissioner. The pitch must be instantly interesting, informative and original whilst also being correct, concise and persuasive. It must be clear what the angle is, why you are the best person to produce the story and what your access is to relevant sources. Crucially it must fit the audience who will consume it and leave the editor wanting to know more. Not too much to ask then.

The vast majority of pitches are made via email. It is a definite no-no to pitch via social media, and it is rare that you will get a face to face with an editor or producer. Many editors set their phones to voicemail or screen their calls to enable them to manage their busy workload without distraction. It has therefore become the norm for editors to like, and expect, pitches via email. But that doesn't mean you should never pitch via the phone, especially if it is an editor you have built up a relationship with. Freelance journalist Anna Codrea-Rado is a huge advocate of telephone pitching and believes many editors are too. In her weekly newsletter The Professional Freelancer she explains why:

> The huge benefit of pitching over the phone is that you'll get an answer straight away. You can hear it in their voice, get that instant reaction of 'oh wow that's a great idea!' If it's not quite there yet, you have an opportunity to hash out why with them and get it over the line. And if they do say 'no', they'll have to give you a reason for declining; a vital piece of feedback you'll rarely get via email.[1]

However, if you are cold pitching to an editor particularly if they have put a shout out for pitches, then it is usually best to stick to normal practice and send an email. Pitch writing is an art form, but there are many ways to increase your chances of sealing a commission and not ending up in the email trash. Susan Grossman of susangrossman.co.uk who runs pitching clinics in London says it's important to remember that a pitch is a conversation. "Imagine you are sitting next to the editor in the pub. You reveal a fact, a figure, a quote, to which the response is 'I didn't know that, tell me more'".

A fundamental starting point is to understand what you are pitching, in particular whether it is a news story, feature or comment piece. This will influence the tone and content of the pitch and make it clear to the editor what you are proposing. It is possible for one story to be all three, but you need to make it clear in each pitch what it is you are selling. It may be that you initially pitch a news story, which once published you can pitch a feature about and then once it has gained some traction you can pitch a comment piece on the same topic. Some commissioning editors will only commission a feature if the topic has been in the news recently, so sometimes it is worth pitching to news desks first even if it is a feature that you really want to focus on.

Where to pitch

You can have the best pitch in the world, but if you don't get it in front of the right person it is a non-starter from the off. Knowing who to contact takes research and is covered in depth in Chapter 5. There are two keys ways to find pitching opportunities. These are cold pitching and responding to callouts on social media, in newsletters and on job websites.

It is important to keep on top of editor call outs for pitches by not only following them on Twitter but also closely monitoring key words such as 'pitches', 'submissions', and 'freelance writers' and using advance Boolean searches combining phrases like 'call for pitches' AND 'paid'. Setting up a third-party app such as Tweetdeck will help you to monitor all of these key words, because you can set up a column for each one. Being quick to respond to a callout for pitches will give you a definite head start.

As outlined in Chapter 5, having good networks and signing up to newsletters and job sites such as Cision, Mediargh and MediaBeans will keep you abreast of the commissioning editors actively seeking pitches on particular topics. Make sure you are on the key freelance Facebook groups for your country and/or specialism and set up email notifications around key words such as 'freelance journalist' and 'freelance writer' on LinkedIn.

For cold pitching, before you even identity an individual to pitch to you need to decide upon a relevant publication or broadcaster. There is much to be said for aiming high and targeting the big media brands. Just one commission from a national newspaper or magazine can open up opportunities elsewhere and make commissioning editors sit up and notice you. However, thinking beyond the mainstream media also has its benefits. The internet has opened up a wealth of media start-ups; many of which rely on freelance contributions. It might be a niche sports website, an online parenting magazine or a political news site. Think about where your story would fit best and target accordingly. It might be a publication that you would never read yourself but that should not stop you swotting up on their content before sending in a pitch. Also think local and regional. There are thousands of local and regional publications in each country, and advertising heavy magazines will often have a budget for freelance features. And if you are a specialist writer seek out the business-to-business and trade magazines and websites which are more likely to commission a niche idea.

Always start by doing your homework and researching the market. Read back issues of magazines and newspapers and check online archives to get a feel for the tone of articles, topics covered and intended audience. Most publications will have a media pack on their website for advertisers or you can order one for free. These often contain a wealth of information about the reader demographic, interests and lifestyle which will give you a good sense of the type of stories and issues they cover and the age and background of their readers.

It is essential that your idea matches the publication you pitch to and you are aware of the age, sex and lifestyle of the reader. There is no point pitching a story about the menopause to a publication targeted at millennials or sending an idea for a story about sustainability to a website whose audience is more interested in money saving deals at McDonalds than making reusable toilet paper. It is also wise to find out if your idea has been covered in some fashion already, which is where an online archive comes in handy. If it has, find a new angle and justification for covering the topic again or drop the idea. And if a magazine is subscription only, then contact the editor and explain that you would like a copy so you can pitch appropriately to them or ring the sales team and ask to buy a single back issue.

Box 4.1 Author's experience

Emma works mostly for business-to-business publications for health professionals as well as medical journals. In her experience, knowing the title well is key for pitching. The editors working for these publications know their specialities inside out, so you need to properly understand the type of articles they do and who they are aimed at. They are often ahead of the national media so always check they have not already done something before you pitch it, Emma advises. And it is always worthwhile thinking how you can reframe an issue for a publication with a different audience. For example, Emma wrote a number of articles for pharmacy publications on medicine shortages. She guessed (correctly) that if pharmacists were having headaches sourcing medicines, then it would also be affecting GPs (primary care doctors) who would have to rewrite prescriptions. After spotting a doctor complaining about just this issue on social media, she successfully pitched the story to a magazine aimed at GPs. Emma has also found that if specialist magazines are impressed with a pitch, even if they don't commission, they will often keep you in mind for other articles. It's all about showing that you know what you are talking about, she says.

Pitching to broadcasters

Broadcasters rely less heavily on freelances and often expect their contract staff to pitch ideas to them instead. However, if you work freelance shifts at a radio station or a television news programme this is an ideal opportunity to pitch ideas.

When pitching a radio or television news story to a series producer or editor, you must be able to demonstrate that you can do everything from beginning to end. Essentially you need to hand the product to them on a plate. This means not only being able to source a good story but also having the ability to record and shoot it before editing it on any software. You are pitching the idea as a producer as well as a reporter to front the story. Since you are unlikely to get any research assistance it is vital that your pitch makes it clear that you understand the production process. You also need to be honest with yourself about your skills to ensure that you are able to deliver what you pitched.

A pitch should contain details of background research, who you are going to talk to, what you are going to record or shoot and the length of the story or documentary. You need to ensure that all of your speakers are lined up in principle and that logistically you can put the piece together in your given timeframe which is usually a few days. If you have to shoot at opposite ends of the country then you need to factor in travelling time. You also need to account for editing time at the end for both radio and television stories.

Another way of getting work commissioned is via pitching rounds. These are held by BBC news programmes and documentaries each year and the various television channels such as Channel 4, and streaming services also have their own annual processes. Information about the commissioning rounds can be found on the channel's websites, and the commissioners will be looking a year ahead so ideas need to be timeless or linked to a future event.

These broadcasters will expect pitches to come via an independent production company, so you will need to find one to work with and pitch your ideas to them first. By listening to the end of a radio programme or viewing all the credits on a television production, you will be able to spot who the production company is. Look at the types of programmes they make and what they are interested in before sending them relevant ideas. Send them a brief email outlining your idea in 250 words, including why it is newsworthy, who you would speak to, what your experience is and why they should work with you. The production company will then decide on your role, which could be as a researcher, producer or person who conducts the interviews.

What a commissioning editor wants

The following pointers come directly from commissioning editors who we spoke to for this chapter.

Editors want to be intrigued and feel confident that you can pull off the whole package, but that doesn't mean sending them the full story. Never send a written story on spec and the only attachment on emails should be one or two example photos, where relevant. You may actually prefer to embed photos at low resolution into the pitch, so the editor can scan through and see them without having to open anything.

A great pitch is all about how quickly you can convey the key information to a busy editor. Brevity is vital and if an editor is interested, they will ask for more detail and develop the idea with you. If they have to wade through a big dense email, they are more likely to end up deleting it than finishing it. Instead make sure your pitch is snappy and concise and leaves the editor wanting more. Sum up the hook of your story in a couple of sentences and lead straight into it, there is no time for waffle.

Although you need to be concise, you also need to have done your research. Don't send a pitch saying 'I would like to look into this' or 'I plan to submit a Freedom of Information Request on this topic'. Make sure you have the data first and include it in your pitch to show you know what you are talking about and are ready to go.

Having a good grasp of the media outlet you are pitching to is extremely important, and the editor will want to know you have read and understood their publication and have a good sense of their audience and where the piece would sit. It is also bad form to criticise the publication's previous coverage of the topic in question, and instead you should highlight why it is timely to cover the subject now. Also make sure you don't pitch a topic that has already been covered recently, why would an editor commission the same piece twice? Some editors also like to know when the story needs to run and if there are any competing pieces likely to be published first.

Getting the tone of voice right is also important, and it is always best to err on the side of caution and be formal rather than come across as too cocky, demanding or personal. This means never pitch via social media.

Always ensure that you have a clear angle rather than sending a pitch stating that you would like to write about a certain topic. You need to be clear what the piece would look like and what a potential headline could be rather than just giving a bunch of statistics on a subject.

You also need to demonstrate to the editor that you are the right person to commission for this particular story. Do you have experience writing about similar topics that you can link to or is the topic something you have experienced first-hand? Do you have privileged access to a source or several case studies? And can you write a compelling story? A good pitch will be compelling evidence that you are a capable writer, so make sure everything has perfect spelling, punctuation and grammar. And always get the editor's name right. Pitch to Sara Smyth and spell her name Sarah Smith and she will never, ever commission you.

How to write a pitch?

There is no formal pitch procedure and each editor will have their own set of quirky expectations and pet hates, but there are some key pieces of information you should include. This section outlines how to structure a pitch and the type of content to include. The next chapter (Chapter 5) will explain how to find the correct person to send it to.

Style

It is important to strike a balance between a polite, professional email and one that sparkles with personality. The tone should be direct without being rude and should immediately get to the point. Avoid waffle, hyperbole and forensic detail at all costs. It is appropriate to open an email with 'Hi Mark', rather than 'Dear Mr Jones' but at the same time don't include slang, acronyms such as LOL or emojis in your pitch unless it is directly relevant to the story content.

Length

The shorter the better. Editors scan emails and won't read an 800-word pitch. The only exception is a pitch for a long read which might require you to submit a detailed proposal. In short, a good pitch should be able to convey all the required information within 200 words or less. Don't send a whole article, just an idea which grabs the editor's attention. Once you have been commissioned by the same editor a few times, you will find your pitches tend to get shorter as they know you are reliable and have good access to sources so you won't have to spell everything out.

Email subject

In the email subject heading you need to spell out what you are pitching. Be as explicit as possible and include a potential headline. For example: PITCH: "Hackers stole my £100,000 retirement pot" or EXCLUSIVE NEWS STORY: Breast milk can cure cancer, say scientists. For magazine pitches you may want to head your email SIGNED: "I'm jealous of my sperm donor husband" or SECURED: "I gave birth to triplets in a Nandos' toilet" to let them know you have the interviewee all lined up or have already got the story. This will grab the editor's attention, increase the likelihood that they will open your email and give a strong impression that you know what the angle of the story is.

If you are sending multiple pitches in an email then perhaps choose the strongest one for the subject heading for example: 3 PITCHES: How to overcome procrastination and more…

Content

After a brief introduction about yourself you need to get straight into the pitch. Start with a headline which sums up the story in 10 snappy words or less. It is fine to repeat the headline given in your email subject; in fact, if you change it this may confuse the editor or imply you don't know what the angle is.

Follow this with a summary of the story idea which outlines the key issues it will cover, relevant topical angles, headline statistics and a list of who you will speak to including identifiable case studies and experts. In effect, this summary should tell the editor why this story should be covered now and why it is relevant to their readership or audience. You should be able to convey all of this information within three or four sentences.

After the summary you need to indicate any photographs you have or if the people in the story are willing to be photographed. If it is a case study-led story, then it is worth attaching one sample photo at a low resolution, so it doesn't clog up the editor's inbox.

At the end of the pitch include a brief biography of yourself and links to relevant experience and publications. Alternatively, if you are pitching on spec to an editor for the first time, then you might want to put this information at the top of the email – there is no hard and fast rule. This information could also be permanently embedded in your email signature, so you don't need to input it each time. Make sure you also include a link to your website and your professional social media profiles. If you have limited publications then link to blog posts or any quality content you have written online.

Think about the presentation and scannability of your email and include lots of paragraphs, so it is quick and easy to read. Also make use of bold, italics and bullet points to highlight specific points but don't get carried away with these. Use the pitching templates in this chapter as a starting point to structure your own pitch.

Withholding key information

Most editors are lovely people, but as a freelance you have to protect yourself and your work. Since there is no copyright on ideas, the last thing you want is an editor stealing yours. When you include content in a pitch be careful not to give so much away that they could produce the story themselves. If you have a particularly strong case study or exclusive data, then don't hand this over before you are commissioned. Refer to a case study as a '29-year-old woman' rather than 'Christina Jewey, 29, from Nether Edge, Sheffield'. Give sample statistics or data but not an entire spreadsheet so you are able to pique the interest of the editor without doing yourself out of a job. And if you do find that an editor or reporter runs off with your idea and tries to do their own version of your story, politely confront them about it and seek external advice (see Chapter 8). You may find that when pitching an idea to a news desk a reporter contacts you asking for contact details. In this instance explain that you are seeking a commission to produce the story yourself and do not hand over any contact details or data, or negotiate with them for a tip-off or contacts fee.

Box 4.2 Template: On spec pitch

This is a template which can be used as a guide for contacting a commissioning editor for the first time, also known as on spec.

Dear (*insert first name*),

    I am a freelance (*insert specialism*) journalist with experience writing for (*insert names of publications/websites here and hyperlink to your stories*).

I have an exclusive story which I would like to offer (*insert name of their section/publication*) first.

I have secured interviews with (*insert details of case studies/experts*) who are happy to be photographed/provide photographs (*delete as applicable*).

(Insert suggested headline in bold text here)

(*Summarise story in 3 sentences here including relevant statistics, key findings, juicy quotes, sources, why relevant for this editor, etc.*)

I am happy to discuss this in more detail if you are interested.

I look forward to hearing from you.

Regards,
(*insert your name*)

Quantity

As a general rule of thumb, it is best not to send more than three or four ideas in one email. You might have one really strong story that you want to pitch on its own, but quite often you will want to send multiple ideas to an editor so they have a few to choose from. This is particularly the case when you have been commissioned by the editor before. Any more than four ideas and your email is going to be too long for the editor to scan through. It is also worthwhile holding back ideas and not blowing them all at once. The editor may only be looking to commission one feature from you, so you may want to save some ideas for the following week or month. Conversely, it can be really stressful if an editor commissions several or all of your ideas in one go, as it may be difficult to complete them by the deadline. Before the panic sets in, make sure you negotiate realistic deadlines. It is better to manage expectations and say you need an extra week at the beginning rather than find yourself in a position where you let the editor down because you can't meet the agreed deadline.

Box 4.3 Example: Multiple pitch

This is an example of a list of ideas sent to a commissioning editor which the journalist had an existing working relationship with. All three ideas were commissioned.

Hi Liz,

Here are some Money feature ideas for May. Or if you have anything else in mind that you would like me to do, then just let me know.

Turning opinions into cash

Most people love to voice their views, whether it is ranting at the television or comparing their favourite brands with friends.

But what if you could be paid to give your expert opinion and how much cash could you make?

A round up of the main ways to make money, top websites and how much you can earn:

Surveys – e.g., YouGov
Market research – e.g., Shop Scan

Studies – e.g., Prolific
Mystery shopping – e.g., Marketforce
Watching TV – e.g., Amazon Preview
Photograph adverts – e.g., Jobspotter

Case study of someone who has made money to supplement their income doing a mixture of these.

Is being vegetarian good for your wallet?

May 14 is National Vegetarian Week. I thought this would be a good opportunity to look at the financial cost of being vegetarian and comparing it with carnivores. Or alternatively the focus could be on being vegan and the cost of this.

I would look at comparing:

Food shopping costs
Wine and beer
Clothes and shoes
Accessories (bags, wallets, phone cases)
Cosmetics
Hidden items containing animal fats – plastic bags, condoms, soaps

Case study of a vegetarian/vegan and their monthly spending

How to give generously when you have no money

A round-up of the more unusual and less well-known ways to give to charity if you are short on cash. For example:

Car scrapping
Donating hair/milk
Dog walking for an animal rescue shelter
Milling flour
Online shopping and searching (Open a Tab, GoodSearch, Give as you Live)
Online quiz (Free Rice)

Thanks,
Lily

Exclusivity

There is quite a bit of debate amongst freelances over how many editors to pitch an idea to at any one time. There is no right or wrong approach, but it is good etiquette to pitch to one editor at a time, even within the same publication, and ask them to respond within a designated time frame so you are able to pitch the story elsewhere. If you don't hear anything within the given timeframe, then either chase the editor or move onto a new one.

However, if it is a time-sensitive piece, you might want to pitch to several editors at the same time with an outline and then offer the exclusive details (names, photos, contact details, best quotes) to whoever offers you the best commission. It really depends on the type of story and whether you are cold pitching or if you already have a relationship with an editor. If you are cold pitching then a savvy editor will ask you if you have pitched it elsewhere and it is best to be honest. If they really want the story then they will still buy it. And don't worry if you find yourself in a bidding war position. This is fairly common for real life stories within women's magazines, and you just need to be up front to each publication about how much you are being offered. In broadcasting, the general rule of thumb is not to offer an idea to more than one person at a time. So, for example, try BBC Radio 1 and if they decline or don't get back to you within a given timeframe try BBC Radio 4.

Box 4.4 Example: Pitch

This is an example of a successful on spec pitch which resulted in a commission for the *South China Morning Post*.

Dear Cathy,

I am a freelance journalist in the UK and I have been given exclusive access to a health story based on research in China.

Would the following story be of interest to the health and well-being section of the *South China Morning Post*? I have a photo and interview with the lead researcher, and statistics specific to China.

What you eat in pregnancy DOES affect your baby's gut health, scientists claim as they reveal diet, climate, antibiotics and birthing method all impact the infant immune system

Research of breastfeeding mothers in China, Spain, Finland and South Africa reveals that prenatal lifestyle influences good bacteria and fungi in baby's gut.

A low-fat, high-fibre diet improves quality of microbes passed from mother to baby via breast milk.

Antibiotics in pregnancy dramatically reduce the amount of microbes transferred to baby.

C-section can disrupt microbe colonisation, leading to higher risk of obesity and allergy in child's life.

This is new research, which for the first time makes the link between the external environment during pregnancy and what is passed onto newborn babies via breast milk.

This has not been published anywhere in the media to date.

Many thanks,
Lily

I am a freelance **money, health and lifestyle** journalist with experience writing for <u>Moneywise</u>, <u>Metro Money</u>, <u>This is Money</u>, <u>Guardian Money</u>, <u>The Times</u>, <u>The Telegraph</u> and <u>Vegan Living</u>. I also work as a senior lecturer in journalism at <u>Sheffield Hallam University</u>.

Changes to your idea

Think of a pitch as the start of a conversation. Even if it is commissioned it is likely that an editor will want their own input and will have a clear picture of how it will fit in their publication. As a freelance you have to be prepared to be flexible and respond to your editor's needs. This may mean changing an objective news feature into a more personal first-person piece or writing a scientific research story from the perspective of a case study. Your story is likely to change and evolve through the process but don't be too rigid about sticking to your original pitch. The only time you should put your foot down – politely – is if you are uncomfortable with the direction the story is heading in and you feel it is unethical or inappropriate. In this case be prepared to stick to your principles but be aware that this may mean losing a commission.

Your story may also evolve as you do more research and interviews, which is to be expected. Keep the editor in the loop and as long as your story is still interesting, engaging and relevant, they should stick with it (see Chapter 6). However, if a story dramatically changes from the original pitch because a case study pulls out or you can't secure the interviews you promised, then the editor is likely to drop it. The worst thing you can do is pitch a great idea which you can't follow through. This means you have to ensure the people involved have agreed in principle to be in the story and be identified before you pitch the idea. This is certainly the case for case studies or celebrities, but you can usually guarantee that you can find a relevant expert to speak to without having to line them up first.

Also make sure that your case studies are aware of the publication you are pitching to as they may be fussy. Appearing in Good Housekeeping may be an attractive prospect for a case study, but if you don't get a commission there and then pitch the same story to Real Life magazine without checking with the case study first, they may pull out. This could leave you in a potentially embarrassing situation if the story is commissioned and you suddenly have no case study, making you appear unreliable to the editor.

Timing

Getting an editor to read your pitch is not all about catchy headlines and juicy titbits. Much of it is to do with timing. There is no point crafting an amazing pitch if the editor never reads it because it is lost amongst a sea of press releases or comes at the wrong time of year. Try to find out when the regular feature meeting is held (phone up and ask!) and the time of month or week that work is commissioned. Once you have made reciprocal contact with an editor ask them when they like to receive pitches. Ideally you want your pitches to fall into their inbox just before a planning meeting, so it is fresh in their mind.

Monthly magazines tend to work three to six months in advance and newspaper supplements may work several weeks ahead, so you need to understand their production schedule. There is no point pitching Christmas features to a magazine in November as these will be planned in the late summer. You always need to be thinking ahead and be sure to mention the particular issue and section you think your idea is particularly well suited to. That means you'll need to pitch Mother's Day ideas in January and back-to-school subjects no later than May.

There are also advantages to pitching timeless pieces. These can be attractive to editors because they come in handy if something else falls through or there is a slow news period. The disadvantage is they may commission the piece but then hold onto it for a long time before publication, which can delay your payment (see Chapter 7). It can be worthwhile giving an editor a nudge to remind them of a forthcoming hook to attach your story to if they have been sitting on it for several months.

The other timing trick is the time of day and day of the week that you email out a pitch. Try to avoid Mondays as these are usually the busiest day for editors and they may end up mass deleting emails that have clogged up their inbox over the weekend. Mid-week can be an opportune time, particularly first thing in the morning. If you send an email at 7.30 am to 8.30 am, it is likely that your pitch will be at the top of their inbox and therefore more likely to be read and responded to, before the phone starts ringing and staff start coming into the office.

If you send a pitch to an editor following a shout out on social media then there are two tactics you can try. Either fire off a pitch straight away in the hope that you beat others to it or alternatively wait a week or two for their inbox to calm down and then send a pitch.

Money

Most freelances hate to ask about money, but it is vital that you understand the terms of the commission from the very beginning. Once an editor has expressed an interest in your story, whether they have commissioned it yet or not, it is perfectly reasonable to ask about their rates before going any further. Read more about negotiating fee rates in Chapter 7.

Multiple bites of the cherry

A good way to maximise your income is to repurpose and reshape pitches for different media outlets. Even if your story has been published already it doesn't mean you can't use it elsewhere. For case study stories there may be limitations around the rights (see Chapter 8), meaning you can't sell the story elsewhere but for general news and features there is often lots of opportunity to exploit a good idea. You could pitch a news story to a newspaper first, follow it up with a feature in a magazine and then write an opinion piece for an online news website. As long as you don't use the word 'exclusive' in your email you can pitch ideas which you have had published elsewhere if you ensure you have a different angle and rewrite the content, usually with fresh quotes and some new interviews.

Box 4.5 Author's experience

Lily learnt early on that repurposing story ideas and case studies for different publications was an accepted practice. Her first experience of this came when she broke a news story on stealth childcare costs in *The Times*. Realising there was more potential for the story she pitched it with a case study angle to This is Money (Mail Online) before writing an opinion piece for Novara Media. And a story about her father, a criminal psychologist, losing £18,000 to fraudsters was so strong that she wrote about it for This is Money, Moneywise, The Sun Online, loveMONEY and The Pool. Each time the piece had a different hook and was written from a fresh perspective. For example, she originally wrote the story as a breaking news piece for This is Money but two years later wrote a reflective first-person article for loveMONEY on the lasting impact of the scam. Meanwhile the story for The Sun Online money section focused on how her father's banks responded to the crime and subsequent changes in bank compensation policy. The Sun Online approached her to write this story having seen her father's story as a case study in Moneywise magazine.

Chasing editors

This is one of the trickiest things to get right and something which freelances agonise over. The conundrum is how soon and how frequently to chase an editor over a pitch without seeming desperate or annoying them. If you are sending out pitches cold to an editor, you have not contacted before then the most likely response you will get is none. Get used to the wall of silence. It's not you, it's their overflowing inbox. In most cases if an editor is not interested in your pitch, they won't reply to let you know, they simply haven't got time.

However, it may also be the case that they just haven't seen your email or they have deleted it alongside 100 dull and irrelevant press releases. It is therefore always worth chasing up a pitch within a reasonable amount of time. If it is time-sensitive then this could be the next day, but if it is for a magazine with a long lead time, you may want to wait a week. If you still don't get a response after chasing two or three times then it is best to move on and try somewhere else or ditch the idea. There is a fine line between knowing when you have a genuinely good idea that just needs to find the right home and when you are flogging a dead horse. It will depend on your personal commitment and passion for a story and how much time you can dedicate to pitching the same idea.

If you have been commissioned by an editor before, then it is usually worth having a chat with them on the phone or via email after your first commission to ask how much of a freelance budget they have, the type of stories they are looking for, when they like to receive pitches and if they want to be chased. Once you have established a relationship with them, they are far more likely to respond to these types of questions. Usually editors are happy to be chased because they do miss emails and many will actually insist that you do keep pursing them. This might mean emailing five or six times over several weeks before you get a response, but persistence will usually be worth it as it keeps you on their radar.

When you send an email asking if an editor has seen, or is interested in your idea, make sure you include the original pitch again. The editor will not want to go hunting around in their inbox for it and may have accidentally deleted it anyway. Some editors will respond even if they do not want to commission your story to give feedback and encouragement. This is gold dust in itself and shows you have grabbed their attention and they are interested in your ideas. Seize this moment of interaction by asking more questions about the kinds of things they are looking for and send more ideas as soon as possible.

Box 4.6 Case study: Nina Hendy

As a freelance business journalist based in Hobart, Australia, Nina Hendy regularly contributes to some of the country's best-known business mastheads, including *The Age*, *The Sydney Morning Herald* and the *Brisbane Times*.

She has a network of editors that she pitches ideas to several times a month.

"I don't do anything face-to-face. All of my relationships are over email. I never phone pitch as editors mostly don't like being hassled on the phone".

Nina keeps her pitches brief and sends a suggested headline with a short three-line synopsis based on a news hook.

"I also give a sentence on why I think it is a useful article and I check it has not been published somewhere else. I am quite light and breezy in my pitches as I have existing relationship with editors", she adds.

In order to maximise her earning potential, Nina spends minimal time writing her pitches, allowing her to dedicate more time to writing commissions.

But she says this comes with experience and is more effective when you have developed a relationship with an editor over time.

"Fifteen years ago, I was pitching in more detail. These days, I constantly feed the same editors over and over again and they are grateful for the content. If I have an idea, I try to make it work for an existing editor I work with rather than cold pitching a new publication".

Her advice to those new to freelancing is to make sure your pitch stands out by offering something unique.

"In your pitch say I have been offered this exclusively or it is a first look at this research and I really want to offer it to you first. Put that at the top.

Or if you already have quotes put in a couple from an expert. If you have a case study it is worth putting this in the pitch. And say why it is the right story for that particular editor".

Nina also advises subtly making yourself known to the editor prior to pitching.

"Just start liking a few of their tweets and get on their radar. If you look up their profile on LinkedIn they will get a notification and see your name".

She also says it is best to wait a couple of days before following up on a pitch.

"I will send a follow up email saying 'Hi, just checking if you are interested in this one. Let me know if you want more information' and then I leave it. If they are not interested, let it go and give them something else. There are no rules on how soon to pitch to the same editor again".

Nina also says it is vitally important to make sure your online presence is strong before you start firing off emails.

"Take a step back before you start pitching and make sure all the basics are in place. You need a really great website with samples of your work and to ensure that a quick Google search will find you, so you are not pitching blind. Be conscious of your online reputation".

ninahendy.com.au
@NinaHendy

Getting started

- Choose one story idea and identify your case studies, experts and key sources of information
- Research potential publications or broadcasters to send your pitch to, paying particular attention to their audience demographic
- Create a strong, concise headline for the story idea
- Write a pitch using the template in this chapter as a guide
- Read the next chapter to identify who to send the pitch to and then email it at the optimum time

Note

1 Codrea-Rado, A. 2019 "Why you should pitch over the phone" *Newsletter* June 28 2019 www.annacodrearado.com/newsletter.

5
Contacts and networking

OBJECTIVES

In this chapter you will learn:

- How editorial departments are structured
- Tricks to track down the correct person to pitch to
- The best way to use social media and directories to make contacts
- How to take advantage of awards and events
- The value of press cards and gaining access to events

So, you have created the perfect pitch and you know exactly who your target audience is. All you need to do now is find the right commissioning editor and convince them to buy your story. This might seem like an impossible task but once you have sealed one commission you are on the road to securing many more.

The trickiest part at this stage is finding the correct person to send your pitch to, as media organisations are notoriously slippery when it comes to telling you whom to contact for what. In an ideal world, news organisations with a freelance budget would publish the email addresses of commissioning editors online, making it a relatively straightforward task to get hold of the right person. But very few companies do this and instead prefer you to use your journalistic skills to hunt down the appropriate editor, as a way of demonstrating your tenacity and insight into the organisation.

Company websites will usually give you a generic email address for a news or features desk, but this inbox will be inundated with hundreds, if not thousands, of press releases every day and will be checked by a variety of different staffers. If you are lucky, the website may have a list of staff or section editors, but it can still be difficult to know who commissions pitches and whether an editor is effectively the most senior journalist in that subject area or a commissioning editor. And even if someone has the title 'commissioning editor' they may not have a freelance budget as all their commissioning occurs in-house.

So how on earth do you find out who has the power and budget to commission you as a freelance? It helps to know how organisations are structured and to be prepared to put in the groundwork to identify exactly the right person to send your pitch to. Without it landing in the inbox of that One True Editor you have almost zero chance of being commissioned because your email will be ignored or deleted and at best forwarded onto someone else, before they ignore or delete it.

Who does what?

Each company will be different, and a lot depends on the size of the organisation as well as the platform. Monthly magazines tend to operate on a much smaller staff ratio than national newspapers, and news websites can overlap with their offline counterpart but not always – so here is a brief guide to some of the organisational structures and hierarchies you might come across.

Newspapers

The structure of a newspaper tends to run along the same lines whether it is a local weekly paper or national daily; the main difference is the scale. There will be reporters (trainee, senior, specialist, chief) at the bottom of the hierarchy and section editors (news editors, features editors, sports editors, specialist editors) in middle management who work alongside sub-editors and copy editors. But these all sit under the editor, who may also delegate roles to a deputy editor and/or assistant editor. Above the editor there are strategic roles such as executive editor, editor-in-chief or managing editor, but responding to pitches is well above their paid grade. The people you need to familiarise yourself with are the section editors who are responsible for the day-to-day content.

You need to be clear from the outset whether your pitch is a news story, feature or opinion (also known as comment, op-ed or opinion editorial) piece. This will dictate whom you pitch to and the amount you are paid. News and features are run as separate departments with separate budgets, and you may have more than one person working in the same role on news, particularly on a news desk where staff work on a rotating shift pattern. It is therefore good to know who all the news editors on the news desk are, or if you build up a rapport with one person, find out what days or times they tend to work. The news editor (other possible titles are content editor, head of news or commissioning editor for news) is responsible for managing all of the stories each day and allocating them to reporters. Most national newspapers will have a freelance budget, so they can pay for tips-offs, case studies and stories written by freelances.

Make sure you understand the different sections of the newspaper as much as you can. Usually there will be health, money or personal finance, business, education, and comment sections and possibly also social affairs, environment, lifestyle, culture, travel, science, technology and so on. Be aware that some section editors may look after a number of topics; for example, a Lifestyle or Life and Style editor may cover health, fitness, women, fashion, sex and parenting or may only cover one or two of these topics.

Sometimes, it will be the section deputy editor who filters all of the pitches because the editor is too busy with other responsibilities. If you don't get a response from a section editor, a neat trick is to contact the deputy editor separately, who may respond more quickly. An even more confusing scenario is when a freelance works as a commissioning editor, as sometimes happens. They will usually do this work using the newspaper email address but can be a bit trickier to find. A hunt on social media is usually the best way of deciphering whether they are the most relevant person to contact or not.

It can also be helpful to make contact with specialist reporters or correspondents as a way to secure a commission. They can lobby the news desk on your behalf, and they may be more likely to respond to an email than an editor with an overflowing inbox. There are pros and cons to this approach. It may mean that you are paid a lower fee, as your story is treated the same as agency copy, but it is more likely to be picked up and get your name known. The reporter may also get a joint byline with you and edit your copy to put their own stamp on it, but they will be more eager to champion your story if they have a vested interest in it. One way to identify relevant reporters to contact is to see who follows up on previous stories you have published.

Box 5.1 Author's experience

Whilst researching a food story for the *Metro* newspaper, Lily made contact with the editor of Vegan Living magazine via a journalism Facebook group. The editor was happy to be interviewed for the article and gave her opinion on the financial cost of a vegan diet. At the end of the interview Lily asked the editor if she was accepting pitches for Vegan Living and the types of content she was looking for. The editor gave Lily lots of helpful advice and encouraged her to pitch via email. Within a few days Lily sent a list of ideas to the editor and several of these were commissioned. It was the start of a fruitful relationship and Lily continued to write for the magazine for over a year. The process of writing this book has also proved an excellent networking experience. In Chapter 11 Lily spoke to freelance

Marissa Carruthers who writes for publications in South East Asia. She found Marissa through a Facebook media network and following the interview asked her for a contact at the *South China Morning Post*. This contact was then able to put Lily in touch with the health and well-being editor, and Lily has been writing regularly for the newspaper ever since. Lily takes advantage of any opportunity to speak directly to editors or be recommended via peers finding this more effective than emailing editors she has no prior connection to.

In some circumstances, like the given example, but also when pitches are sent to section editors, you may need to wait for confirmation once the story is discussed at news conference. This is the daily briefing where all the section editors discuss the content for the next day's paper and the week ahead. It is at this meeting where stories are given the go-ahead, so it is quite normal for a reporter or news editor to say they like your story and they will 'take it to conference'. Section editors tend to be more autonomous and may commission features directly without going via conference.

Websites including digital only

Newspaper websites tend to operate in a similar fashion to their print counterpart, and section editors may be responsible for commissioning content for both platforms. However, in large organisations you may have two completely different people doing the same job, one for print and one for online. There may be an online money editor and a newspaper money editor who commission different types of content. It is always worth pitching to both, but not at the same time. Similarly, there may be an online news editor as well as an offline one, so it is worth knowing who covers which.

Newspaper websites may also have sections that do not appear in the print edition, so you can pitch on a different range of topics. The UK *Guardian* website has a running blog within its Life & Style section but no equivalent in the newspaper. Getting commissioned by this section may also mean that your content is shared on the *Australian Guardian* website, although there is no extra payment for this.

And then there are websites that are digital native like Vice, HuffPost, MEL magazine and The Overtake, and have no legacy media attached. These are often looking for fresh, dynamic content particularly on niche subjects or targeting a specific audience such as millennials, LGBTQ+ or ethnic minorities.

Many of these websites have helpful guidance on how to pitch, so it is always worth digging it out and following their recommendations.

Be aware that contact details are not always kept up to date on websites, so you may be pitching to a section editor who has moved on to another publication. Once you have a potential name of a section editor it is always worth checking them out on social media to see whether they are still working there.

Magazines

Once you have got your head around the structure of newspapers, then magazines are relatively straightforward. They tend to run on a much smaller scale and have fewer staff and sections. Niche consumer or trade publications may have less than five editorial staff so it is likely that you can identify the correct contact quite easily. On a small publication this may be the editor or deputy editor, and as the publication becomes bigger, you are more likely to find that there are features editors or section editors. Magazines tend to rely heavily on freelance content, so it is always worth contacting a relevant editor or section editor rather than a writer because they may be freelance themselves and will not be in a position to champion a story for you.

How to track editors down

The first step when you have your pitch is to identity a list of publications you would like to ideally place it with. Never have just one in mind even if it means you have to tailor the idea to fit different outlets (see Chapter 4). Then you need to send it by email to the right person. Even for seasoned journalists who have a good understanding of how newspapers, magazines and websites are organised, it can be difficult to track down the right person, especially when pitching to places for the first time. Publications you have previously worked for have a moveable feast of staff, structures, departments and budgets and what works one time may not the next.

You will find that every organisation will have a generic email address to send stories to, and this is often promoted as the place to send scoops or exclusives. For example, exclusive@the-sun.co.uk is the advertised inbox for *The Sun* daily, tabloid newspaper in the UK. It is possible to receive a commission after pitching to this kind of email address, but it is pretty rare. This will be an inbox glanced over by a number of different people to whom every man and his dog, plus his dog's publicist, will email. You are far more likely to grab the attention of a named individual, so it is vital that you track their email address down.

Do your research

Spending some time finding the right person at this point can save a lot of wasted time waiting for a response to an email which has been ignored, deleted or simply missed in the fog of press day. It is not necessarily a bad thing that media organisations want you to flex your investigative muscles and figure out whom to contact rather than handing it to you on a plate. After all, this kind of digging is what journalists excel at. Once you have got the hang of the process and built up your contacts and networks, it will get easier.

Have a look at the information provided by the publication you wish to pitch to about its staff to help build a picture of how it is organised. What sections does it have and where might your article fit within that? Are there any details about who works in those sections on their website or in the print publication? Larger or more established outlets will have a masthead listing staff details.

Have a look at regular bylines to pick out job titles of staff members. And do not forget to Google – sometimes the most obvious investigative method can pay off even if, on the face of it, the publication does not seem to want you to know who works there. If you find a name but no contact details, try to figure out their email address. Most organisations email addresses follow a basic convention (i.e., firstname.lastname@organisation.com). The generic email could give you a clue, and a quick Google search can often prove if your guess is correct.

Social media

The best way to find out who commissions content is not via a news organisation website but via social media. If you think you have the name of the relevant section editor, run it through Twitter and LinkedIn to check whether they are still in that role or have moved to another publication. Chances are their Twitter profile will be updated before the company website.

Twitter can be a particularly useful tool for tracking down a section or commissioning editor at a publication, because people tend to include at least some job information in their bios. Have a go at using Twitter's search tool to identify people using 'editor' and the handle of the publication you want to pitch to (e.g., editor@buzzfeed), as this will bring up section editors or deputy editors who would in most circumstances be in charge of commissioning if they have a budget. Using the advanced search can help you drill down to specific subjects. Some editors and journalists even helpfully provide email contact details in their Twitter bio.

Other social media platforms, such as Facebook, offer very helpful freelance journalism groups (see more detail below), which can be an invaluable source of information on whom to approach for commissioning requests, and even other potential publications you may not have heard of. But ask carefully. Do not expect to be handed information readily. Make sure you have done the groundwork first or you may not be taken seriously. If someone has moved or you are getting no response, it is reasonable to ask if others have faced the same barrier.

Newsletters

There are an emerging group of freelance journalists who are setting up newsletters to share words of wisdom but also freelance jobs of the week. In the UK, Sian Meades-Williams writes an informative and witty free newsletter which sends out details of all the latest freelance journalism and communications positions and editors seeking pitches on specific topics. Sian scours the internet for the latest opportunities, and subscribers can buy her a virtual cup of tea to say thank you, if they wish. Even if you don't have anything to pitch at the time, the newsletters are worth saving for the contact details. Another newsletter resource is The Professional Freelancer written by Anna Codrea-Rado, who offers one free post a week and a brief call for pitches, or you can pay to sign up for more detailed content. Journo Resources also has a free newsletter which lists jobs, freelance opportunities, grants and awards. Meanwhile Sonia Weiser writes an opportunities of the week newsletter, which is US focused but there is a small suggested fee of $3 a month. Find out what newsletters exist in your country and if they don't, start one and earn some supplementary income (see Chapter 11).

Pick up the phone

It seems obvious, but really the best way to find out whom to pitch an article to is to ring the switchboard or news desk and ask them directly. While commissioning editors themselves may not answer or have their phones going straight to voicemail, there will be someone who will be able to answer your question in a couple of minutes. This approach can help you collect a wealth of information not only on the right person to pitch to as well as their contact details but also on the best time of day to get in touch or when in their news cycle a pitch is most likely to get attention.

You can also ask how they prefer to receive pitches so you can tailor it exactly to their needs and include all the information they want to see. If a weekly publication goes to press on a Thursday, anything sent on Wednesday or Thursday is likely to get ignored. In fact, your best bet would be Friday when they will discuss what they have for the next issue. Better still, ask for the timing of the editorial or news conference so you can send any pitches a couple of hours before, reaching the commissioning editor's desk just at the point they are thinking about what fresh, new ideas they have to offer.

Ask around

Journalists have always relied on other journalists for useful contacts. There is a certain amount of give and take here, and no one is going to hand over hardwon commissioning contacts to someone they do not know without getting anything in return. But by building up relationships and hooking yourself into journalism networks, you will have access to a wealth of advice and wisdom.

If you have never written for a certain publication or if you have a good idea on a topic that is outside your usual area of interest, first have a think if you know any journalists who work in that area who may be able to provide some guidance. Ultimately, as you build up your career and your peers and colleagues move around different publications, you will have a wealth of information at your fingertips.

Directories

There are many online media directories that promise the freelance journalist a flood of commissions. They may also prove a useful tool for finding a commissioning editor or picking up some work. Just as there are many routes into freelance journalism, there are differing views on how useful such directories can be. Once you have built up your address book, you may find they become obsolete. But some experienced journalists say they routinely pick up new work and contacts through sites such as journalism.co.uk. In the US, mediabistro is a media jobs listing site that also has a freelance marketplace available to subscribers and offers career advice and insights for freelances.

But here's the downside – they are not all free and it is important to consider whether it is worth paying a fee for those that charge. The key is probably quality not quantity, signing up to trusted sources of information about those working in journalism and not throwing away cash to get access to contact details that could be found through a Google search or that may be out of date. Or being tempted to sign up to directory services promising the earth but actually are more of a PR tool than a must have for the average freelance. You need to consider carefully what you are getting in return that you would not be able to get elsewhere.

What may be most useful are websites that enable you to develop a profile as well as providing a tool to find useful media contacts when you have a really attention-grabbing idea for an article. We would point out that for getting work, nothing beats pitching over and over and there is no doubt it can be a thankless slog. Be wary of expecting regular or well-paid work from websites where you can bid for work. They may be worth checking out but in most cases are unlikely to provide a regular (or even fair) income despite the claims to the contrary. This is by no means a comprehensive list but are some examples of media directories and what they offer.

Journalism.co.uk

Journalism.co.uk offers job listings, press releases, event and award listings as well as a series of useful 'how to' guides. It also contains a searchable freelance directory of journalists with over 400 members. Freelances listed on the site pay a fee and in return are offered a branded email address and discounts on training courses.

Journalisted

This is an independent not-for-profit site run by the Media Standards Trust which you can use to search for articles published in UK national newspaper sites and BBC news by journalist, news outlet or keyword. It also contains more information on particular journalists, including in some cases an email address.

Gorkana

A media organisation that essentially connects journalists and PR professionals. There is a strong focus on business-to-business (b2b) publications. It is a free directory which offers a media request service and has a daily email round up, jobs listings and a database of thousands of journalists, bloggers, writers and media influencers.

The Chartered Institute of Journalists, Muck Rack and National Union of Journalists all have a freelance directory for members. Similarly, in the US, the Society of Professional Journalists has a freelance community which includes a directory among its resources. The Australian Associated Press offers several directories (for a fee), including a media contacts database, as does also the MEAA (the Australian union for media, entertainment and creative professionals). For specialist journalists, there are various organisations which offer directory listing and message boards or online communities as part of membership, for example, the Association of British Science Writers, the Medical Journalists Association and the Sports Journalists Association.

Social media networks

The authors cannot stress strongly enough the importance of social media networks for cultivating ideas, finding sources and gaining new contacts and commissions. The trick is to take a tiered approach to maintaining these networks.

First pick one social media platform that you want to focus on and treat this like a high maintenance garden. You will need to give it lots of attention in order to make it grow, which means checking through posts every day and following up on requests for pitches, case studies and feedback. Then select one or two other platforms which require much lower level maintenance. Check in on these once a week, or even once a month, make sure they are up to date and post on an ad hoc basis when you really need to.

And like with any garden, make sure you have a good cull once a year and get rid of everything you don't need. Don't be afraid to unfollow people, leave groups and unsubscribe to accounts that are no longer useful.

You can have dual professional and private accounts on social media, but this may get confusing and time-consuming. It may be best to decide which ones you want to use professionally and which ones privately, and stick to that. Or you join some groups as a professional and some as a private individual. Again, it is whatever works for you and there are no set rules.

If you do get into a conversation with an individual on social media, make sure you take it into a private space such as a direct message once it starts to directly relate to a story. This means you won't bore everyone else following you, or the post, and you can talk more candidly.

The most commonly used social media platforms for freelance journalists are Facebook, Twitter, LinkedIn and to a lesser extent Instagram. They are great, to varying degrees, for the following:

- Finding commissioning editors
- Gaining commissions
- Promoting your work
- Finding case studies and experts

- Sharing advice with other freelances
- Spotting trends and gauging opinion

As hard as you may find it, it is really important to promote your work on social media and gain some traction from your stories. This will help you come to the attention of editors and also public relation workers who can help you find experts on future stories or add you to their relevant press release mailing lists (see Chapter 9). The Twitter hashtag #journorequest can also come in handy when trying to track down case studies and experts.

It is also important to have a support network, somewhere to rant and complain, and gain advice from people going through the same thing. This is where private Facebook groups really come into their own, and each country has its own set of freelance journalism communities, such as The Society of Professional Journalists' Freelance Community in the US and A Few Good Hacks in the UK.

Having a profile on several different social media platforms even if you are just a lurker on a couple of them will give you a good sense of what people are talking about and the topics that matter to them, which is perfect fodder for pitches. Instagram can be a great place to lurk and keep track of trending topics, social influencers and relevant businesses.

Facebook

Facebook is a brilliant way to find work opportunities if you join the right journalism, media or freelance groups. Some of these will be hidden and you can only be invited by a member and others will be searchable, but you may have to answer questions to join and demonstrate you are a freelance by linking to your website or articles online. Others will be completely open and anyone can join. The more closed the group, the more useful it tends to be, because commissioning editors will also join as they know it is a reliable place to find experienced journalists rather than a free for all.

Once you have been admitted into a group, it is important that you read and follow the rules, and act professionally. Some groups will encourage you to pitch ideas and will even share contact details of commissioning editors or publication pay rates. If you help out fellow freelances with a comment or guidance for free, then they are more likely to return the favour and even pass work your way.

The best groups will be spaces where commissioning editors ask member to pitch to them on particular topics and supply their direct email address, or where employers post job or project opportunities. There are also plenty of shout outs for case studies, many of which come with a fee attached. Make sure you read the posts carefully, and if an editor is asking freelances to email them with a CV or pitches, make sure you follow these instructions and don't just reply to the post saying you are interested.

If you need to find a specific contact name or email address, the search box on a Facebook group is extremely useful. Groups which have been active for years are a bountiful unofficial archive, so, for example, if you need to find the name and email of the health editor of the *Daily Mail*, chances are you will find it via a search on one of these groups.

If you find the group that works for you, then less is more, so put all your effort into keeping track of posts in this one place rather than trying to keep track of several groups at once.

Twitter

This can be a fruitful place for finding information and sources, but it is also worth keeping abreast of commissioning editors' posts. If they are in need of content, they may post asking for pitches with a link to their pitching guidance. Twitter can be very difficult to keep track of, so it is crucial that you create lists to categorise your feed or use a third-party app like Tweetdeck. You may want to create lists for commissioning editors, news feeds and different specialist topics, so if you are short of time you can always make sure you know what a commissioning editor is doing and thinking about.

Twitter is also the best place for promoting your work, so always make sure you tweet out a link to your story and @mention sources in the article and include relevant #hashtags. This way users are more likely to retweet your original post, and you will gain more followers in relevant fields and build your network. And remember to reciprocate by sharing or commenting on tweets by people you follow particularly if you want to work with them in the future.

LinkedIn

Having a specialism and flagging this up on LinkedIn can be a fantastic way to secure work. Individuals and organisations will search for journalists with experience in niche areas and may approach you directly with a specific project or reporting assignment in mind. It is also another convenient place to find commissioning editors and check on their current job status. By making as many relevant connections as possible, you can build up a network and look out for relevant opportunities.

As with all social media it is important to keep your profile and CV up to date, have your skills endorsed and keep communicating so your account looks fresh and active. LinkedIn now has a newsfeed similar to Facebook so you can post your latest achievements and highlight unusual or interesting aspects of your CV.

Awards and events

Attending events is a great way to network, share tips with other freelances and get your name and face out there. But this needs to be balanced against the time and money involved in attending. If you do go to an event, make sure you are armed with business cards, your social media and website is up to date and you have lots of ideas to hand for a range of publications.

Conferences

Conferences are a productive place to meet other journalists and very often the key speakers will be section editors or upstart founders, whom you can introduce yourself to in the coffee break. As a conversation starter reflect upon something in their talk that sparked your interest and then gradually introduce your own background and expertise before handing them a card. Politely ask if they would be open to you sending them pitches and ask for their contact details or the relevant person to pitch to. Then make sure you send your pitches as soon as possible, that very day even, to demonstrate that you are keen, committed and reliable.

It is also really handy if the conference has a delegate list and Twitter handles (i.e. usernames) available in advance so you can pinpoint people to contact on the day or follow up after the event. The main thing is to come across as interested in their organisation, ideas and ethos and to share stories and experiences rather than directly plugging your own work. It is about setting a lasting impression so they remember you when you send a pitch and are more likely to respond.

Networking events and online communities

Dedicated journalism networking events can also be a great way to make new contacts and gain advice from other experienced freelances. Always make sure you know who the event is likely to attract and look at past attendees to see if they are relevant to your area. You may find that such events are capital city centric and, if you live in another part of the country, are too expensive to travel to. It is always a calculation between getting to the event, the entry fee and the potential contacts you will make, which will help you secure future work. If there is nothing in your area then think about gauging interest, setting up your own network and inviting commissioning editors.

Unions, accreditation bodies and societies such as the National Union of Journalists, Royal Television Society and the Media Society all hold events, so it is worth signing up to their emailing lists for notifications. Different countries will have their own physical and virtual networking groups; for example, the Deadline Club in New York operates as a chapter of the Society of Professional Journalists and hosts workshops and talks whilst also offering scholarships and award programmes. Meanwhile Hostwriter is a Berlin-based collaborative network which enables journalists to connect and communicate online, whilst TravMedia is a global online network connecting journalists and PR professionals across the travel industry.

Festivals

Believe it or not there are now festivals dedicated to journalism. In the UK Byline Festival is an annual three-day event in Sussex with speakers, workshops, live music and camping all dedicated to independent journalism and free speech. Here you can rub shoulders and share a pint with the likes of Hacked Off campaigner and British actor Hugh Grant and learn from journalists with decades of experience. There is also the Radio Festival held each May in London.

Or if you fancy a more grandiose setting there is the International Journalism Festival held in Perugia, Italy, each April, which is the biggest annual media event in Europe and free to attend.

And if you can't find a festival solely for journalism then there are many writers' events, such as the week-long Sydney Writers' Festival and the Melbourne Writers' Festival, which feature internationally renowned journalists alongside novelists, screenwriters and musicians.

Awards

Entering awards can be a fantastic way to meet other journalists, get your name out there and hopefully get some recognition for your work. In addition to the big, prestigious journalism awards including the British Society for Magazine

Editors, Professional Publishers Association, and British Journalism Awards in the UK, the Pulitzers in the US, the European Press Prize or the Walkley Awards in Australia, there are multiple smaller organisations, charities or foundations who honour the best in journalism.

There are separate awards for health, science, travel, sport, music, financial and political journalism. Look out for categories specifically related to freelancing or journalists at the start of their career. Some may not even be solely about journalism; for example, the Association of Independent Professionals and the Self Employed (IPSE) has annual awards for freelances. Some are only open to members or there may be a fee to enter for non-members.

There are even regional awards for journalists and bloggers and most of them come with a cash prize. In the US, there are multiple awards set up to honour the best young journalists, excellent reporting in areas of special interest or in the public interest. And keep an eye out for awards that celebrate certain groups, such as ethnic minorities or women in journalism.

Make sure you carefully read the entry criteria and pick the category most suited to your work. Even if you miss out on the top prize many will publish shortlists or give out commendations or special mentions. And if you get to go to the awards ceremony, it can be a useful place to meet other journalists and put a face to the name as well as find out the people that make up those editorial teams you have been trying to pitch to.

Box 5.2 Author's experience

Early in her career Emma entered *The Daily Telegraph* BASF Science Writer Awards with a piece written especially for the occasion. She did not expect to get anywhere but was pleasantly surprised to receive a highly commended. It gave her the confidence to enter more awards, and she has since been a finalist in both the Medical Journalist Association Awards (MJAs) and Guild of Health Writers Awards as well as a highly commended in the best newcomer category for journalists early in their career at the MJAs. But perhaps more usefully than the awards themselves, it was at one of these ceremonies where she met a fellow reporter who would lead to her first freelance job at BBC News Online where she went on to work for four years. It is unlikely she would have found out any other way that the freelance position on the online health team was up for grabs.

Press cards and access

One issue freelances often procrastinate over is whether they need a press card or verified journalism credentials in order to secure work. The answer is yes, no or maybe. It really depends on the type of stories that you produce and who for.

Staffers, or those employed by a media organisation, will usually receive a press card via their company who will have their own press card scheme or be affiliated to a recognised body. Freelances don't have that option, but there are plenty of alternatives. The advantage of having a press card is that it is a quick and easy way for people to identify you and allow you access whether it be onto the press bench in court or into a private area of a hotel where a celebrity waits to be interviewed. It also helps when contacting sources for information because they can quickly see that you are a bona fide journalist and can be trusted. However, it is quite possible to have a successful freelance journalism career without ever holding a press card.

For a start, gaining access to events or high-profile people is almost always arranged in advance via email and press accreditation, for example, to cover a sports event or attend a festival. When you arrive at the agreed location you can give your name and provide another form of identification, such as a driving licence. Or you may be asked to provide an assignment letter or email from the editor before access is agreed, again without the need for a press card. And if you have your own website and social media links on your email signature it is very easy for someone to verify who you are and who you have experience working for, without the need for a press card.

However, you might find yourself in a situation where a press card would come in really handy particularly if you are working internationally and trying to gain access to restricted areas like conflict zones. Also press cards are often an added bonus included in membership of a union or guild so you need to consider the wider benefits (see Chapter 8). In the UK, the National Union of Journalists offer a press card to freelances as part of membership as does the Pacific Media Workers Guild in the US. In Australia, you can join the Media, Entertainment and Arts Alliance trade union and as part of their Freelance Pro package receive a media access card.

If you do not want to sign up to a union, then press cards are offered by a range of different institutions and usually require you to provide a letter from an editor or commissioning editor confirming that you regularly work for them as a freelance. There is usually a small fee for the card and it will need renewing regularly. The UK Press Card Authority oversees all legitimate press cards in the country, of which there are 19 gatekeepers. Meanwhile the International Federation of Journalists International Press Card has official recognition within the European Union and agencies of the United Nations. However, you must be a member of a union or national association of journalists in order to apply.

But be aware that there are bogus press cards out there that go through no verification process such as the International Press Card by WireNews+Co.

Box 5.3 Case study: Nic Fleming

Nic Fleming is a freelance journalist based in Bristol, UK who specialises in science. Having once worked at both *The Daily Express* and *The Daily Telegraph*, he has been self-employed for the past decade, writing regularly for New Scientist, *The Guardian*, *The Observer*, BBC Future and Nature.

Despite being freelance for 10 years, Nic makes a point of hunting out new publications to write for and says the hardest part is often finding the right contact.

"The most important thing is to pitch to the right person, because if you're not careful you will end up sending it to someone who doesn't have a budget. Really it is just about using those journalistic skills to track people down".

And ideas can come from anywhere, he says. And that means sometimes writing outside your comfort zone or on a topic you have not covered before. Once you understand pitching, the process is pretty much the same whatever the idea or type of publication, he adds.

"A friend of mine who is an architect designed a school that transformed results and behaviour, which is not a topic I would usually write about but the impact the design of the building had on the kids was really interesting and I ended up pitching to *The Times* Education Supplement and got commissioned".

But there is no sure-fire way for hitting the right person and getting a commission that works every time, he points out.

"Social media can be quite useful for finding the right person but sometimes you just need someone to give you a bit of insight. I was recently pitching to BBC Culture and not getting anywhere but I emailed an old contact who had worked in this area and he helped me identify who I needed to send the pitch to".

"Also don't forget to pick up the phone. Ask the news desk how they like to get pitches and when. New Scientist magazine publishes on a Wednesday so Thursday is basically my day to pitch because I know that is when they are going to be looking for new ideas".

Although he suspects it is easier to have a specialty – a unique selling point – Nic works hard to make sure he is not relying on the same publications to commission his work.

"I do keep trying to find new outlets because if you're not careful you can become a bit comfortable and if an editor moves you can suddenly lose a third of your work".

"When I lived in London I would go to a lot more science journalism events and they can be really useful and help remind people that you exist".

"But work can also come from the most surprising sources. A few years ago, I went to a book launch with a friend and his partner had just started some editing work on a section called Nature Careers which I had never heard of. That conversation has led to five years of work through four different editors".

@NicFlem

Getting started

- Make a list of ten news organisations/sections you would like to work for and find the relevant contact details for the commissioning editor in your subject area
- Join three relevant Facebook groups and engage in them for a month before making a decision on whether to continue or not
- Create a basic CV profile on LinkedIn, make connections and pilot it for a month
- Make a list of 20 commissioning editors on Twitter and check their posts daily, try this for a month
- Research and identify three awards you would be eligible to enter each year

6
Providing great copy

OBJECTIVES

In this chapter you will learn:

- The importance of getting and sticking to the brief
- How to achieve the right style and tone
- Why you should fact-check, proofread and meet the word count
- How to source a great case study
- What to do when the words won't flow or things go wrong

You have been commissioned, congratulations! You have now unlocked the next level in freelancing and all you have to do is provide the material you have been asked for. Seems easy right? But there are plenty of aspects to consider and things that can go wrong. In order to get more work in the future and build a good relationship with your commissioning editor, you now need to deliver on that promise of a moving first-person account or hard-hitting investigation. Whatever the idea, whatever the job, there are vital steps to take to ensure you provide exactly what your editor wants.

In this chapter, many of the examples focus on written articles, but the information given below is transferable to a radio or video package. Essentially this is about making sure you provide what is asked of you whether that is written copy, or sound and images, in the style and structure expected by the commissioning editor.

Meeting the brief

Before you start anything, make sure you are clear what you are being asked to do. The type of piece the editor has in mind may differ quite a bit from what you had initially envisaged. And a rushed editor, dashing to an editorial meeting, may not always provide the level of detail you need at first. On the most basic level, make sure you know what type of article you are writing and what section it is destined for. For example, is this news, features, opinion, analysis, first person account, ghost-authored piece (i.e., the journalist is writing up someone else's words as told to them) or backgrounder? Is it for a supplement or specialist section of the publication? This is important to understand from the beginning because it will make a difference about the level of detail required, the style of the writing and how the article is presented.

Equally you need to know how long the piece should be and when you need to file it by. This is all minimum information that should be provided when a piece is commissioned. As the authors can attest, the level of detail that is given at this point can vary widely. Some editors will send standard forms filled out with so much information on what should be included in the article that there is little room for ambiguity. This can even extend to suggested experts or spokespeople to contact and how to format the article before submission. Others will have a far more informal system which will consist of a quick line in an email, saying can I have 1,000 words on x topic by Monday.

The brief you will get will depend on a variety of factors, including the editor's personal preference, the type of publication and whether or not you already have a working relationship with them. Some may not give much information specific to your article but will send general guidelines on how to write for the publication, including details on the style guide, which will outline information such as how to address people quoted in the piece, or their style for numbers and abbreviations.

From the journalist's point of view, any of these approaches is fine as long as you understand what is expected. This is the time to speak up if you are unsure about any aspect of the article. If the editor has been particularly vague, it may be useful to reply with a short outline of what you understand the commission to be, so any potential misunderstanding can be picked up at that point. A detailed brief can make it easier for the journalist to deliver exactly what is being asked and prevent a lot of frustrating back and forth down the line. It also gives you proof of what you were asked to do in case there is any disagreement about whether you met your end of the deal once it has been submitted.

Getting the style and tone right

Pick the top story in the news today and look at how it is presented across different newspapers or online news sites. All publications have their own way of telling a story. A more austere, serious publication may report on an event in a very different way to a publication intended for a younger audience. Headlines, style of intro, length of story and how events are described will all noticeably differ. Now think about how a local news outlet would cover the same story, or one intended for a specialist audience. Take the example of a report that found too many patients had been dying at one hospital. Some outlets would report the facts just as they were in the report, while others would focus on patient stories, putting that emphasis first. A newspaper in the town of the hospital would probably do multiple stories throughout the paper. A medical magazine might focus on the views of doctors or discuss regulation.

Whoever you are writing for or whatever the type of article you have been commissioned to put together, your article needs to match the style and tone of that publication. The only way to really get a handle on what that means in any given circumstance is to do your research. You need to have an understanding of what this publication is about, who their audience is and how they present information. Hopefully you will already have a good idea of this from putting your pitch together. Are they chatty and relaxed in their writing? Or do they prefer a more formal style. What do their intros look like? Straight to the point or perhaps they favour a drop intro. Are their features heavily centred on a case study or is that separate to the main article? What level of understanding do they expect of their readers? If you are writing an economics story for a business magazine, there may be a certain level of basic knowledge that does not need to be spelt out, whereas more detail or context might be needed for a publication aimed at a more general audience.

If the piece is for a series or type of article that runs routinely in, say, a magazine or online section, then there is plenty of guidance right there in the other articles they have done. Read them in order to be clear on the tone. Perhaps this particular type of article is always written in the first person, or as a question and answer piece. It is important to retain your own voice and writing but to do that within the scope you have been set.

Some articles will require more colour and description. It may be that the hardest part of your job in this case is developing the right prose. Setting the scene and taking the reader into the world you are writing about may be vital in a certain style of magazine feature or long-form article. This can involve descriptions of people, places or the location of an interview. Make sure you take note of those details at the time so you can use them in your final piece. This may also involve more background research to take the reader on a journey than would be the case for a straightforward news story.

When writing, it can be useful to get into the mindset of your audience. Why do they care about this story? What will be the most important part of the article to them? Try and keep that in mind when making decisions about what to include, what to discount and how to present the information you have.

Also make sure your final work is presented clearly with components such as headlines, subheadings and any additional fact boxes carefully labelled. Break up paragraphs. Make the editing process as easy as possible for the next person looking over your piece.

Spelling, punctuation and grammar

One of the most important aspects to get right is spelling and punctuation. For some publications the copy will go through a hefty sub-edit before going to press, where errors will be picked up, but for others, especially if they have a small editorial staff, there may be nothing more than a quick read through. Some journalists will be self-publishing their work. Whatever the scenario, it is vital that the copy you submit is not littered with mistakes.

If errors do get published and your byline is on the top of the article, it will look unprofessional. But more importantly, the commissioning editor who receives your copy will notice if you send them sloppy work and will be less inclined to commission you next time. If the publication or website has to spend hours trawling through your copy correcting your mistakes, they will be less likely to offer you more work. It shows you have not put the time and care into the piece and throws doubt on the validity of the information you have included.

If spelling and punctuation is not your strong point (with the best will in the world, we all make mistakes), then employ tools to help you. Do not leave it to others to tidy your copy up. Use the spellchecker on your computer. Double check you have used capital letters and full stops correctly. The same goes for grammar. There are computer programmes and apps that can guide you if you are unsure of the best way to phrase something. It is your responsibility as a journalist to make sure that this part of your work is just as professional as interviews you may carry out or fact-checking or research you may do. There are plenty of re-sources available to help you in this area. Have a dictionary or thesaurus (or make use of the online version) to hand. One guide that many journalists swear by is *Essential English for Journalists, Editors and Writers* by Harold Evans.[1]

Style guides

Many publications will have their own style guide and will be able to send you a copy on request if it is not freely available online. This will outline how they spell certain words, whether they use US or UK English, how to refer to people, use job titles, treat numbers, etc. Some style guides are in common usage, and they are seen as the gold standard, even available as weighty books. This includes, in the UK, the BBC, *Economist*, *The Guardian* and *The Times* style guides or in the US, Associated Press, *New York Times* or *Wall Street Journal* style guides, sometimes also known as stylebooks. Buzzfeed also has a style guide which they have made available online. For some of these there will be quite a bit of crossover and they are worth a look just to get a sense of the sorts of decisions you may be expected to make when writing.

Box 6.1 Author's experience

Emma writes for a variety of specialist medical magazines and websites, and they all have slight differences in key style points, including whether they use single or double quotes, how they use job titles, what hyperlinks or expert comment they expect and even how formal the writing should be. Frequently she will find herself simultaneously writing for a handful of titles and it has the potential to get confusing. To help keep track, she has pinned a notice on the wall behind her computer with the key style points she has to remember for each of her regular publications. This way she can take a quick glance to remind herself without having to open separate style guides or hunt through a load of emails to find her instructions. Mistakes will always creep in from time to time, says Emma, but most editors will happily forgive the odd slip up as long as you have clearly made the effort to stick to the brief you have been given.

If you want to get repeat commissions, you need to do everything you can to hand in neat copy that will require little editing, and that includes sticking to the style of the publication you are writing for. It can take a little extra work, and if you are writing for many different publications at once it can get a little confusing but it is worth doing. Some editors will spell out in the brief what style they expect you to stick to and may automatically send you their style guide especially if you are a new writer for that publication. If that does not happen and you are unsure, use your initiative and find out.

Building the article

It will help immensely if, from the beginning, you are organised and clear about what you need to do in order to write the piece you are working on. Who do you need to interview? What research is needed? What components will make up the article, for example, main body text plus case study plus fact box? Are there any figures, infographics or images that you are responsible for sourcing or compiling? Those aspects can be easy to put to one side and may get forgotten about.

With all this detail in mind, make a plan based on the length of time you have before deadline. Get interviews set up early to account for difficulties getting hold of people or arranging suitable times. This is particularly vital when a piece centres on the opinion, story or statement from one individual. At the same time, start to collect any data, facts or figures you may need. Bear in mind, there is likely to be a certain level of research or information you will need before embarking on interviews.

Even with years of experience, all journalists will sometimes struggle to get an article going. The strongest angle may not be clear at first. Or you have collected so much information you do not know where to start or how on earth you are going to condense it into a meaningful form. Call it writers block, or just a routine part of the job, there are some handy tricks that can help to overcome this problem.

First, avoid staring at a blank piece of paper. Get something, anything down on the page. It could be notes, bullet points, or some key quotes you have collected, but it will get the creative juices flowing. This will likely need some intensive copy editing before filing, but this approach can overcome the mental barrier of worrying there is nothing to say or that it will not be any good. If you have a basic structure in mind or points you absolutely have to cover, write those details in a list at the top to remind you not to miss anything out.

An alternative method is to use your brief as the guide, which works especially well if you have been given a detailed outline. Copy and paste that into a Word document and fill out blanks with quotes, facts and figures. Most journalists would agree that the intro can be the hardest part to write, and it is a perfectly reasonable approach to perfect this last once the other information is down on the page. This avoids the scenario of trying and failing to get a feature started because the perfect opening line escapes you. A similar technique would be to write down a series of subheadings to help you order your thoughts. Once you have a loose shape, it can be helpful to take a break, or do another task, and come back to it with a fresh mind.

Alison Kerr, a freelance journalist based in Glasgow, Scotland, who has written for all the Scottish broadsheets as well as *The Independent* and *The Times* says she tends to mull over possible intros when she is working on other things but if she is struggling will return to her original pitch for the piece. "Often the pitch is sparky and fresh whereas what you might come up with after you've been immersed in research can be a bit tired sounding", she says.

It is important to point out that everyone works differently and it can depend on the type of article you are writing. Some never write in a linear fashion, starting off with the easy bits, background or key quotes, using that as a base to build the rest. Others say they can never really get going until they have a good intro, and once that is in place the rest of the article flows naturally. Whatever your approach, it can be very useful to consider other techniques to keep your writing at its best. Keep an eye on what others are doing. Read widely and when you come across a piece that kept you hooked from start to finish, make a note of how it was structured in order to employ that approach in your own work.

A deadline is a great motivator and can help to focus the mind. If you are one of those people who work best under pressure, it may be useful to set mini-deadlines as you go along, especially if it is a larger project or the final submission date is far away. For other tips on staying motivated, see Chapter 10.

Fact-checking

You need to be able to stand by the information you have included in your piece, not just hazard a guess and hope someone else will check it further down the line. *The Washington Post* ended up having to produce an embarrassing (by their own admission) 579-word correction with 15 bullet points to an article about black families being able to hold onto family farms.[2] You do not want your byline on a piece that ends up with multiple post-publication corrections.

This means asking questions, trusting your sources of information and taking good notes or recordings of phone calls. Depending on how quickly a publication turns your copy around, you could find yourself faced with questions about your article weeks or months down the line and memory alone will not suffice at this time. If your article is complicated with lots of quotes, it can be worth having a separate document with all interviews transcribed so you can refer back to it if an editor has a question about a quote or asks for more. If you can quickly find the right file, because you have a sensible system, this part of the process will be much simpler.

One of the most important things to get right is the name of people who you have included in your article. Check things like spellings, where they are from and job titles. You would be amazed how common it is for the wrong person to be quoted in a piece. Double check unusual spellings of names in case the auto-correct function on your computer has taken over. Make sure you have offered a right of reply where appropriate.

Some publications employ fact-checkers as an extra line of defence against misinformation sneaking into a story. This does not mean that you can take less care relying on someone else to pick up errors. That fact-checker will come to you with questions about sources of evidence, if figures quoted are correct and so on, and you will need to provide those answers. This can also happen as part of the sub-editing process. You may be asked to verify an aspect of your piece, or if you have a quote supporting a certain view. Sloppy journalism will be found out and a piece can quickly fall apart if you do not take care with the facts you are presenting. There may also be a legal stage that a piece has to go through which again can throw up more questions and requests for evidence. More detail on legal issues can be found in Chapter 8.

Word count

When you are commissioned to write a piece, the first thing you need to find out, if you have not already been told, is the word count. How long is this expected to be? And then you need to stick to it. Depending on the type of article, there may be scope for going slightly over the word count. For long features, an extra 100–200 words may be neither here nor there. You will need to apply some common sense. If this is for a print publication and you submit work that is under the word count, the editor may be left with a blank space to fill. For online articles you may be given a bit more flexibility; for example, please file a news story on 'x' topic of between 350 and 400 words, with at least one expert comment.

Some editors may like to have more words to work with in the editing process. But, unless they specify otherwise, it is probably better to stick to the commissioned word count and leave a note saying there is much more information on this aspect or lots of additional quotes from the interviewee if you need more. Otherwise you are essentially handing them way more work because they have to find a way to edit out all the superfluous information.

It can be tempting, when you have spent hours on the phone interviewing several different people for an article you are passionate about to try and get everything in there. As the journalist you want to hang on to your precious words and interviews. Yet handing in 3,000 words when you were commissioned for 1,500 is usually a sure-fire way to irritate the person who has taken a chance on you. It is vital that you are ruthless and cut everything that does not help tell the story or keep it moving. If the copy is vastly over the word count, there are inevitably dense or slow sections that could easily be cut if you cast an objective eye.

One simple way to cut extraneous words is to avoid having lengthy paragraphs of direct quotes that go on and on. Breaking up the best quotes with reported speech, paraphrasing the interviewee's words to create shorter and more fluid prose, will create a far more readable piece in the end.

If you have a lot of factual information that is taking up much needed space, how about using some bullet points or creating a box of key points. As long as that fits with what a publication would usually do, they would likely welcome the creativity. If you're not sure, propose your solution and get the editors approval. Trying to get in everything that you think is important when words are at a premium can be most difficult with your own writing. It is always easier to hack away at articles written by others, but it is an important part of the journalistic process and with practice can become easier.

Finding case studies

Securing a top case study can be essential to providing good copy. This is an identifiable individual who has first-hand experience of the topic you are writing about. A case study is different to a source or quote because their experience is shared in more detail usually with a photograph. A story can also be centred on a single case study, can use a case study as an example in a separate section to the main story or be made up of composite case studies with each individual telling their personal story to the reader or viewer.

Finding a case study that meets the specific requirement of a story can be tricky and time-consuming. It might be someone who bought a horse after getting a divorce or a pharmacist who has a side hustle using their pharmaceutical skills. There are several methods you can take to track down the right person/people, and it is best to exhaust all options rather than choosing one single tactic.

Twitter can be a good place to start particularly using the #journorequest hashtag or tagging relevant companies or public relation firms. But often these requests can get lost amongst thousands of other obscure callouts so you cannot rely on Twitter alone. Niche Facebook groups around the topic you are researching can be a goldmine for case studies particularly if it is an issue people are angry or concerned about. There are also services like FeatureMe, JournoLink and ResponseSource which will put notifications out to their networks on your behalf.

Friends and family are another tactic but one you should tread carefully with because it could backfire if their expectations are difficult to manage or they are unhappy with the final story.

Using public relation officers can be a really effective way to find someone with minimal time and effort of your behalf. If you receive a press release on a topic of interest, tell the PR you can only run it if they can find a suitable case study. Over time you will develop a relationship with this PR and find that they start coming to you with ready-made case studies. Similarly, if you are looking for a case study, reach out to PRs in relevant areas and ask them who they have access to. They will usually bend over backwards to help accommodate your request.

Once you find a case study, make sure they are happy to be identified and photographed before spending time interviewing them. An editor will not accept an anonymous case study unless it is a particularly sensitive topic and this has been agreed in advance. Nor will they accept someone who is unwilling to provide key details such as their full name and a photograph.

Box 6.2 Author's experience

Finding strong case studies is often part of the brief when Lily writes stories for *The Sun*, *Metro*, Moneywise and Vegan Living. In order to make sure she provides exactly what is needed, she asks potential case studies up front if they are happy to be identified and provide a photograph of themselves, before any interview has taken place. In order to find case studies Lily uses social media, particularly niche Facebook groups on the topic she is writing about. For example, on an investigation about doubling ground rents she found case studies on the page National Leasehold Campaign, whilst she found people with vegan pets on a regional vegan and vegetarian Facebook group. And when she receives press releases from PR agencies, she will only consider them if the PR can find a related case study. This saves her time and puts her in a better position when pitching the idea because a case study is already attached.

Hitting problems

However organised and clear you are about the article you are writing, there will be bumps along the way. A case study pulls out at the last minute, the original angle intended for the article is not standing up to scrutiny, or you cannot get anyone to talk on the record about the issue in question. When this happens, do not panic or bury your head, but think practically about what you need to do to solve the problem.

Jaimie Kaffash, editor of UK B2B magazine Pulse, an award-winning online and print publication for general practitioners, stresses that even if he has provided a detailed brief, if a reason to go in a different direction emerges, he welcomes that feedback from a freelance. "I would much rather have a 10-minute conversation about it than something going wrong further down the line when it's harder to solve", he says.

There are times when you have rung all the right people and they do not agree with the premise of the article or have nothing to say on the topic. As long as you have not given up at the first hurdle and made a reasonable effort, an editor will usually understand. Have the conversation early to avoid that awkward scenario on deadline day when you have nothing to deliver. Being honest and asking what leeway there is or whether an alternative article is possible is by far the better solution. It will not be the first time this has happened to the editor, and they may have been in this situation themselves.

Yet when you do hit a barrier or a story is not working out as expected, the best way to get in the editor's good books and ensure repeat commissions is to work out an alternative direction or way to get the article done. Busy editors will truly welcome anything you can do to ease their workload. "One thing that I see more and more with young journalists is they don't think of ways around problems. As an editor I want you to be proactive and think of solutions", says Jaimie.

Deadlines

Hitting a deadline is important and turning in copy early, if possible, will definitely get you in the good books. For some publications, particularly magazines or pull out sections of newspapers, there will be some leeway built into a deadline and if you need that one extra interview to really make the piece stand out, have that conversation with the editor. Most of the time, where possible, they have built in unforeseen circumstances to the deadline they gave you. That said, never take it upon yourself to decide a deadline is flexible.

The editor may well be up against their own deadline and be relying on your copy to fill a last-minute space. And if your article is a planned front-page exclusive in tomorrow's edition, that deadline will be non-negotiable. Apart from anything else, by accepting the commission, you have entered into a contract with the editor. Fulfilling your end of the bargain on or ahead of time is what separates a good from a mediocre freelance. If you think a deadline is unachievable at the point you received the commission (e.g., 24 hours for an in-depth investigation) do not be afraid to ask at that point whether more time can be given.

Technology fails

At some point, technological disaster will get the better of most journalists. Imagine the scene, you have just completed 1,000 perfect words when all of a sudden the computer crashes and that well-crafted feature disappears, never to be seen again. It is the stuff of Sunday night anxiety dreams. There are journalists who only work in Google docs or Dropbox for this very reason. Whatever programme you use, make sure you save as you go along and any autosave function is turned on, working and can be trusted. Get into the habit of naming and saving a document as soon as you open it. Backing up your work to a cloud can also prove useful should the device you are working on suddenly fail. Spilling a full glass of cola or cup of coffee onto a laptop can be its death and you need access to your work should that hard-drive be unrecoverable.

Some journalists use shorthand to take notes; others rely solely on audio recordings of interviews, or a mix of the two. You do need to be aware that the more you rely on technology, the bigger chance a glitch can come along to ruin your day. For long interviews, or those where a recording of the interview may be useful for legal purposes, always check and double check your recording device is on and working. It is not unknown for journalists to use two devices to record a conversation. Then once the interview is complete make sure you save the recording immediately. You will not have to search far to find a journalist who has sheepishly had to ask to redo an interview because they have got back to their desk to find an inaudible recording or corrupted file.

One of the most recently available tools to ease the boring admin work of journalists is the automated transcription app (see Chapter 10). It is worth noting here though that should you use this option to ease your workload, you will still need to check that the final transcription makes sense and embarrassing errors have not crept in.

Box 6.3 Case study: Jennifer Karchmer

Jennifer Karchmer started out in the 1990s working at local radio stations, before going mainstream working for the Associated Press and CNN in New York.

Having worked as an independent journalist and copy editor since 2006, she is currently focused on reporting on Freedom of the Press and reporter safety in addition to offering a mentor service for aspiring journalists.

Having a clear idea of who you are writing for is a key aspect of delivering good copy, she says. It is a skill that also means you can write the same story – with different angles – for several outlets.

"Part of any reporting is getting familiar with your audience and that is going to dictate your lede [or intro], the organisation of the story, all of it. One of the ways I recommend people do that is to talk your story out before you sit down and write it. It will help you develop the mind-set of having an audience member in your head".

And getting a clear brief at the start is half the battle, she adds.

"If it's a freelance assignment you need them to be as clear as possible, get the guidance before writing something then they can advise you if that is not the angle they are looking for or they've already covered a certain aspect. Don't be shy in double checking".

One thing that you don't get too much guidance on at university, she says, is how to be organised to ensure that you can back up everything you have written.

"I am a notebook-based writer but it is essential that you come up with an organisational method that works for you. Ignorance is not bliss. It is your responsibility to have some sort of system in place so you can be accountable to what you have written".

This will differ depending on the type of work you are doing, but Jennifer's approach is to have a document for each article called notes where all details and quotes from interviews can be recorded as well as any research with clear annotation on where information has come from.

"I can then highlight things I think I will want to use, then in a new file that I call draft I can start transferring my notes over. You are only as good as your notes. When you are asked questions, you need to show you have credibility as a journalist and be able to find those answers".

Ultimately, she says the freelance must take responsibility for the quality of their work and good copy editing and good writing go hand in hand. It is no longer the case that you can rely on newsrooms or editorial teams to have all of the resources to do this for you.

"Even a silly typo, over time, can erode the credibility of the publication or outlet and if you have spelled something wrong, people are not going to take your work seriously. Proofreading is one of the most important steps you need to take in all of your work".

jenniferkarchmer.com
@journalist_jk

Getting started

- Check you have been given and understand the brief for the article you are writing
- Identify the key components you need to complete before submission
- Create a list of all potential sources of quotes and information
- Make sure any technology you are using is working and you are saving as you go
- Get any case studies in place and have a back-up plan should problems arise

Notes

1 Evans, H. 2000 *Essential English for Journalists, Editors and Writers* (2nd revised edition). London: Pimlico.
2 Smith, S. 2019 "Washington Post adds 15 corrections to story on black families & southern farmland" iMediaEthics www.imediaethics.org/washington-post-adds-15-corrections-to-story-on-black-families-southern-farmland/.

7
Finances

OBJECTIVES

In this chapter you will learn:

- How to set yourself up as self-employed
- What rates you should be paid and how to negotiate more
- How to invoice, chase payment, keep records and file a tax return
- Other factors to consider including maternity and paternity leave and pensions
- Whether you should ever work for free

One of the most daunting aspects of being a freelance journalist is getting to grips with being self-employed. Whether freelancing is your first taste of working life or you have only ever been in a job where all your tax was calculated at source, you are likely to have lots of questions about how it works. Even for experienced freelance journalists, finances can be hard to manage. One survey of journalists carried out by the Press Gazette found that freelances were happier than employed journalists with 94.2% saying they enjoyed their job compared with 87.6% of employed journalists. But pay was one of the most prominent concerns with freelance respondents citing falling rates and exploitative and unfair practices.[1]

A big part of combatting the potential precariousness of freelance income is to know your rights and to ensure you are paid swiftly at industry standard rates (or above) for work you have done. The authors know full well that this process is not always a smooth one. Having constant work but large fluctuations in actual income landing in your bank account is a very common complaint from freelance journalists. This is made even more problematic when you take into account the creeping and infuriating practice of payment on publication where you have delivered the goods but an editor is sitting on your work and will not pay until publication or broadcast. Even worse, in some cases, they never use it and offer a kill fee instead. This can leave journalists waiting months or even years before they receive payment for work they have done and then only ending up with 50%.

It paints a somewhat depressing picture of a career where you have more freedom and flexibility but at the expense of a certain amount of financial control. Yet there are many things the freelance can do to mitigate these issues. Knowledge is power, and the first key step is to educate yourself on your rights, what information needs to be agreed at the start of a commission and how to be organised so that you receive the money you are owed and avoid being suddenly hit with an unexpected tax bill.

Self-employment

Wherever in the world you are working as a freelance, it is fairly likely that you will need to register as self-employed with the relevant authority or authorities. This means that you are responsible for declaring your income and paying your own tax. The rules on how this works differ between countries. However, in many places, including the US, UK, Canada, Germany and Australia, you must register as self-employed if you are earning income from providing goods or services and this requires you to set up a business.

One thing to bear in mind before taking this step is to consider whether you are truly freelance. If you declare yourself as self-employed but in reality only work for one company, the tax authority may start to ask questions to assess whether a company is trying to bypass their obligations to their employees, for example, around holiday, maternity and pension rights. With increased scrutiny on the legitimacy of some zero-hour contracts, employment rules are changing all the time, and you will need to check how your personal circumstances match up to the most recent requirements. Generally speaking, a self-employed person would control the what, where, when and how they do their work and they hold the financial risk. For example, they can make not only a profit but also a loss, they provide the equipment, such as a computer, and they are able to work for multiple clients.

As a self-employed person it is, in theory, much easier to move to a new country and is sometimes encouraged with tax breaks, etc., for those who show they can support themselves. But this will still mean learning a whole new set of requirements for the country you move to, some more stringent than others. Do not assume the set up will be the same as the one you are used to. A case in point is in France where, in 2009, new rules were introduced to simplify tax payments for small businesses or self-employed workers with a micro-entreprise category for those earning under around €33,000. Under these rules, you pay a fixed percentage in tax based on your income. However, freelance workers who earn more than this or who want to avoid tax on expenses would instead need to set themselves up as a sole trader or 'Entreprise Individuelle'.

Setting up a business may sound a little overwhelming, but in reality it is fairly simple and there are several options to choose from. The most straightforward route, especially for the freelance journalist just starting out, is to set up as a sole trader, also known as a sole proprietor. As a sole trader you have full control of your business, but it also means you are legally responsible for any debts and tax or other liabilities you may incur (see Chapter 8). Generally speaking, although again this will vary between countries, there is much less paperwork and reporting requirements for sole traders than other types of businesses.

In the UK, you need to set up as a sole trader once you have earned more than £1,000 from self-employment in a year. You can be both employed and self-employed. So, if you have a part-time (or full-time) job, you will also need to register as self-employed if you have additional income on top of those earnings. The first job in registering your sole trader business is to choose a name. This can be your own name as the authors both chose to do when registering their respective businesses. Or you can be more creative as long as you do not break the rules around not being offensive or the same as a registered trademark. This is then the name that you need to put on any official paperwork such as invoices that you send out for payment.

Another potential option for a freelance journalist is to set up a limited company which can be more tax-efficient arrangement, but the administration is more complex and is likely to require advice from an accountant. As a limited company, you are still in charge of your business as the company director, but it is a legally separate entity with separate finances. In the UK, setting up a limited company means registering with Companies House, submitting several documents agreeing how the company will be run and completing an annual return with details about your business. Tax returns also become more complicated, and you will need to keep detailed financial records. It is also mandatory to register a company for VAT (sales) tax once you hit the threshold of £85,000, which means you have to charge VAT on goods or services but you can also claim VAT back. Some companies opt to register for VAT even if they are below the threshold.

Rates

Knowing what rates to accept or charge for your work may feel like a bit of a stab in the dark at first. But there are plenty of guides out there on what you should expect to be paid, and it is important that you do not fall into the trap of underselling yourself. It is far from an exact science. The same journalist working for the same publication can be offered two completely different rates from two commissioning editors working on different sections. Even when you think you have a handle on it, it is not uncommon for journalists to find others have been offered higher rates of pay for the same work.

A rate should always be agreed when accepting a commission alongside details of what you will be expected to deliver. Most articles will be paid per word or a flat fee for a certain number of words. Or you may be paid a project rate for a bigger piece of work, such as an investigation or broadcast, video or audio package. The rate can vary depending on several factors including whether it is for online or print or both and what is included in the brief. The same outlet can offer one rate for news stories and a second rate for complex features. Articles in supplements can attract a different rate again. Alternatively, you may be paid a day rate for doing a shift – be it as a journalist, editor, producer or broadcaster.

There are several key resources to help guide you in either setting a rate or deciding if a rate you have been offered is fair including the National Union of Journalists (NUJ), Journo Resources and The Freelancer Rates Database, and some information is available from the Society of Professional Journalists freelance resources page. The NUJ, while noting that rates can vary widely, suggest the following as a minimum:[2]

- Online writing – £160 for a reporting day shift, £275 per £1,000 words or £350 per 1,000 words for intense research or background
- National print newspapers – £185 for a reporting day shift or £200 a day on supplements, at least £1,000 for page lead, exclusive or large spread, from £500 per 1,000 for a feature and £430 per 1,000 words for news
- Large circulation glossy magazines – £240 per reporting day shift, £750 per 1,000 words or as much as £2,200 per 1,000 for prestige US magazines
- Trade magazines – £165 for a day shift, £335 per £1,000 words
- Broadcast – from £139 for a BBC reporting or producing shift through to £1,400 for a three-minute television feature shot and edited on own equipment

These are just a few examples and the NUJ have an incredibly detailed breakdown of what rates should be expected based on the work done, covering everything from a blog post or review to books, from photography to editing to appearing on a podcast. This does not mean that this is the rate that you will definitely be offered, but it at least helps to have an idea of the industry standard. There is wide variation and not just in the UK – in the US rates per word can vary from $0.03 to upwards of $3 per word. Some freelances are taking steps to be more transparent about the rates they are paid (see Chapter 12) to try to prevent exploitation as well as calling out poor rates or those who expect journalists to work for free.

One way to determine if you are being paid a fair rate is to calculate how long it will take you to write or produce the work in question. For example, if a piece requires a lot of in-depth research or numerous interviews, it will take much longer than a first-person article. A standard word rate may not be appropriate for an article that required days, weeks or even months of investigation. And some of the best, independent journalism can take a huge amount of work to put together. The authors both have experience of negotiating rates that take into account additional time or expertise required for a piece or project. Rates should also take into account that the freelance is not working 24/7, 365 days a year, and has to provide their own equipment, pay tax and pension and so on.

Negotiation

Negotiation is a key part of accepting a commission, and it should be at the forefront of your mind whether the commissioning editor has offered a fee or asked for your rate. Some rates will be set in stone and the publication or outlet will have a standard offer, for example, per 1,000 words or per five-minute piece. That said, if you have worked for them for a while without the rate increasing or are providing regular pieces, it is perfectly reasonable to ask for a pay rise as you would in a salaried position.

Box 7.1 Author's experience

As is often the case, Lily is paid in a variety of ways by different publishers. Some pay a set rate per word which is non-negotiable, whilst others rely on editors to negotiate a fee per story. Over the years Lily has learnt how to negotiate better rates by becoming bolder with editors. Recently, she was offered £150 from a national news website for a story she sensed would go viral. She politely challenged the commissioning editor explaining that she was usually paid £200 to £300 by other sections of the same website and expected the same for this story. In the end she secured £225 for herself, £150 for the case study and an additional 18 hours to write the story. Now whenever she is offered a one-off fee for a story or photograph, she always negotiates higher as she realises the figure given is the lowest – but not final – offer. She always has a figure in mind that she is happy with but goes in slightly higher until a compromise in the middle is made and everyone feels they have a good deal. Treat fee negotiations like haggling at the market and you won't go far wrong, she says.

From a bargaining point of view, it is generally easiest to ask what the client pays and work from there. It can be quite a heart-sink moment to state a rate which is all too quickly accepted, making it very apparent they would have paid more. The freelance needs to take into account the budget the organisation is likely to have, how much bargaining power you have (e.g., is the work based on an exclusive interview that a rival publication would snap up) and how much work is required. In addition, there may be room for manoeuvre over certain aspects of the article such as payment for providing photos or travel expenses. You may also need to consider negotiation over fees for extra uses, such as online or overseas editions of the publication (see Chapter 8).

Try to avoid being rushed into a decision over accepting a fee. Taking a step back to plan whether the money on offer is reasonable for the work under discussion is a sensible approach, as is giving yourself time to check if possible what others have been paid by the same outlet. Depending on the type of work, the rate the freelance is offered may also include any payments to case studies who have taken part. When negotiating a higher rate, remember if you don't ask you don't get, and a client is unlikely to open with the most they would be willing to pay. Be polite but firm and provide clear reasons for why you believe a higher rate is required. If they say no, you then need to decide if the rate on the table is acceptable. The freelance should always keep in mind that they can reject the commission if there is inadequate compensation.

Negotiation is not just about rate but payment terms. Standard practice is discussed below, but if you are working on a long project, then requesting a series of payments, for example, broken into monthly payments or a third up front, a third halfway through and a final payment, would be a good approach.

Invoicing

It may not be the most enjoyable part of the job, but in order to keep a steady stream of income into your bank account, it is vital to keep on top of invoicing. There are several different ways in which companies process payments to freelances. Some may not need an invoice instead operating an automatic self-billing system. Others will have specific documentation to supply or online systems to fill in instead of a standard invoice. The onus is on the journalist to find out this information – never assume this will be forthcoming. In addition, the first time you work for a publication or outlet, they may need to set you up on the system before payment, which can be an onerous process involving multiple forms and proof of identification. In theory, this should only be needed once, that is, until they change systems or lose your details.

First, you need to set up a system to record what payment was agreed when you accepted the commission, the date that this was filed, the date the invoice or payment details were sent and the expected date of payment. The authors include this information in their general commissions spreadsheet, so any outstanding payments can be spotted with a quick glance.

There are various invoice templates to download online, but it is a simple matter to create your own. In a Word or Google doc, list your details at the top including your name or company name, address, email and phone number. Include a space for the commissioning editor's name, company and address. Every invoice needs to clearly include the date and an invoice number. There is no one format for invoice numbering, but you will need to set up a system and remain consistent in order to track payments, for example, your initials/year-invoice number/company. This would look something like JS19-08Guardian. Underneath, the work should be listed with a title, the agreed rate, any agreed expenses or extras and a total. For payment directly into a bank account, for example, through the UK BACS system, bank details will also need to be included. For international payments, this may need to include the International Bank Account Number (IBAN) and the Bank Identifier Code (BIC) or SWIFT code of the bank to make sure the money goes to the right place (see below for more detail on cross-border payments).

Box 7.2 Template: Invoice

INVOICE

[insert your name here]
Freelance Journalist

123 Cherry Tree Lane London,
SW3 1AB
me@freelancejournalist.com
[insert phone number]

[Name of commissioning editor]

[Company name]

[Address]

[email]

Invoice number: JS19-08 Guardian

Invoice date: 20th September 2019

Description of work	Agreed Rate	Total
1,200-wd feature on freelance rights	£350 per 1,000	£420
350-wd news story	25p per word	£87.50

TOTAL	£507.50

Please pay: [insert name]

[insert bank details including account number and sort code]

This payment is due 30 days from date of invoice unless agreed otherwise

We understand and will exercise our statutory right to interest and compensation for debt recovery costs under the late payment legislation if we are not paid according to agreed credit terms.

Before sending the invoice, make sure you have included all the details the client requires. For example, some may need to set up a purchase order number that has to be on the invoice. Or there may be a particular address needed for invoicing purposes. Finding out the requirements at this point can save a lot of headaches down the line. It is preferable to save and send the invoice as a PDF file.

In the first instance, unless informed otherwise, send the invoice to the editor who commissioned you for the work, as they are likely to be the ones processing it initially. You may be asked to deal directly with an accounts department, but the commissioner should provide this information.

On the bottom of the invoice, it is important to include payment terms – that is the period by which you expect this payment to land in your bank account or for a cheque to appear. For example: *This payment is due 30 days from date of invoice unless agreed otherwise.* It is always better to spell this out rather than use terms such as NET30 which may be misunderstood. Some freelances also choose to include information about fees for late payment on invoices. But you do not have to include this detail in order to charge late fees. A late payment directive put in place in the EU in 2011 included an automatic entitlement to interest for late payment and €40 minimum compensation.[3]

In the UK, by law a payment is considered late 30 days after the invoice is sent unless previously agreed otherwise. After this you have the right to charge statutory interest of 8% plus the Bank of England base rate for business-to-business transactions.[4] Increasingly, freelances growing frustrated with poor payment practices are applying interest to invoices which have not been paid. The government suggests the following wording for invoices:[5]

> We understand and will exercise our statutory right to interest and compensation for debt recovery costs under the late payment legislation if we are not paid according to agreed credit terms.

International payment

Freelances are not tied to working in the country they live, which means they have to get to grips with international payments. While it might seem the most sensible and safest option to use your bank account for all payments, this route can be the most expensive, thanks to a myriad of hidden fees. The authors both have experience of being paid by companies based overseas and there are a number of ways this can be done.

If you opt to be paid through your bank account, you need to be aware that there are additional fees that may be added for varying reasons and these can be far from transparent. In addition, the currency rate may not be the best one on offer or even made clear until after the process is complete. The EU is bringing in legislation to require online and card providers to be up front about fees and rates associated with sending money but that will only apply within the EU.

PayPal and TransferWise are two of the most popular alternatives at the moment for making overseas payments, and the authors have used both in order to avoid incurring any fees. As the biggest online payment system, PayPal operates in more countries and currencies than others such as TransferWise and is well known. However, as some freelances will attest there can still be fees for currency conversion and accepting money from abroad. TransferWise is becoming increasingly popular in the UK because it bypasses expensive international payments and claims to be much cheaper than High Street banks. XE, Moneygram and Western Union are other potential alternatives for making international payments.

Late payment

Freelance journalists tend to accept a certain amount of late payment with a world-weary sigh. Some are starting to fight back (see Chapter 12). The authors would like to see more freelances taking a strict approach on timely payment, especially those experienced journalists with more clout who can set expectations for the profession. Late payments are not accepted in many other trades and professions who would have no qualms about putting penalties in place for those who have not stuck to their end of the deal. Dealing with late payments can be a real financial and emotional burden. There are bills to pay, and it can take up huge amounts of time for a freelance who does not have the administrative staff to manage this side of the business.

The clock starts ticking the moment an invoice is delivered (or their forms are submitted if they have a particular process to follow), which is the main reason it is important to keep on top of the invoicing process and do everything at your end on time. In the UK, penalties and compensation are enforceable by law, apply to businesses of any size and kick in after that 30-day window. Automatic compensation of £40 can be applied to late payments up to £1,000, £70 on payments between £1,000 and £9,999 or £100 over that. Interest of 8% plus the Bank of England Base Rate can be applied on top. Helpfully the NUJ have an online calculator which works out the penalty as does the EU. In the US, the principle is the same in that you are within your rights as a business to apply late fees as long as the client agreed to your terms but states have different laws on how much interest can be applied.

You will only know if a payment is late if you keep accurate and up-to-date records. After 30 days you are within your rights to apply compensation. But you may feel a more reasonable step is to chase the payment with a call or email to the editor or the relevant accounts department (at this stage, the authors would always recommend getting hold of the contact details of the accounts department to keep this process separate from any relationship you may have built up with a commissioning editor) to remind them of their responsibilities, and ask for a date by which the payment will be made. If nothing has materialised in a reasonable period, for example, two weeks, then it is time to send another invoice with late fees applied.

For companies who are refusing to pay or even acknowledge your demands for payment, a legal letter may be the next step. Most businesses will pay up if you write an official letter setting out your intention to take legal action. This does not have to be complicated, just stating how much is owed, attaching copies of the outstanding invoices and informing the client that unless payment is made within seven days, legal action to recover the debt will be taken. It is a way of putting them on notice. In the UK, the NUJ will provide this service for freelance members who are struggling to recoup a payment. The next step after this is court, but it is worth taking legal advice before starting this process as it may be prohibitively expensive depending on the case or amount owed.

If the company who owes you money goes bust, you may never be paid and of course you may have no prior warning this is going to happen. One way to protect yourself is to never let a client run up large bills. If an organisation is failing to pay repeatedly (as happened before the collapse of The Pool in the UK), it can be a real warning sign, and if the business goes under you may never get what is owed to you. Do not keep working for an organisation that is not paying you in the hope they will eventually get their act together. It is good business savvy to always check out who you are working for. If it is a publication or organisation you have never heard of, do your due diligence and, as you always should, make your payment terms clear at the outset.

Payment on publication

Imagine how infuriating it must be to be commissioned to do a piece of work, which you deliver to time as per the brief you were given, only to be waiting for payment a year down the line. Unfortunately, most freelance journalists have had this sort of experience at some point. Sometimes due to incompetence or a company going bust but more often than not, the delay is down to a practice called payment on publication. It means that the freelance is not paid at the point they deliver the work but only once that work is published or broadcast. And that date is something that the freelance has no control over. The record for the authors is 14 months for a feature for a national newspaper.

Payment on publication can be most problematic when working for monthly magazines who may drop an intended feature in favour of something more time-sensitive. Most of the time it will get used eventually, but it can be months down the line. And while the journalist is waiting for an invoice to be paid because their article is nothing more than a headline on a commissioning list, any other professions who may have been used in putting it together, such as photographers or make-up artists sent to make case studies camera ready, are likely to have been paid. In 2018, the practice received widespread condemnation after Eugene Costello wrote in Press Gazette about how payment on publication was making life a misery for freelance journalists.[6] Then, in 2019, French and British journalists joined forces to demand the end of payment on publication.[7] The #fairpayforfreelancers campaign launched on Twitter in February 2019 included an open letter[8] calling for pay reform, which at the date of writing this book had more than 1,000 signatories (Chapter 12).

Those who have worked as freelances for decades say that this practice is becoming more commonplace. There is no getting around the fact there is a power imbalance at the heart of it – that potential threat of 'if you kick up a fuss we will give the work to someone else'. The only way to counter this is to set your terms at the start of the commission. Some journalists refuse to write for anyone who pays only on publication and stringently set out their terms in advance. Others say this is unrealistic as the practice is so pervasive. There is less room for argument if a freelance sets out their terms on their website or in fine print at the bottom of pitching emails, for example, that they expect payment within 30 days of supply. And wherever possible ask for confirmation of those terms in an email when accepting the commission.

Kill fee

If a publication decides not to run a piece they have commissioned, the freelance may be offered a kill fee, most likely to be 50% of the original agreed fee. Again, this is difficult territory for the freelance who is attempting to both keep a potential future source of income happy and protect their rights and income. Whether or not you accept the 50% can depend on a variety of factors, including the likelihood of placing the piece elsewhere and if you have to pay case studies, etc., out of that money.

Do not be afraid to negotiate when offered a kill fee; in fact, the authors would advise this should be your first response. And again, refer back to the terms set at the time of commission (see Chapter 8). Bear in mind that in the UK, the NUJ recommend that any work delivered on time and to specification should be paid in full. This principle also stands for any shifts you have agreed to do which have been cancelled at short notice (within a week). If you have turned down other work to fit that shift in you are perfectly within your rights to charge the full day rate. Again, the approach needs to be one of professional negotiation. They may be able to offer you different work.

Tax returns and record keeping

As a self-employed journalist, whether a sole trader or limited company, you will be required to keep a record of your income and file a tax return at least once a year. It is possible to do this yourself, especially if your income and expenses are a straightforward affair, or you can hire an accountant to do it on your behalf. But whichever route you take, planning and organisation are essential.

Box 7.3 Template: Commission and payment

Month	Client	Commission	Deadline	Notes	Word count	Agreed rate	Total	Invoice number	Date invoiced	Date paid
September	Guardian	Feature on freelance rights	16/9/2019	Needs at least two case studies	1,200	£350 per 1,000	£420	JS19-08	20-09-2019	
September	Guardian	News story on freelance campaign launch	17/9/2019		350	25p a word	£87.50	JS19-08	20-09-2019	
September	Moneywise	Making your side hustle pay	30/9/2019	Five examples needed	1500	30p a word	£450	JS19-09		
							£975.70			

Step one is to have a document which records all your income. As already mentioned in this chapter, this can be one spreadsheet which lists all commissions, invoices and dates. At the end of the tax year, calculating your gross income is a simple task of adding up the invoices paid as listed in this spreadsheet. It is vital you do this as you go along. Otherwise you will hit two problems, first that people may not have paid you and you have not realised and second that come the end of the tax year you waste hours and hours trawling through emails and invoices trying to work out how much you actually earned.

Step two is to plan for the fact that at some point down the line you will be expected to pay tax on your earnings and you will need to put some money aside for that eventuality. How much you need to put aside will depend on local tax rates in the country, which may also depend on how much you have earned that year if a progressive tax system is in place (i.e., taxation rates are higher for higher earners). As a rule of thumb, it is always better to save more than you think you will need so you are not caught out by any unexpected bills. By tracking income as you go along, you will have a rough idea of how much you should have been holding back rather than getting a big shock when it comes time to do that tax return.

It can be useful to open a separate bank account to keep your freelance income and expenses separate from your personal finances. Again, this will enable you to keep better track of the financial side of your freelance work and will aid you in your record keeping. It can be a business account (for some types of business this will be a legal requirement), which may have some benefits but may also come with additional fees, but does not have to be and a current or personal account may be suitable for a sole trader keen to avoid the expense of a business account. Some banks offer accounts for sole traders, and it is important to shop around to find the best option for your circumstances.

In the UK, freelances in their first year are often caught out by a system called payment on account, where you are expected to pay 50% of your tax bill for your second year up front, once your tax bill is more than £1,000. This is calculated on the previous years' earnings, and if you expect this to drop dramatically, you can apply to reduce the payment on account. For example, if you owe £2,000 in taxes for the first year, you will be expected to pay £1,000 on top of that towards the next year's tax bill (this is usually paid in July). This will reduce the amount you will be required to pay in year two as you have already contributed but can be a bit of a hit initially.

Other systems will apply in different countries; for example, in the US a sole proprietor would calculate their business income tax through filling out a Schedule C form before adding this to their personal tax form which would take into account any employment earnings that had already been taxed and any deductions they were eligible for. Calculations also take into account self-employment tax which covers social security and Medicare, and estimated tax payments must be paid on a quarterly basis.

It is common for tax authorities to have tax calculators available online so you can work out roughly how much you would be paying based on your income or your estimated income. Some back of the envelope maths taking into account the basic rate – say 20% taxation – would also help guide you in knowing the sort of tax bill you may get. However, this would not take into account any deductions or tax breaks an individual may be eligible for or any additional business taxes a self-employed person may be expected to pay.

Box 7.4 Author's experience

After too many years finding it hard to properly track payments into her bank account, Emma set up a separate account just for freelance income and expenses. After researching her options, she decided that as a sole trader she did not need a dedicated business account which tends to come with additional charges but opened an extra personal account which had several important features, including a low rate overdraft and associated credit card. It is now much easier for Emma to track when payments have been made and keep money aside for tax bills. She also uses this account for expenses such as her website. Emma tends to move a proportion of her income into her regular account for paying bills and so on. At the same time, having got frustrated with late payments, she had an overhaul of her administrative processes, so she can quickly flag when an invoice has not been paid on time. Once a week she sets time aside to manage invoicing and payment, which she does in an Excel spreadsheet, to ensure as smooth a cash flow as possible and updates all her records as she goes to avoid forgetting about any expenses she can claim.

The tax rules and how you declare income will differ depending on what sort of business you are. As already mentioned, if you choose to become a limited company, the paperwork is more onerous and that includes tax returns because you will have had the option to pay yourself a regular salary from the company accounts or take some money out as a dividend, all of which has tax implications and is likely to require an accountant. Likewise, in the UK, if your turnover is more than £85,000 a year you must register for VAT (sales tax), which means you can charge 20% VAT on your invoices but for journalism means paying a reduced rate back to the treasury.

In addition to being organised to make sure you have sufficient detail to file your tax return and have enough funds to pay the resulting bill, you need to ensure you get all paperwork in on time. If you miss deadlines for filing tax returns or paying what you owe you are likely to get stung with a fine or interest on late payments. The deadline for filing a self-assessment tax form online in the UK is the 31st January for the previous tax year which ended on the 5th April. You will then receive a bill made up of income tax, Class 2 and Class 4 National Insurance contributions (essentially state pension contributions) and any payment on account readjustments. As boring as filing tax forms can be, getting them in early avoids any unexpected bills and saves stress from trying to get it done last minute.

Expenses

Having a record of your income is just one part of filing a tax return. As a self-employed freelance, it is likely that you will also be able to deduct certain expenses from that income before the tax is calculated. What is allowed as an expense varies between tax authorities or countries, but it can include travel, office equipment, cost of phone calls and internet, promotion or marketing material, which would include things like website fees and the cost of running premises or an office. In the UK, the definition of a business expense is that it is 'wholly, necessarily and exclusively' incurred in the running of the business. So, if you earned £30,000 in total but had £2,000 of allowable expenses, the tax you owed would be calculated on your 'profit' of £28,000. That is, of course, taking into account the personal allowance (currently set at £12,500) on which you pay no tax at all.

It can be complicated, for example, if you have a phone that you use for both personal and business reasons, you can only deduct as expenses the proportion you use for business. For working from home there are two ways you can work out the expense for UK tax purposes. You can calculate what proportion of your home you use as an office and how many days you work from home and claim that proportion of your electricity, heating, internet and phone use. Or you can use a simplified expenses approach where someone working more than 101 hours a month from home can claim £26 in expenses per month.

All expenses claimed need to be supported by receipts or documentation. You will need to keep accurate records and ensure you have proof to back it up including bank statements. If you buy something that is classed as a business expense, for example, a printer or printer cartridges, you will need to keep the receipt. Likewise, for trains, buses or taxis taken for work-related journeys. If you use a car, you will need to record mileage for work-based journeys so you can claim the travel expenses. Training courses may also be an allowable expense so again careful records are required. You will not be able to conjure all this from memory at the point of filing a tax return or when it comes time to send all your records to your accountant. It is also advisable to keep everything that may be relevant even if it turns out later down the line it is not an allowable expense.

To find out what is an allowable expense for your business or circumstances, you will need to refer to guidance published by the tax authority to which you file your return. In the US, 'ordinary and necessary expenses' are set out under Internal Revenue Code section 162(a). Likewise, the Australian Tax Authority lists deductions that you can claim again stipulating this must be for business purposes and not private use. Note that there may be a distinction between capital expenses such as a computer which will be used over a long period of time and operating expenses which occur in the year you use them.

As with income, expenses can be recorded in a simple spreadsheet. If you want some extra help in this department, there are many apps and cloud-based accounting software packages available. Quickbooks is one of the most well known, but there are many other options, including Xero, EasyBooks and Sage. This option will come with a fee, but this in itself is most likely tax deductible (as is hiring an accountant). As long as you have accurate records, the way you do it is up to you and how comfortable you feel using the various options. It is worth bearing in mind that if you do choose to use an accountant, keeping an up-to-date accurate record of your income and expenses will help keep that bill down by making their job easier.

Maternity and paternity leave

For the self-employed navigating complex maternity and paternity leave, laws and entitlements can prove tricky when there is no human resources department or company policy to help guide you. Of course the amount of leave you take when pregnant or having a baby is entirely up to you when you are freelance, but what you will have to balance is how much time you can afford to take off, depending on what maternity benefits you may be entitled to, or if there is any option for keeping a certain amount of work going. Many countries do make provision for maternity and sometimes paternity pay for self-employed parents.

The rules around maternity and paternity leave vary widely throughout the world. Even in the EU where the law sets 14-weeks minimum maternity leave of which two weeks are mandatory, there is huge variation in what countries

Box 7.5 Template: Expenses

Date	Equipment	Stationery and postage	Newspapers and magazines	Sundries	Travel	Training	Marketing	Broadband	Phone
06/07/2019			Runner's World £4		Train to Manchester £46				
14/6/2019	Phone headset £12	Printer cartridges £32							
15/6/2019							Business cards £8		
31/06/2019			Times subscription £10		Bus to meet client £4				£33.50

offer new parents on top of that, with some countries offering very progressive and flexible options. At the top of the charts comes Sweden where each parent is eligible for up to 240 days paid parental leave, 150 of which can be transferred to the other parent, and some of which can be saved for use years down the line. By contrast in the Netherlands new mothers are entitled to 16 weeks paid maternity leave and are paid 100% of their earnings with a self-employed maternity benefits scheme.

In Australia where maternity leave is 12 months, anyone who is self-employed or owns their own small business is entitled to the same maternity pay as employees, which is $695 per week, for a maximum of 18 weeks, as long as they have been doing that work for 10 months in the past 13. The US falls roundly into the category of countries who have the poorest maternity leave rights for all workers, never mind the self-employed, with no laws requiring paid maternity leave at all.

The UK is at the more progressive end of the scale with 52 weeks maternity leave, some of which can be taken as shared parental leave. If you are self-employed and pay Class 2 National Insurance (for at least 13 of the 66 weeks before your baby's due), you are eligible for a maternity allowance of £148.68 a week for 39 weeks.

Pensions

One important part of your finances to consider is a pension. For anyone employed by a large organisation, a pension is one of those perks that they may not have put a huge amount of thought into. For a self-employed freelance, a pension can be easy to overlook or push to the bottom of the to-do list. No one else is going to research or set this up for you, and it can be harder to make regular contributions when cashflow may be up and down. Many countries do have state pensions, some which have a flat rate on reaching retirement age, which can also depend on how many years someone has paid into it, and others which calculate your pension based on earnings, such as in Spain, Germany or France. What you need to consider is that on its own a state pension is unlikely to provide you with the income you would like in your later years, and the sooner you start paying into a pension, the better off you will be.

In the UK, all employers now have to provide a workplace pension scheme which they also pay into to boost the amount available upon retirement. While self-employed workers miss out on this type of top up, there are tax breaks to encourage pensions savings. For self-employed basic-rate taxpayers for every £100 paid into a pension, the government will add £25 in tax relief. The UK government has also made provision for self-employed people to use the National

Employment Savings Trust (NEST) – the workplace pension scheme – which can be a relatively simple way to start saving if you are eligible. There are a myriad of different pension schemes available for the self-employed, and there are pros and cons to all of them. A financial advisor will be able to talk you through the best options for your circumstances. It is up to you to work out how much you reasonably want to contribute to a pension scheme, which will also depend on how old you are when you start, but most will have upper limits.

Working for free

One of the phrases you are likely to come across when working as a freelance is 'we have no budget to pay you but this work will be good exposure'. This essentially means work for us for free and it will help build up your portfolio and reputation. For the most part, this is absolute nonsense, and by agreeing to work for free, you undermine your value as a skilled professional and pull down rates for everyone else. 'Exposure' does not pay the bills. And whoever is asking you to work for free will be making money out of your hard work. While you are spending time on this work that will supposedly lead to more opportunities, you may be missing out on work that will earn you an income. Have confidence that you deserve fair pay for the work you do. Sometimes an organisation will claim they have no budget or are just starting out to tug on your heartstrings, but it is worth questioning any business model that is built on exploiting others.

There are some limited circumstances where you may consider working for free. Where you feel passionately about an issue or campaign, for example. Or if you really want to support a local grass roots organisation or a friend's project. Ask yourself how much time should I donate to this, what experience or skills will this help me with, will it legitimately lead to other work or opportunities and how does it fit in with my future goals. One of the benefits of freelancing is its flexibility, which may offer you time to pursue projects that are important to you. And it may be a two-way street. You write some copy for a friend's website and in return they do some graphic design for your business. That is very different than agreeing to write, teach or speak for free for an organisation who can afford (and should) pay for your expertise.

Beware companies that ask you to do a writing test or certain amount of work for free as part of an interview process or to check you are right for the job. If you are an experienced writer you will have plenty of examples of published work you can send them. If you are just starting out, you may feel that a request to do a writing test is more reasonable if it is not too time-consuming or onerous. But you should ask to be paid for your time. There are numerous examples of journalists submitting work as part of an application for work and then never hearing from the company again. If enough applicants have given them all this free time, they may have all the copy they need and will not need to hire anyone. Likewise, do not be talked into handing over contacts or any other information which is yours to keep.

Box 7.6 Case study: Chandni Doulatramani

After working for the 24-hour news channel Times Now and as a financial journalist at Reuters, Calcutta-based journalist Chandni decided she wanted a new challenge and took the leap into freelancing in 2017. She now writes about anything other than finances, including culture, travel and lifestyle, having had bylines for *The Guardian*, Al Jazeera, Foreign Policy, HuffPost US, VICE and National Geographic.

The first bit of advice she has for new freelances is to keep a detailed track of invoices including the expected date of payments, so you can spot when the money has not appeared in your bank account.

"Indian publications often pay very little, some want you to write for free and others can take eight months to clear small amounts of money so that is why I prefer working for international publications because they are more likely to pay on time, they are more organised and you can trust the money will come through".

She adds that keeping on top of the different processes that companies have for payment can further complicate the issue.

"Recently there was an organisation that wanted me to send a copy of the invoice by post and they also wanted me to sign the document digitally but apparently my digital signature was an image and not according to the format they preferred and so they sent me a 12-slide Powerpoint presentation just so I could sign the document".

Working for international publications means that Chandni is quite often paid in dollars, and there can be additional fees involved, for example, if the organisation insists on paying by PayPal.

"It does feel sometimes that from a financial point of view there is very little that is in my power to change but I always make sure that I do all invoices and send everything from my end on time", she says.

At the beginning of her freelance career, Chandni says she was reluctant to chase late payments but she soon realised she needed to take a different approach.

"I thought they would pay sooner or later but I realised that's not how it works so I'm now much more proactive – the onus is on me to chase them".

She says freelance journalists in India do not have any organisation or union who are fighting their corner on payments, but there are things individuals can do when they are not paid money they are owed, including being selective about who they work for and publicly calling out the worst offenders.

"You can name and shame on social media and I have done that before on Twitter".

Chandni adds that sometimes a journalist may want to write for a low or no fee if it is a cause they believe in, including freedom of the press.

"It is a very complicated situation because we have to support the cause of journalism. There's so much more to journalism than it being just a source of income and that is the challenging part".

porterfolio.net/chandnidoulatramani
@itsnotChandni

Getting started

- Research what is your best option for self-employment (e.g., sole trader or limited company)
- Create a spread sheet to track commissions and income
- Decide how you will record your expenses
- Design an invoice for your business
- Consider opening a dedicated bank account for freelance income and expenses

Notes

1 Turvill, W. 2016 "Press Gazette survey finds freelance journalists are happier than staffers – but pay is falling" Press Gazette www.pressgazette.co.uk/press-gazette-survey-finds-freelance-journalists-are-happier-staffers-pay-falling/.
2 National Union of Journalists. "Freelance Fees Guide" www.londonfreelance.org/feesguide/index.php?language=en&country=UK&section=Welcome.
3 EU law on late payment.
4 Gov.UK. "Late commercial payments: charging interest and debt recovery" www.gov.uk/late-commercial-payments-interest-debt-recovery/charging-interest-commercial-debt.
5 Credit Protection Association. "Late payment compensation" https://cpa.co.uk/late-payment-compensation/.
6 Costello, E. 2018 "How payment on publication is making life a misery for many freelance journalists" Press Gazette www.pressgazette.co.uk/how-payment-on-publication-is-making-life-a-misery-for-many-freelance-journalists/.
7 European Federation of Journalists. "In the UK and France, freelance journalists stand up for their rights to fairer, better and faster pay" https://europeanjournalists.org/blog/2019/02/08/uk-and-france-freelance-journalists-stand-up-for-their-rights-to-fairer-better-and-faster-pay/.
8 #FairPayForFreelancers. Open letter. https://docs.google.com/document/d/1BvCJbsaLVlNkgCPCqiyBxnqHtFincmCyvIOvRiw5LOo/edit.

8
Law, safety and ethics

OBJECTIVES

In this chapter you will learn:

- How to ensure you are legally protected
- What your rights are as a freelance
- Whom to turn to for legal support
- The importance of risk assessment
- How to work ethically and responsibly

Working as a freelance means the buck stops with you. Your job title may be journalist but you are also your own lawyer, advocate, health and safety officer, and moral compass. Unlike a staffer who has colleagues to turn to and processes to follow, the freelance journalist has to work out most things for themselves. It is therefore imperative that you are able to protect yourself legally, physically and psychologically. Working ethically and responsibly are also essential for your brand in order for you to be recognised and relied upon as a professional.

Fair working conditions for freelance journalists are gradually being eroded, so now more than ever freelances need to insist on their rights in order to enact change. This means equipping yourself with the knowledge and skills to challenge and negotiate with commissioning editors and having the right legal and safety protection in place.

Media law

As a freelance journalist it is your responsibility to learn and understand the law. It is also important to seek advice when you are unsure rather than assume any legal issues will be 'picked up' at the other end. If you are covering court cases, then you must seek professional media law training in order to ensure you operate legally. Even feature and opinion writers need to have a comprehensive grasp of the law if they don't want to end up in civil or criminal court. The key legal areas to learn inside out are defamation, copyright, data protection and protection of sources, but you will also need a firm understanding of how to avoid contempt of court and the identification of children and sexual offence victims.

Social media networks have become host to a series of legal breaches in recent years, due to a lack of media law knowledge by the public. Tommy Robinson, founder of the far-right English Defence League, was jailed for 13 months in 2018 for contempt of court. He broadcast an hour-long video via Facebook from outside Leeds Crown Court and made comments that risked causing a trial to collapse. Meanwhile, ten people were ordered to pay £624 to a woman who claimed she was raped by UK footballer Ched Evans, after they admitted naming her on Twitter and Facebook.[1] Under the UK Sexual Offences Act 2003, victims and alleged victims of sex crimes are given lifelong anonymity. The Sheffield United and Wales striker was jailed for raping the 19-year-old but was later acquitted.

It is also vital that you understand the types of laws that cover different countries and regions, particularly those with limited press freedom. For example, India ranks low in the Reporters Without Borders 2019 World Press Freedom Index, positioned at 140 out of 180.[2] Countries like these often allow SLAPPs which are a strategic lawsuit against public participation. This kind of lawsuit is intended to censor, intimidate and/or silence critics by burdening them with expensive legal defence costs to force them to abandon their criticism. SLAPPs are not illegal in India unlike other parts of the world which are higher up on the press freedom rankings.

As a freelance journalist your knowledge of the law and what you can and cannot publish or broadcast will be your best defence against fines, settlements and imprisonment, so make sure you have adequate training and resources at hand before embarking on a freelance career.

Defamation

Any individual or company can sue for damages to their reputation caused by material broadcast or published to a third party, including material published online, as long as they are identifiable. Libel is a permanent defamatory publication or broadcast which can include written material in books, newspapers, magazines, websites and social media platforms, or allegations appearing in television or radio. Slander relates to the spoken word which is more transient in nature such as defamatory remarks made at a public event in front of an audience but not recorded in any manner. In the UK under the new Defamation Act 2013, claimants need to demonstrate that the content would tend to lower them in the estimation of right-thinking people generally and cause serious harm to their reputation. Companies can only sue if they can prove serious financial loss. A defamation case can be brought against an author, editor or publishing company and even distributors of defamatory material such as website owners and internet service providers.

British defamation law is regarded by journalists as the harshest in the Western world because of potentially massive legal costs and the high amounts awarded for damages particularly since the loser of a trial pays both sides' costs. But it is possible to be sued for defamation in most parts of the world even in America, which has the first amendment right of freedom of the press.

If you are working as a freelance journalist, it is essential that you understand the law surrounding defamation and what you can and can't say about people and organisations. Never rely on sub-editors or editors to fill in your media law gaps, as your work may not always be meticulously edited and you could be held liable for anything you produce. If you are in any doubt, discuss it with the commissioning editor or ask to speak to the company lawyer if there is one.

Copyright

This law gives the creators of literary, dramatic, musical and artistic works the right to control the ways in which their material may be used. It is an automatic right when an individual or organisation creates a work that is regarded as original, and exhibits a degree of labour, skill or judgement. For work to be protected by copyright law, it must be tangible and expressed in a physical form, meaning you cannot copyright an idea. The period of time a piece of work is protected for depends on a range of factors, such as what type of work it is and when it was made. Each country has its own copyright law, but most will protect works created in other countries in the same way. Some forms of creativity are also protected by Intellectual Property laws.

In journalism, issues of copyright breach arise when contents, such as photographs or entire sections of news text or broadcast footage, are used without permission. However, in the UK it is lawful to use or reproduce work without permission under the fair usage, or fair dealing, rule. This is allowed when the use of the work is for research or private study, is used for the purposes of criticism, review or quotation, or is utilised for the purposes of reporting current events – although this does not apply to photographs.

As a rule of thumb, always ask permission if you want to use a piece of work, such as a photograph, graphic or video, created by someone else. Never copy and paste something you have found on Google images or anywhere else online. There are plenty of copyright free resources online where you can find photographs, music, sounds and moving images to legally use under a creative commons license such as Unsplash, Pixabay, Freesound and ZapSplat. Check the conditions of using the piece of work as it may require you to credit the creator.

Re-using written content is a slightly more grey area because as soon as you rewrite a story it becomes a new piece of work with its own copyright. However, it is bad practice and legally dubious to copy and paste an entire story verbatim, especially if you are reproducing quotes. A professional, ethical journalist will do the legwork themselves by fact-checking, obtaining new quotes and following up rather than repeating a story.

Data protection

As a journalist you will often hold a lot of personal, sensitive and/or confidential information about the sources you speak to. Under data protection law, you have a duty to ensure that this information is held securely, not kept for longer than necessary and is fairly and lawfully processed.

In the UK, the Information Commissioner's Office has a detailed guide on how the Data Protection Act 1988 applies to journalism. There are exemptions for journalism except in the area of keeping information secure. If you hold information about sources or anyone you work with, such as press officers and commissioning editors, then you must ensure that you only collect information that you need for a specific purpose. You also have an obligation to ensure the information is relevant and up to date, you only hold as much as you need for as long as you need it and you allow the subject to see the information if they request it.

A lot of confusion has been created by the implementation of the General Data Protection Regulation (GDPR) in Europe, with people mistakenly thinking that journalists cannot contact them or hold their information. In simple terms, the regulation is an updated version of UK data protection laws and exemptions for journalism apply. Generally speaking, journalists do not need to gain consent to process personal data or contact sources. However, caution needs to be applied when sending out electronic marketing, such as events ticket sales or electronic newsletters. Unsolicited marketing cannot be sent to individuals without their consent, meaning they have to sign up for these services independently rather than being approached directly. This falls under the separate but related law, the Privacy and Electronic Communication Regulations 2003. Additionally, personal data gathered for one purpose cannot be used for another, so if a freelance found an email address and contacted a source for a story, they then could not use those contact details for marketing purposes.

The key obligation for freelances, who are likely to be classed as the data controllers, is to make sure appropriate security is in place, such as encryptions on devices, locked filing cabinets and passwords and two-step verification on email accounts.

Protection of sources

Journalism could simply not operate effectively or democratically if journalists were not able to protect their sources, many of whom are risking their livelihoods – and sometimes their lives – by coming forward with confidential information. The protection of sources is, therefore, well recognised in international law as a key principle underpinning press freedom. As such it is recognised by the United Nations and human rights organisation, the Council of Europe. In the US, state laws vary in scope, but they generally uphold reporters' rights to resist demands to reveal their sources.

When a source provides information to a journalist on the basis that they will not be named or identified, it is a fundamental rule of journalism that this will not be breached. However, the right of protection of journalistic sources does not attract absolute privilege against disclosure as it would for a doctor or lawyer. Protection of sources can clash with other laws although courts are usually reluctant to order the disclosure of a source. In some situations, the court will order disclosure of sources in the interests of justice, national security or for the prevention of disorder or crime. There has been an increasing number of laws introduced in recent years which set out conditions under which police and intelligence agencies can seek to obtain confidential journalistic source material. In the UK, these include the Investigatory Powers Act, of 2016, and the Police and Criminal Evidence Act, of 1984, whilst in the US these are covered within the Espionage Act, of 1917, and the Patriot Act, of 2001.

Journalists should, therefore, tread carefully when promising complete anonymity to sources. Offering unqualified protection never to disclose the identity of a source is not recommended, but it is reasonable to pledge not to disclose their identity unless ordered to do so by a court.

Your copyright protection

Byline banditry or creative cannibalism is a largely untested legal area but is a practice that has spread like wildfire across the internet. It is common practice for news organisations to take content from one another's websites in the interests of reporting current events known as fair dealing and repackaging it as their own content with their own reporter's byline. Since copyright lies in the expression and not the idea itself, once a story is 'stolen' and rewritten, there is no real redress for the original journalist. It is certainly highly unethical to rewrite someone else's story and even more unjust to remove their byline, but it is currently not illegal.

Photographs are a different matter, however, as these are not protected by fair dealing and freelance photographers have become more vigilant in pursuing media organisations for breach of copyright. In the US, there were more than 200 private settlements in 2017 for copyright infringement as a growing number of independent photographers launched lawsuits against moguls such as AOL, CBS, NPR and Yahoo!.[3] In one peculiar case, a photographer and online media company found themselves locked in a counter legal battle. Jon Tannen filed a lawsuit accusing CBS Interactive of using his copyrighted photos in an article on 247 Sports without his permission, demanding $150,000 for each infringed photo. In response CBS filed its own copyright infringement lawsuit against Tannen accusing the photographer of posting screenshots from a 1958 CBS TV series on his social media accounts without permission, seeking $150,000 in damages. CBS later dropped the lawsuit.[4]

Although it is difficult to maintain ownership over a piece of journalistic work, there are steps that freelances can take to minimise exploitation. Selling a story and/or images for single use in single media only means that the commissioning organisation cannot sell them on and make a profit from your work without your permission, for which you should ask for payment. This may not be appropriate for every story that you sell, but it is always worth making an informed decision about how much you may need to control the spread of the story.

Since there is more restriction over the use of photographs, a savvy way to maintain ownership and make additional money from a story is to take your own pictures and insist on a photo byline watermarked on the image. If media organisations approach you asking to reuse the copyrighted images they have spotted on your original story, then negotiate a fee rather than handing them out for nothing. Again, state that the images are for single use in single media and must have your photo byline. Similarly, if a news organisation reproduces the image without your permission, contact the picture desk and highlight the unauthorised use and ask for a payment per photo. In most cases they will hold up their hands and pay out. If they do not respond then send a cease and desist letter asking for payment or for the images to be removed. Explain that if this does not happen within a specified amount of time they will be contacted by your solicitor or attorney.

If you are using photos provided by a case study which they took themselves (meaning they own the copyright), ensure the images are private on social media and watermark them with the individual's name. You can then pursue payment on the case study's behalf for unauthorised use of the images and agree a commission with them for doing this.

Syndication

When you sell a story or are commissioned to produce a piece of work, you need to be aware of who else may reproduce the content. This is particularly vital for digital content, which spreads quickly online. The first time the work is distributed will be under primary rights, so, for example, if you write an article for a newspaper website, the contract you have with the publisher will be a payment for that single piece of work.

Secondary rights involve secondary use of work which has already been distributed to the public. So, if another website or a magazine reproduces the article this is secondary use. As a freelance, it is important to try to maintain ownership of your work and licence other people to reuse it for a fee rather than let it be copied over and over again for free.

One of the difficulties of this is that many media organisations have syndication deals agreed in advance, and this can be part of the contract or terms and conditions you are commissioned under. This means your work is licensed for publication or broadcast elsewhere in return for a fee. In some circumstances the author of the work will receive around 50% of the syndication fee, but in some contracts, there is no additional fee as it is built into the original commissioning rate.

A freelance journalist commissioned by *The Guardian* website could find their story reproduced word-for-word on the *Irish Times*, *Sydney Morning Herald*, *South China Morning Post* website or newspaper a day later, as these are syndication partners with Guardian News & Media. These outlets pay a regular syndication subscription to receive all of *The Guardian* and/or *The Observer* news and feature feeds in their territory. The journalist will receive no remuneration for this syndication because their commission fee is an all-inclusive one covering syndication rights as set out in the Freelance Charter. A freelance will only receive additional payment if the story is a spot sale syndication, which is an ad hoc selling of an individual article.

To try to maintain ownership of your work the best approach is to ask the commissioning editor to agree in an email that your work is not to be syndicated. You can also have the wording 'no syndication without my express permission' in your terms and conditions. This may not always be possible, but it is always worth trying to negotiate the best deal for yourself.

Box 8.1 Author's experience

Lily was able to control the unsolicited spread of a news story by being savvy with the photographs. The body shaming story, which she originally sold to The Sun Online, included photographs from the case study who owned the copyright. The case study ensured the photographs were not publicly available on her social media networks and agreed to direct all media enquiries to Lily. When two newspaper websites contacted Lily asking for permission to reuse the story and photos without offering a fee, Lily asked for payment before releasing them. She also asked the organisations to agree to give the case study a photo byline and only gave permission for single use, in single media. This meant that when a third newspaper website reproduced the images without seeking permission first Lily was able to approach the picture desk and ask for payment for unauthorised use. Using photography copyright laws, Lily was able to receive payment for the same story four times, making three times as much money from the resale as she did from the original story. She split these payments with the case study.

ALCS

To ensure that you receive the money you are entitled to as a writer, it is worth signing up to ALCS. This not-for-profit organisation collects money from all over the world when someone copies or uses your work. This includes the photocopying, scanning and digital reuse of electronic and online publications, such as articles, book chapters and scripts. It is free to sign up to the service, but you will be charged a 9.5% commission on any funds paid out to you. This commission is a tax deduction against the income you receive from ALCS, so in effect it is an expense against your business income. There is also a lifetime membership fee of £36, and this is taken off your first payout. However, if you are a member of one of the unions listed on their website, your membership is free.

Although ALCS has a UK focus the organisation has agreements with over 55 collecting societies around the world. It is well known amongst freelances as being a great source of 'free money', and twice a year journalism networks are filled with the chatter of rejoicing writers who have just received a surprise payment sometimes for thousands of pounds.

Contracts

Trading under your own name or brand name means you have responsibility for adopting reasonable business standards and acting in a professional manner. This means working to an industry standard, adhering to ethical codes and operating like a business. At the heart of this is understanding your own worth and having the confidence to value your work.

Many 'contracts' between freelances and commissioning editors are set out through an exchange of emails. This is often the most efficient way to operate rather than signing endless, lengthy contracts. Before starting any work, you need to agree in an email what work will be conducted (word count/package length, number of sources, photo sourcing, etc.), the deadline and the payment. If you make an agreement in person, over the phone or via social media, then ask the editor to send you an email confirming the details. An acknowledged email is a contract.

Many businesses are not forthcoming with offering a contract particularly if you work for them on an ad hoc basis. The benefit of this is that you can set your own terms. Some news organisations, however, have fairly detailed terms, so always check with the editor if there is a standard freelance charter or terms and conditions that are online, as this will be their fall back if you query anything. Guardian News & Media publishes on its website lengthy terms and conditions for the supply of contributions: www.theguardian.com/info/guardian-news-media-freelance-charter. This sets out fees, syndication rights and expenses paid but that does not prevent you from coming to an agreement with the commissioning editor for different terms, particularly around syndication rights.

To protect yourself from unfair treatment, late payments and unlicensed use of your work, it is important to set out the business terms you are willing to work under before you agree to any commission. This will also be much more effective than trying to get a busy commissioning editor to read and sign a contract or terms and conditions sent via email. Setting out your terms can be as subtle as having a link in your email signature which says 'See my terms and conditions here' – which then links to the full list on your website. This will put you in a much stronger position if you ever have to challenge an employer or take them to court (see Chapter 7).

The terms should set out payment and licensing terms with wording such as '*Payment of my invoices is strictly within 30 days. Payments later than this will be subject to a charge and interest*'. You can also state that unless explicitly authorised, you only license your work for single use in single media. A useful example of business terms can be found on the website of freelance journalist and executive member of the National Union of Journalists, Tim Dawson http://tim-dawson.com/.

If you are asked to sign a contract for a publication, platform or broadcaster, then make sure you read it cover to cover, rather than quickly scrolling through it. And don't be afraid to ask for clauses to be removed or changed. Things to look out for in particular are clauses around copyright, payment, indemnity and non-competing. Who owns the copyright for your work and are you able to sell the story at a later date? Will you get paid on publication or on completion of the work? What happens to payment if your story is axed? Are you liable to pay the costs of any potential law suit because you have agreed to an indemnity clause?

In most cases, it is strongly advisable not to sign an indemnity clause because this can be financial suicide. An indemnity clause is a contractual transfer of risk between two parties to compensate for a loss which may occur as a result of a specific event. If you sign an indemnity clause you are taking on the risk – and cost – of a potential lawsuit from the organisation you are working for, which will have far more resources to fight a legal battle than you as an individual.

The overarching advice is to proceed cautiously with contracts, make a judgement and balance your relationship with the editor with the conditions you are happy to work under. Keep your eyes open and know where to turn for support and how to protect yourself.

Unions

As a freelance you can be quite isolated and don't always have colleagues to turn to for advice. Joining a union serves the dual purpose of providing you with support whilst also contributing to the collective lobbying of government and industry in order to affect change. There is no obligation to join a union and certainly many freelances don't, but you should at least be aware of what they can offer.

Unions will charge an annual membership fee and often have a tiered structure for freelances, which corresponds to their income. Once you become a member you will have access to support such as legal advice, experts to read contracts and representatives to initiative legal action on your behalf. There are often additional services such as relief funds to give financial support to members and their dependents in times of need, free or discounted training, press cards, discounted dental and health coverage, access to networking events and a regular magazine.

In the UK, the National Union of Journalists (NUJ), nuj.org.uk, has a temporary freelance membership scheme for those trying to establish or re-establish themselves as a full-time freelance journalist. If you do not yet earn half of your income from freelance journalism and don't have another full-time job, you can apply for this special membership for up to three years at a reduced rate, starting at £60 per annum at the time of writing. Freelance membership thereafter is based on salary and ranges from £180 to £300 a year. The NUJ also offer student associate membership for £30 for the duration of your course. On graduation, students automatically qualify for temporary freelance membership and receive a 50% discount off their first year.

In the US, there are a range of freelance unions, including Guild Freelancers guildfreelancers.org, which is part of NewsGuild, the largest journalism union in the country. Membership is $12 a month. There are also broader freelance unions such as Freelancers Union freelancersunion.org, which offers support and advocacy to independent workers from graphic designers and contractors to entrepreneurs and writers. It is free to join and represents 450,000 members. It is able to provide insurance benefits appropriate for freelances and access to freelance hubs in 25 major cities.

The Media, Entertainment and Arts Alliance in Australia, meaa.org, is the largest union representing freelance and staff journalists. Membership fees, which are fully tax deductible, are based on income and start at $7.25 Australia dollars a week, with the average being $14.35 a week. Benefits include free entry to the Walkley Awards ($260 to non-members), which has a freelance journalist category. Discounts are also available for companies and services including cinemas, theatres, insurance firms, travel agencies, restaurants and banks.

But be aware that some countries including India do not have professional unions or membership organisations with enough clout to challenge the media. In this situation knowing the law inside out and having the right insurance in place is even more fundamental.

Insurance

As a freelance you could be liable as an individual and will not necessarily have the protection of your commissioning organisation. A particularly litigious and wealthy person or someone with a business interest to protect could sue you in civil court for damages. The mostly likely lawsuits are for defamation or breach of contract. Both of these could leave you with eye-watering legal costs and crippling pay outs forcing you to declare yourself insolvent and/or sell your home.

For any risk you can't afford to cover yourself, it is worth considering insurance. As outlined above, many contracts include indemnity clauses, meaning you are liable to pay legal costs if you are commissioned to do a piece of work which subsequently leads to a lawsuit. Indemnity insurance offers a good amount of protection and will pay out for losses or damages sustained by another party. There are a number of insurance firms that offer specific professional indemnity insurance for journalists, or it can be purchased via trade unions. Another option which is popular in the US is omissions and errors insurance, a type of professional liability insurance that protects against claims of inadequate work or negligent actions. This can protect freelances against million-dollar lawsuits that media firms may be able to afford to settle but individuals cannot.

Public liability insurance is particularly useful for freelances who regularly visit different premises to conduct interviews or take photographs. The insurance can cover legal costs and compensation payments if you are held responsible for injury or property damage to a client, contractor or member of the public. For example, if you permanently stain the new cream carpets of a glamour model's home by accidentally walking on them with dog poo on your boots (as happened to a Wiltshire photographer once) or spill coffee over a case study's laptop whilst interviewing them, then public liability insurance can cover compensation for this damage. Some organisations, particularly corporate clients, will only hire freelances with public liability insurance, so don't be surprised if it is something you are asked about.

Check your home insurance to see if equipment you use for work purposes, such as a computers, cameras and microphones, is covered inside and outside the home. You may need to include personal possessions protection, and any high value items may need additional cover.

As with all insurances, make sure you weight up the pros and cons, and the likelihood of being at risk and the subsequent consequences. Buying every single relevant insurance is probably unnecessary, impractical and too expensive, particularly when you are starting out, so think about what you need to prioritise. Make sure you shop around to get a competitive price and always read policy documents carefully to see what they include and exclude.

Health and safety

As a lone worker is it vital that you continually assess your health and safety. This does not mean filling in endless risk assessment forms, but it does mean taking a common sense approach to protect yourself. Even if you are not working in a conflict zone, it is important to take sensible precautions and not put yourself at unnecessary risk of physical, psychological or digital harm. This can be as simple as telling someone where you are going when you go out to conduct an interview or making sure you talk to a friend, partner or family member if you are working on a distressing story.

Journalists face a range of threats and hazards whether working from home or out in the field. Environmental hazards can range from being in a car accident to covering a natural disaster whilst in the eye of a storm. Journalists are generally more at risk then others because they go into these hazardous zones to report on them rather than escape them. Conflict zones and politically unstable countries are also a great danger to journalists, particularly those who are not embedded within military forces. Not only is there a risk of becoming collateral damage by being caught in the crossfire, journalists are also frequently becoming direct targets themselves. Northern Ireland journalist Lyra McKee was shot whilst covering rioting in the Creggan area of Derry in 2019, in an alleged assassination by the New IRA.[5] There is also the increased risk of kidnap, as terrorists are acutely aware of the media storm created by the capture of a journalist.

As a result, story-related threats are on the rise with the number of journalists killed worldwide in retaliation for their work doubling in 2018 according to the Committee to Protect Journalists. Reporters Without Borders recorded 49 journalists killed in 2019 along with 389 imprisoned and 57 held hostage.[6] These threats are global with journalists – many of them freelance – losing their lives in the UK, Mexico, Somalia, Afghanistan, Ukraine, the Philippines and many more countries.

And greater democracy and freedom of the press does not necessarily equate to a safer environment for journalists as the deaths in the UK and Philippines demonstrate. Some countries such as India do not have press card schemes, meaning journalists are more at risk of harassment and physical abuse and can be readily detained or arrested by the police because they have no effective way of proving they are a journalist. This is even more risky for freelance journalists.

Where there is financial or political corruption, there is a potential danger to journalists who try to expose it. Indeed, politics kills more journalists than wars. And sensitive topics such as organised crime, gender issues, prostitution, gambling and elections can put journalists at risk of physical attack but also online harassment. Digital bullying and trolling are another way in which journalists are continually under attack, and the emotional damage this causes can be just as traumatic as physical abuse. Journalists also need to protect themselves from security breaches, in order to protect their sources and confidential data they may be storing.

Risk assessment

The key to protecting your safety as a freelance journalist is to consider the potential risks before entering a situation. Are you carrying expensive equipment which could attract unwanted attention? Are you more vulnerable because you are on your own? What is the potential impact of your gender, ethnicity and/or culture? Are there any environmental hazards such as adverse weather conditions? Are you meeting someone whose life is in danger? Are you travelling with sensitive data on your laptop or phone? Are you going into a zone where you will need a bulletproof vest and helmet?

Once you have identified the risks you can prepare yourself for the unexpected. But don't make the mistake of weighing the importance of the story against the risk. These two elements should be kept apart and the risk should be assessed on its own merit and not balanced against anything else. If you balance one against the other, you will make an emotional rather than practical judgment, which could put you in danger. With this in mind always make sure you conduct a risk assessment whilst in a neutral frame of mind rather than when you feel overtly optimistic or conversely guilty or stressed. Sleep, nutrition, alcohol and fitness will all impact upon your decision making so try to make a judgement call when your well-being is at its best rather than at its worst.

Preparation

Whenever you leave the house to cover a story make sure a colleague, close friend or family member knows where you are going and how they can contact you. Think of it as being similar to going on a first date. Meet in a public place whenever possible and only conduct an interview at someone's home if you feel comfortable doing so and give the address to someone who will check up on you.

If you are travelling abroad or going into an unfamiliar community, make sure you understand the local customs, traditions and cultural norms. Be prepared to dress appropriately, use non-threatening body language and know when it is best to stay silent rather than antagonise a situation. In some circumstances, it may be appropriate to learn self-defence skills and be able to react quickly to threatening situations.

When entering a potentially dangerous or hazardous location, continually assess the situation and make a mental note of escape routes and identify when it is best to step away or make a run for it. When it comes to digital safety make sure you travel with encrypted memory cards which are kept hidden away and also consider protecting your personal data and what details you publish about yourself online.

If you have a confidential source with a potentially explosive story, then choose your communication methods carefully and understand that there is no such thing as a 100% safe digital platform. Skype calls can be monitored by security services[7] and you can be tracked via your mobile phone so download a map rather than using a GPS signal. The Reporters Without Borders website rsf.org has a wealth of checklists, guidelines and advice which can help you to prepare and make informed safety choices. The International Association of Women in Radio and Television also has a safety handbook for woman journalists, which is free to download online from iawrt.org.

Debriefing

The psychological impact of covering a story can be extremely damaging, and since mental health issues affect one in four people, it is highly likely that as a freelance journalist covering potentially distressing stories you will be at risk at some point in your career. Journalists can suffer from post-traumatic stress disorder, fatigue, anxiety and depression, which can lead to burn out, poor personal care and heavy drinking so it is important to be able to recognise the warning signs but also to talk through a difficult experience.

Having a mentor, colleague or loved-one to discuss an interview, eye witness account or experience with post event is crucial for a freelance who does not have a line manager or human resources department. Don't be afraid to talk to someone about how you are feeling and how a story has impacted you or raked up forgotten memories. It is normal for journalists to react to stressful events by experiencing intrusive memories, interrupted sleep and mood swings, and normally these will fade within a few weeks particularly if you have someone to talk to. However, if these reactions do not fade, it is important to identify them and seek professional support, such as counselling. Relaxation techniques such as yoga, meditation and tai chi are also useful coping mechanisms.

Meeting deadlines and juggling multiple commissions can be very stressful for freelance journalists. Looking after your mental health is as important as taking care of your physical well-being so make sure you take time out to relax. This is where it pays to be organised and planning in breaks, exercise, and 'me' time is essential (see Chapter 10). There is also useful advice on coping with stress on the National Union of Journalists website, which is relevant to freelances working in any country nuj.org.uk/documents/nuj-stress-factsheet/.

Ethics

What a journalist can and cannot do within the rule of law is set out in legislation and can be easily learnt from media law textbooks. The ethically conduct of a journalist, however, is less clear cut as it is not legislated for, and unlike the medical profession, freelance journalists can operate without signing up to a code of conduct.

The ethics of different publications and broadcasters will vary, and as a freelance you need to have a strident understanding of your own moral compass and what you are, and are not, prepared to do, within the law. Joining a union and/or declaring on your website that you follow a professional code of conduct (with a link to it) will strengthen your brand as an ethical, trusted freelance. This is particularly important if you work in a part of the world with no or limited professional press codes. In this instance, it may be appropriate to draw up your own code of practice or align yourself with an international journalism body such as the International Federation of Journalists, which has a Global Charter of Ethics for Journalists.

In the UK, newspaper and magazine journalists are guided by the Editors' Code of Practice and the National Union of Journalists Code of Conduct, whilst broadcast journalists follow ethical guidelines set out in Ofcom Broadcasting Code. Breaches of these codes can lead to fines and force a media organisation to publish or broadcast apologies, corrections or clarifications. Similar codes exist around the world, with journalist members of the Media Entertainment and Arts Alliance in Australia being bound by the Journalist Code of Ethics. Meanwhile in America, the Society for Professional Journalists, the Investigative Reporters and Editors non-profit organisation and the National Writers Union all have their own code of conduct which members sign up to including freelances. The German Press Council, Media Council of Kenya and National Union of French Journalists also have their own ethical codes.

These codes set out guidelines around honesty, fairness, independence, accuracy, public interest and privacy as well as the treatment of children, vulnerable adults and victims of crime. As a freelance, you should be fully aware of all the clauses and operate within the boundaries of these codes.

Sources

The treatment of sources is a central part of working ethically, and there is always a balance to be struck between protecting them from harm and serving the public interest. It is not your job to save a source from saying something unwise or embarrassing, but at the same time you need to consider whether the comment was made off the record (an agreement that the information is not to be reported) and if it will damage any potential ongoing relationship with the source. This is where a judgement call has to be made, and if you are unsure, it is worth discussing it with fellow freelances and/or your editor whilst protecting the person's identity.

When dealing with any sources, it is useful to run through a checklist in your head – or on paper – to ensure you have dealt with them fairly. Ask yourself whether you clarified with the source what your intentions were and what any potential consequences of speaking to you may be. Autonomy as a journalist is vital but so is maintaining good relations with sources so you may wish to compromise in some instances and agree to allow them to see the copy and amend factual content only.

Relationships with public relations staff can be tricky to navigate particularly if they are demanding the inclusion of hyperlinks or plugging a business or website in return for a juicy case study or exclusive data. Don't be afraid to be firm and explain why you cannot agree to their terms or alternatively be honest and say you can include the information but cannot guarantee that it won't be removed in the editing process. Remember that your story is there to serve the public and not their client and politely redirect them to the advertising department if you feel they are demanding too much.

If you are someone who uses case studies regularly, then be aware that they may ask to be paid. Some publications will pay a case study fee which is separate to your commissioning fee, or they may pay a finder's fee if you pass case study contact details onto them but don't produce the story yourself. Magazines will often pay an all-in fee, which you then split with the case study. There is no hard and fast rule over how much you give to the case study, but you should offer them an amount that you feel is fair. This may be a 70/30 split, 60/40 or even 50/50. The case study will generally get the smaller proportion because telling their story takes less time and effort than recording it and turning it into a story. Freelances tend to offer a case study a fee, for example, £300, without telling their source that total payment amount from the publication is £800 – of which the journalist receives £500. How transparent you want to be with your source is up to you, and again you need to be guided by your own moral compass but don't underestimate the value of the work that you are doing.

Copy approval

Allowing story sources to see or amend your work before it is published is known as copy approval or quote approval. Read back is a similar courtesy where a journalist will read the text to a source over the phone before filing the copy. Journalists are under no obligation to allow their sources to hear, view or read any part of their work before publication or broadcast, and it is certainly frowned upon by many reporters. The practice can also be dimly viewed by editors because it fundamentally undermines the autonomy of journalists and freedom of the press. That being said there may be circumstances where you feel it is more appropriate or ethical to allow a source to view or hear their quotes rather than deny them this opportunity. For example, if you were writing a sensitive story for a magazine about a woman who was raped, and she had consented to lift her anonymity, you, in discussion with the commissioning editor, may decide that a read back is the right course of action. In some cases, you may wish to send quotes or sections of a story to an expert to check for accuracy if you are writing about a particularly complex issue that you wish to fact-check.

Sometimes a source or a PR may directly ask for copy approval and this may be a condition of an interview. It is a slippery slope once you start saying yes to these kinds of demands, so your default position should be to say that it is not your policy to allow copy approval because it breaches journalistic independence. It may be a process of negotiation, however, and it is worth talking to your commissioning editor to find out how hardline their stance is. For lighter stories allowing someone to read through a story and amend any factual errors – but not opinion – may be acceptable. But for hard news stories it should only happen in extremely exceptional cases, if at all. Also be aware that even if you say no to copy approval, it may happen once you have filed the copy anyway. In 2017, freelance journalist Ginny Dougary wrote an expose in *The Guardian* claiming that British TV presenter Clare Balding and her publicity team had allegedly been allowed to remove and rewrite sections of an interview with Saga magazine which Dougary had submitted.[8]

Box 8.2 Author's experience

As a freelance it is important to Emma that the editors she works for can trust in her copy. She is rarely working in the office of the publication commissioning her, so they have no sense of how she operates or the conversations she has with interviewees. This means it is her responsibility to consider and be aware of ethical guidelines around privacy, public interest, conflict of interest and right of reply. Sometimes Emma has been provided with confidential documents or spoken to sources on the condition of anonymity. In these circumstances she has made the editor aware of any potential ethical issues and made a plan about how to deal with them. For example, in protecting your source, Emma says you may have to find an alternative way to back up a story. On the flip side, it also means being aware of your rights and responsibilities if anyone tries to stop you publishing a story that shows them in a negative light.

Conflict of interest

Sometimes journalists can get too close to their source particularly if they have spent a lot of time with them or struck up a rapport. It is important to retain a professional relationship so ethical boundaries are not crossed and you are still able to question what they say and do not become an unofficial mouthpiece for their own agenda. This means not accepting payment from a source or allowing them to dictate the angle or content of a story.

If you write for an advertising-led magazine, you may be explicitly asked by an editor to write a positive review of a product or service or to only use advertisers as sources for your articles. This is where you need to make a personal judgement over whether you feel comfortable doing this or express to the editor that you feel this is not transparent enough to the readers.

If you also have a supplementary income (see Chapter 11), you may find yourself in a situation where you do commercial work for a client and then you have to write about them objectively as a journalist. In this instance, you need to explain to the client that you are operating independently as a journalist under a different set of practices or you need to declare a conflict of interest and decline the journalism assignment.

There may be many other scenarios where you are too close to a story because it involves someone you know, where you live or an experience you have shared with the subject, and you must judge these on a case-by-case basis. In some circumstances it will be appropriate to produce a first-person piece and declare your connection, but in others you may need to declare an interest and simply not cover the story if you feel you cannot be objective.

Reporting death

Reporting tragic events, such as terrorist attacks, mass shootings, suicide and fatal accidents, is difficult for any journalist and must be handled sensitively. There is also a responsibility to local communities to find the balance between honouring the dead – often referred to as a tribute – and avoiding intrusion into grief. Journalists also have a duty to the wider public to report on mass tragedies and analyse the context in which they occurred rather than focus on the graphic or violent details. Objectivity may not always be the most appropriate response to human catastrophe as this may alienate you from participants. In some situations, it is justified for a journalist to bear witness to a horrific event including the expression of subjective emotions. A freelance journalist must also protect themselves from experiencing trauma by seeking help and support as outlined above.

One of the rites of passage for a trainee reporter is the death knock. This is the practice of contacting family or close friends of a recently deceased individual in an attempt to gather their response to the death and additional information about their loved one. This is usually an unsolicited visit to the home of the deceased or their relatives. Often regional freelances are sent on death knocks for national newspapers whose own reporters are located hundreds of miles away. Although it can be viewed as unethical by the public, it is an opportunity to tell a personal story which is often welcome by grieving families. It gives people the chance to pay tribute to the deceased, raise awareness about an issue or expose crime and negligence.

If you are sent to a death knock and are concerned that you may be threatened, then take someone you trust with you. Double and triple check that the family has been informed of the death as it is not a reporter's job to tell them. Always be polite, softly spoken and dress smartly. Offer your condolences and ask if the person would like a tribute to be published or broadcast in honour of their loved one. If they say no then make them aware if a story is going to run anyway. Always leave your business card so they are able to contact you if they change their mind or have any questions. Above all else be sensitive and discreet and do not harass or persist in contacting the family. Be particularly thoughtful if the death involves a suspected suicide. If the person does want to speak to you, then give them time and ask open-ended questions. Do not rush them and leave difficult questions to the end. They may ask to see the copy before the story is printed, so make sure you know the editorial policy before setting out to do the knock. Invaluable resources include the suicidereportingtoolkit.com and journoresources.org.uk/death-knocks-how-tackle-reporter-journalism/.

Box 8.3 Case study: Ruth E. Thaler-Carter

Turning down a dream project due to a liability clause in the contract was the right decision for trade and consumer journalist Ruth E. Thaler-Carter.

The veteran freelancer, who has written for *The Washington Post*, *Baltimore Sun* and *New York Daily News*, among many other outlets, has more than 35 years of experience in working for various media companies and always ensures she carefully reads the fine print of a contract.

"I turned down a project because the contract said I would have responsibility for everything I wrote even after I had submitted it. They refused to remove the clause. It would have been a dream project, but I couldn't sign it. I would have accepted a lower rate than I usually receive, since it was something I really wanted to do, but I wouldn't accept the contract".

Ruth, who lives in St. Louis, Missouri, USA, says freelances should never be held responsible for any changes made to their work after they submit it because it makes them vulnerable to legal challenges for something that is out of their control.

"You need to make sure you have some kind of a contract for each project and client that says, 'I attest to providing accurate, factual information and I cannot be held responsible for any changes after I submit it'".

She says in most circumstances, clients are amenable to changing or removing clauses you are uncomfortable with. Liability clauses, for instance, are often not relevant to individual freelances because they refer to people working at the client's location, subcontracting or operating heavy equipment.

The best way to protect yourself from being sued is to follow a code of ethics and "do your damnedest to only report and publish what you think is true and can be defended", advises Ruth.

With cuts to newsroom staff including copy editors, fact-checkers and proofreaders, it has never been more important for freelances to double and triple check their own work.

"Don't submit or publish opinion or anything you can't back up. If you publish something that is true, it can be defended. It is unfounded allegations that get you into trouble. You have to be more careful than in the past, because we don't have the layers of checking that we had before", warns Ruth.

writerruth.com
@WriterRuth

Getting started

- Get an up-to-date media law textbook for the country you work in
- Add terms and conditions to your website and signpost via a link in your email signature
- Sign up to ALCS or another relevant collecting society

- Print out the code of conduct most relevant to your work and always keep it with you
- Identify at least two confidants to speak to following a stressful or distressing experience

Notes

1 BBC News. 2013 "Ched Evans rape case: tenth person fined for naming victim" www.bbc.co.uk/news/uk-wales-north-east-wales-21123465.
2 Reporters without Borders. 2019 "World Press Freedom Index 2019: India" https://rsf.org/en/india.
3 Torrent Freak. 2017 "'Pirating' mainstream media outlets haunted by photographers in court" https://torrentfreak.com/pirating-mainstream-media-outlets-haunted-by-photographers-in-court-171028/.
4 Torrent Freak. 2017 "CBS drops lawsuit over 'pirated' screenshot of 59-Year-Old TV Show" https://torrentfreak.com/cbs-drops-lawsuit-over-pirated-screenshot-of-59-year-old-tv-show-171215/.
5 BBC News. 2019 "Lyra McKee: 'New IRA' admits killing of journalist" www.bbc.co.uk/news/uk-48018615.
6 Reporters without Borders. 2019 "RSF yearly round-up: 'historically low' number of journalists killed in 2019" https://rsf.org/en/news/rsf-yearly-round-historically-low-number-journalists-killed-2019.
7 Kirchner, L. 2014 "Why Skype isn't safe for journalists" *Columbia Journalism Review* https://archives.cjr.org/behind_the_news/skype_alternatives.php.
8 Dougary, G. 2017 "How BBC star Clare Balding nicked my byline" *The Guardian* www.theguardian.com/media/2017/sep/30/celebrity-interview-bullying-behaviour-balding-saga.

9
Brand Me

OBJECTIVES

In this chapter you will learn:

- How to think of yourself as a brand
- How to define your unique selling point
- The importance of a digital profile
- The best tools for promoting your work
- What you need to do to improve your branding

Whether you like it or not as a freelance you are a brand. From the very beginning, you need to get good at selling yourself, promoting your skills and nurturing your profile. When an editor commissions a piece of work, they are buying into you and your brand rather than simply buying your idea. They need to know that you have the correct skills and experience and are able to deliver as promised. By establishing and cultivating your brand, you will be able to demonstrate this in a few simple clicks. Brand Me simply means marketing yourself, particularly online, in a consistent, honest and positive manner.

Many journalists are uncomfortable with the idea of Brand Me because they want their stories to be their platform, but as a freelance in a competitive marketplace, you don't have the luxury of hiding behind your work (unless you are an undercover reporter). You need to be front and centre, building a professional profile from the very beginning so when anyone Googles your name, they can easily find you and your portfolio. Using search engine optimisation to bump up your name to the top of a Google search is extremely important and is achieved by populating different platforms with your name and profession. It is also vital that you own your brand and the way in which your profile is presented online to counteract any disinformation that may exist particularly as your public profile grows.

Social media plays an influential role in building your profile, but it should not be the focus of all of your attention. Websites and email are key tools in your branding box and require a lot of attention and consideration. However, if you do already have a reasonable following on social media, this is an attractive measure for editors as they can tap into your ready made audience.

Where to start?

It seems that every week a celebrity or public figure is sacked from their job for something they posted online several years ago. Hollywood director James Gunn was fired from Guardian of the Galaxy 3 (only to be reinstated after the cast protested) for something he tweeted a decade ago.[1] And there are also plenty of examples of everyday employees being caught out by inappropriate posts on social media, which have cost them their livelihoods. You only have to look at the Business Insider story 17 People Who Were Fired For Using Facebook to realise that what goes online, stays online.[2]

So, when it comes to creating Brand Me the best place to start is with a purge. Take a systematic approach and go through each of your social media profiles deleting content which could be deemed unprofessional or switch the access to private. Drunken nights out, swearing rants and bikini beer pong should probably be removed from public posts. If you already have a website or blog take a close look at the content and take down anything poorly written or that paints you in a negative light. Be brutal and use a healthy dose of common sense, it will benefit you in the long run.

Once the clean-up is complete, you need to make a decision about your personal and private spaces online. Many journalists choose to keep Facebook and Instagram for their family and friends only but use Twitter, LinkedIn and other social media platforms for their public facing work. Others seem to find a healthy balance between life and work tweeting about stories they have covered alongside cute pictures of their dog on the beach. Everyone will take a different approach, and it is up to you to decide what you are prepared to associate with your brand and how much personalisation you want to offer. There is no right or wrong approach, and it is something which tends to evolve organically. Only tweeting links to your stories is adequate enough, but most editors will expect to see some demonstration of engagement with your followers and an inkling of personality rather than a robot. Whatever you decide to post online, think about how it might appear to potential commissioning editors and sources, before going live.

The next step is to find out how prominent your name is on a web search engine. Google your name and then also search for your name and either the word journalist or your specialism, for example, Daniel Bates Foreign Correspondent. This will give you an indication of how prevalent your name, and your brand, is. As you start to develop your online profile, repeat your name, occupation and specialism on different websites and platforms so that your search engine optimisation improves. Even if you have a common name like Emma Wilkinson, by building up your digital profile you will be easy for people to find if they search your name with associated words such as medicine or health journalist. It is worth regularly checking your position on a Google web search to see how strong your ranking is and acting accordingly to ensure your brand continues to score highly.

Before you begin pitching story ideas, it is vital to have your branding in place so editors can quickly check out your cuttings and scan your (clean) digital footprint. The two most important components are a website and an email address with a signature which links to your website and/or cuttings. These are the must-have basics to have in place, and the rest can be developed over time. Obviously, your profile will be stronger if you have a Twitter presence and can be found on a variety of social media platforms, but if you are time stretched then concentrate on your website portfolio.

Creating a unique selling point

Branding can seem to be all about clever logos, fancy websites and catchy straplines but at the heart of the brand is you. This means you need to understand what your brand stands for and what skills, experience and perspective you are bringing to it. Your brand should reflect your values and your personality and the type of work you intend to do. If you are a hard news journalist covering crime then your branding may be more sober and formal with dark, neutral colours on your website and social media profile. But if you are an entertainment feature writer, then you may need a bit more sparkle and fun embodied in your brand with the use of bright colours, a witty strapline and a bubbly photograph. It is worth defining your brand to yourself by writing down your core values, personality, mission and positioning. This will help to inform an overall brand and guide you towards the most appropriate photographs, backdrops and colours to use.

If you are a generalist then don't be afraid to embrace this in your brand, for example: 'Clare Smith, Freelance Journalist, Writing about the issues that matter most'. In this instance, the key unique selling point is the person rather than their specialism. If you do cover a particular niche and that is unlikely to change, then use it to create your central unique selling point, for example: 'Craig Hill, Hockey journalist' or 'Sarah Brown, motoring journalist specialising in classic cars' or 'Gurvinder Sidhu, news reporter covering South Yorkshire and Humberside'.

Names and logos

Depending on your area of work, you may decide that a logo is an effective way to brand yourself and this may include a strapline or slogan. This will help editors and your audience to immediately understand what you are selling and what your perspective is. This may also involve creating a pseudonym or brand identity. This approach is particularly prevalent amongst bloggers and influencers but is creeping into journalism too particularly as freelances tend to have portfolio careers (see Chapter 11). For example, personal finance writer Lynn James brands herself Mrs Mummypenny with the strapline 'Healthy wealth, body and mind'. Her website is mrsmummypenny.co.uk and her Twitter handle is @MrsMummypennyUK. Meanwhile documentarian Christian Payne is also known as Documentally and has a humorous politically inclined logo which appears across all of his digital profiles under his Documentally brand.

For most journalists using their own name is the best way to build a credible, authoritative brand which sets them apart from bloggers and opinion writers, but it can be worth considering a different approach to allow your brand to stand out. In the UK, Anna Turns brands herself as Environmental Journalist with the website www.environmentaljournalist.co.uk and the Twitter name Environment Journalist with the handle @AnnaTurns.

Box 9.1 Author's experience

As a journalist interested in a range of topics Lily initially found it difficult to brand herself. Taking advice from a career coach, she decided not to be constricted by one specialism and began promoting herself as a money, health and lifestyle journalist. Within the first six months of going freelance she decided to turn her blog into a professional website. She already owned the domain lilycanter.co.uk but was using the free WordPress blogging platform which had limited functions. She hired a new web developer to redesign her website for under £500. More established developers had quoted £1,000 upwards for the same work. The website was designed to reflect her breadth of work with a portfolio page for each of her specialisms (money, health, lifestyle, reviews), which she updates each week with new cuttings. There is also a page which outlines her academic research and publications, but the primary focus of the website is to act as an online journalism resume. After using a variety of social media platforms Lily found that Twitter and Instagram were the most effective and easiest to update on a regular basis. She now uses Twitter to find case studies and promote both her journalistic and academic work. Meanwhile her Instagram profile specialises on veganism and sport as she found these types of posts gained the most reach.

Your literary writing style

Your writing style will be partly determined by the publications that you work for. These will each have an in-house style guide and a particular approach to format and structure which is directly linked to who their audience is (see Chapter 6). However, even within this there is room to create your own literary style which can become a strong part of your brand. The words that you use, sentence formation and figurative language all create a voice through which a story is told. The four typical ways of presenting a piece of writing are expository, descriptive, persuasive and narrative. Journalism can be presented in any of these forms but is often expository in nature, explaining and informing the audience. A narrative approach is more common in human interest features, as the subject of the article becomes a character in an unfolding story. Travel and food writing, on the other hand, tends to be descriptive, whilst opinion writers and columnists rely on persuasive text to convert the audience to their point of view.

As a freelance writer, you may need to be able to switch between these different forms of writing, but if you are particularly strong in one area, then this can be built into your brand. Acknowledging your strengths and weaknesses is a great way to identity what your literary style is, and the type of journalism it is best suited to. If you excel at creating polemic prose that persuades one audience and repels another, like *The Guardian* commentator Owen Jones, then push this to the forefront of your brand. However, if you are better at explaining complex matters in plain English, then your brand may benefit from focusing on a news specialism such as fintech journalism.

Digital profile

Your digital profile is anything that is publicly available online. This includes your professional website, any Tumblr blogs you set up as a teenager, student assignments, social media posts and even your redundant MySpace account. Once you have cleaned up your digital footprint, you want to ensure that your brand is connective and consistent across all public platforms. This means using the same photo and contact information, and keeping them all regularly updated.

Wherever possible, use your own name or brand name as your profile handle and keep it the same wherever you exist online. If your Twitter handle is JoeySmith then don't identify yourself as Joseph Smith on LinkedIn and avoid calling your website Joe the Journalist. Choose a consistent name to use across the internet, as this will help to build your reputation and make your name stick in people's minds. Similarly, all of your online profiles should connect to one another, so however a person finds you they can easily hop between them. For example, if an editor lands on your website homepage they should be able to easily click through to your Twitter, YouTube, Flicker and Instagram page, and if they find you on Instagram, there should be a link in your bio back to your website as a bare minimum.

Website

One of the biggest tasks when initiating your brand is setting up a website. This can be as cheap or expensive as you wish and can develop over time. In the first instance it is important to find and pay for an available domain name using a registrar such as 123reg, GoDaddy or Tsohost. The domain needs to be associated with your brand, which may be based on your own name, such as lilycanter.co.uk or emmawilkinson.net, or your brand name, for example, documentally.com or environmentaljournalist.co.uk. Whatever domain name you decide on, make sure it matches up with your profile name on social media platforms. Domains are relatively low in cost starting at around £10 a year, and this is tax deductible (see Chapter 7).

A website can be built using a free platform such as WordPress, Wix or Weebly, and some companies, such as Squarespace, include hosting and domain services as a complete package. Some specific website builders, such as JournoPortfolio and Clippings.me, offer a portfolio style platform which can work well for journalists who want to regularly update the site with new links and PDFs. Paid for services are offered by Squarespace and Pressfolios. All of the free website builders offer paid-for versions with additional widgets and add-ons which allow you to custom build your site and be more creative with the design, navigation and content.

Whilst they are great for setting up a quick website, free web building platforms can be quite limited in scope and generic in design, meaning you are unable to stand out from the crowd or create striking visuals. However, employing a web designer to build you a website from scratch, including a user-friendly mobile version, could cost £1,000 upwards. If you do decide to go down this route, make sure to shop around and get a range of comparable quotes but also draw on the expertise of friends, colleagues and family members who may offer you a better rate.

There are some website builders that also include a custom email such as Wix but others only offer this through a third party such as G suite. The world of website builders, web hosts domain registrars and email hosts is increasingly complex, so paying a web developer or a tech savvy friend to sort everything for you can be a worthwhile purchase.

Whether you decide to build a website yourself using a free or low-cost template, or enlist the skills of a website developer, there are some fundamental pieces of content that you need to include. Every freelance website should incorporate clear contact details including an actual email address, rather than just a Contact Us box to fill in, plus links to all relevant, public social media profiles and a telephone number if you wish to divulge this. There should also be examples of your cuttings or links to them and ideally these will be updated regularly. A brief outline of your experience and training is necessary along with a clear head and shoulders photo. But be aware that using PDFs or screen grabs of your work, even on your own website, could attract the attention of the National Licencing Agency in the UK, so make sure you are not breaching any copyright law. Where possible use hyperlinks instead.

If you list the titles you have worked for and include their logos in a prominent position, even if you have only been commissioned by them once, this will look particularly impressive. Testimonials from people you have worked with or for, such as commissioning editors or senior reporters, will also give your website credibility and add kudos to your brand. If you have a logo and slogan, then these should feature as a banner at the top of each page, to reinforce your brand further.

Box 9.2 Author's experience

Emma is in a fairly unique position as someone with university degrees in both science and journalism. This has enabled her to carve a very specific niche in her work, writing about health, medicine and biosciences. This specialism is a defining characteristic that makes Emma stand out from many other writers working in the same field and she has used this feature as a 'selling point' to attract new work. Her digital presence clearly states her experience and interests and is consistent across social media and LinkedIn. Twitter has been her most successful route for showcasing her work and letting potential new employers know about what she is working on and what she has published. In addition to finding contacts and stories, Twitter has proven a great way for Emma to promote investigations and in-depth features she has worked on as well as the more routine news stories. Several commissioning editors in medicine and health have come across her through this promotion and offered her work. If you have something that makes you stand out, Emma explains, that needs to be front and centre of your digital profile which is increasingly how new connections are built.

Social media

Some journalists still shy away from social media because they feel it is a largely subjective platform where personalities rather than facts gain the most traction. This is a legitimate position to take, but it does restrict brand presence online. Rather than avoiding social media altogether, an alternative approach is to stop and take stock before setting up a branded profile to consider how you intend to use it. Do you want to maintain a level of neutrality and objectivity and how do you intend to balance this against showing your personality and interacting with followers? Will you post comments and images from your social and family life? Is it relevant and how does it affect your brand?

Whatever you post publicly online should be viewed as your branded content and you should be comfortable with potential editors and audience members viewing, sharing and commenting on it. Taking a common sense approach, and posting when in a calm mood rather than enraged, is probably wise. You don't want to become known for ranting about careless drivers in their souped-up cars when you are about to pitch to a racing magazine.

Some freelance writers create an excellent following on social media due to their witty, insightful or highly personal posts, which in turn attracts editors who know they have an engaged audience to promote content to. But the same approach does not work for everyone and each platform is different so carefully consider whether your posts match with your brand values and perspectives. If you do take a more conservative approach, then try to avoid simply posting promotional material about your work, and mix it up with interaction with followers and sharing posts or helpful links. Think about what you can do for the online community rather than what it can do for you. Even these small measures will help to express your personality and with it your brand.

The platforms you decide to inhabit will depend on your niche and medium. If you are a video journalist then a branded YouTube channel showcasing your work could make perfect sense. However, a travel journalist might make better use of Instagram as a means to share photographs from assignments and build up a following, further enhancing their brand.

The staple social networking and platform sharing sites for journalists tend to be Twitter and LinkedIn, but many writers also make use of Facebook pages, Flickr, Pinterest, YouTube, Instagram and Tumblr. There are also professional networks, such as TravMedia, Muck Rack and Hostwriter, where freelances can create a profile. The key is to select the platforms that work best for your brand and to present yourself in a professional manner with a clear, linked profile and up to date photograph or logo. Profile descriptions are also an excellent way to express the essence of your brand whether that be an outline of your specialism, your strapline or tags and links to publications you have written for. On Twitter it is common for freelances to describe their specialism and then include handles, and links to their website, column or latest book, for example, finance journalist @moneywiseonline @lovemoney_com @thisismoney, author *Money Talks*.

Facebook is often used as a private platform for journalists rather than a professional one and is the only online space where they seek solace from their work. However, freelances can spend a lot of time networking with fellow journalists and editors on Facebook and increasingly use it as a resource to find case studies. Even if your profile is set to private, people that you interact with on Facebook or Facebook Messenger will be able to see a limited amount of information about you and your current and historic profile photos, so you may need to lightly brand yourself in this space as well. Another consideration is setting up a branded Facebook page although the functions of this will be different and more restrictive than a personal profile.

When posting content online it is important to be as interactive as possible by including multimedia content, particularly photos and images, plus hyperlinks, as well as tagging people and topics or words. This will help to spread your post further and achieve brand extension. An Instagram post with hashtags will reach thousands rather than hundreds of users and will highlight your brand to potential new followers. Also ensure that you have consistency across all of your social media profiles by using the same wording, photos and colours.

A handy tip for using social media to your advantage is to gain editors' attention on your chosen platform before pitching to them. For instance, start following them on Twitter and share and respond to their posts a few days or weeks before you send them a pitch. Chances are they will recognise your name, which will make them curious and more likely to read your email.

Email

Plenty of successful freelance journalists use Gmail, Hotmail, Yahoo! or a similar provider for their email account, especially if it is a free and they have been using it for a long time. It can be difficult to keep track of multiple email accounts, and some prefer to have everything in one place rather than separate personal and professional accounts. However, it does look more professional if you have an email attached to your website domain. Most web hosts will offer a free basic email account which will allow you to set up an address like fred@fredfreeman. co.uk or anna@environmentaljournalist.co.uk. There is often the option to have more than one inbox so you could have multiple addresses, such as pressreleases@ fredfreeman.co.uk, invoices@fredfreeman.co.uk and info@fredfreeman.co.uk. This could be particularly useful if you cover a variety of specialisms so you could have fashion@fredfreeman.co.uk and beauty@fredfreeman.co.uk and travel@ fredfreeman.co.uk. Again, there is no best way of doing things, and it is about creating a logistical system which works efficiently and effectively for you.

Whether you decide to use an email attached to your domain or not, it is always advisable to have a sensible address which is not silly or obscure. It might have seemed funny when you were a teenager to set up the email address harlotof-hull@gmail.com but it would not be wise to use this professionally. Most journalists use their full name or their brand identity if it is separate from their name.

Just as important as the email address is the signature embedded into your email. This will permanently sit at the bottom of every message you compose and is a great way to present a mini resume and link to your work. Your signature should include your name, job title/specialism, website and social media links. It should also include links to your latest stories and broadcast clips and showcase the media organisations you have worked for. Having all the information together in a few compact sentences gives editors a snapshot of your experience and quick access to your back catalogue. For example:

> **Fred Freeman**
> **Freelance travel journalist**
> **www.fredfreeman.co.uk**
> **@fredfreeman**
>
> **I have experience writing travel reviews and features for The Times [hyperlink to your most recent article], Lonely Planet [hyperlink to PDF on your website], Traveler [hyperlink to PDF on your website] and Wanderlust [hyperlink to your most recent article].**

Websites such as ZippySig, Signature Maker, and Wisestamp will help you to generate a free professional email signature with graphics and images, which will make your profile stand out even more, particularly when pitching to editors for the first time.

Business cards

They may seem old fashioned but most freelance journalists still swear by their business cards. They are particularly important when you are starting out and attending events to network with potential contacts and commissioners (see Chapter 5). In an era of digital profiles, people love to hold a tangible object and have all of your information in one place – even if they end up taking a photograph of it.

Business cards can be as plain or as elaborate as you choose, and there are plenty of websites, such as Vistaprint, Moo and Solopress, which will design a logo for you based on your initials or using copyright free images. Prices are relatively low, starting at around £10 for printing and postage of 250 cards. Things start to get pricier when you select unconventional card shapes or textured paper. You can spend hours agonising over the design of a card, but the most important thing is that they say what you do and how you can be contacted. Include your website, phone number, email and social media handles. You may want contact details on the back of the card and your name or a strong image or design on the front of the card.

Think about the impression the card gives and try to align it with the type of work you want to secure. If you cover hard news then a neon pink card might not be appropriate, but if you specialise in fashion and beauty then it might be suitable. If you want to keep your options open, then choose a more generic design or focus on your name.

If you have the money to spend and feel it would be beneficial, then you may want to employ someone to design a logo for you. This would usually cost upwards of £50. The logo can then be used on your business cards but also on your website, social media profiles and email signature, ensuring branding consistency wherever people find you. This is particularly useful if you have a particular specialism as the logo can reflect this. You might be able to do a skills swap with a graphic designer friend and ask them to design a logo for you in return for writing copy for their website.

Resumes

It is still important to have an up-to-date resume or CV (curriculum vitae) even if you have a website. Although most editors will simply look at your cuttings online, some will ask for a resume especially if you are a recent graduate with less writing experience. Applications for part-time projects often have a mandatory field to attach a resume, so make sure you always have one which is up to date.

It is important to keep all of your branding consistent, so your resume should include the same logo and image of yourself that you have on your website and social media profiles, and your specialism should be the same. If you describe yourself as a travel writer on your resume but your website banner says you are a sports journalist, this will cause confusion. Similarly, if you have a photo on your Twitter profile with long blonde hair and one on your resume with short dark hair, potential employers may think they are looking at the wrong social media account. Having the same images and key words surrounding your name in multiple locations will strengthen your brand and send a clear message to editors.

The content of your resume should reflect your website with a similar writing style and latest cuttings. Remember that since resumes are usually opened on a device connected to the internet, you can embed hyperlinks to your cuttings to make it quick and easy for people to read or view your work. As a rule of thumb resumes should be no more than two pages and often the best ones condense the information into one page. Instead of focusing on your education and interests, concentrate on selling yourself as a journalist by listing the publications you have worked for, the exciting stories you have covered and the bylines or credits you are most proud of.

Try to avoid creating a resume that is too ostentatious or embedded with animations. Unless you are applying for graphic design work, this is unnecessary and may detract from the content. You want to make sure that the employer can quickly open your resume and if they have to download software to view it chances are, they will move onto the next resume in their inbox. Word documents and PDF files are generally accepted as the norm.

It is worth checking your resume every six months to update it with new links and any new titles, publishers or broadcasters you have worked for. As a freelance you may find yourself working for new clients every month and you want to make sure you capture all of this on your resume. You will also need to do the same for your email signature, social media bios and website.

Additional training

As an authority in your subject area, you may find that there comes a point when additional training is required to extend your brand. If you have saturated the print market or identified that there is demand in another field, then it could be time to upskill. In the digital economy multimedia skills will enable you to impress editors and apply for a greater variety of freelance work. If you can supply high-quality, high-resolution photographs, this might give you the edge over other freelances, but this is usually something that requires training.

You may also need to invest in equipment such as a digital SLR camera or an external microphone particularly if you intend to start podcasting. There is plenty of free information and self-help tutorials online, but to set yourself apart from hobbyists it is worth investing in training. This could be a one-day course to give you the basics to build upon or paying a broadcast or photography colleague to give you some hands-on lessons.

Podcasts are a booming medium and relatively straightforward to produce. But don't assume that you can create a quality programme with just a smartphone and an idea. A low-quality product with poor sound quality and/or content will damage your brand. If you are taking the plunge into broadcasting, then ensure that you can create an engaging, useful product rather than a self-indulgent one. Study current podcasts to see where there is a gap in the market and make sure you are clear what makes an effective episode. Audio writing, editing and recording skills are vital when creating a new podcast as you want to create a great impression from the start. You also need to create or commission eye-catching cover art that will stand out in a podcast library and adapted versions for an associated website and social media profiles. If the podcast is connected to you and your brand, then it has to be every bit as professional as all of your other freelance work. There is a wealth of free information on podcast branding at podcastsuccessacademy.com.

Becoming an expert

Another way to establish yourself as a brand in the public domain, rather than simply within the industry, is to put yourself forward as an expert. This could involve speaking on a particular topic on the radio or a television news show, becoming a talking head in documentaries or public speaking. Don't be afraid to offer your opinion if someone is looking for a guest on a show and contact broadcast producers to make them aware of the subjects you can speak to. Contact relevant conference organisers with suggestions of presentation topics and attach evidence of cuttings to illustrate your expertise in given areas. Getting yourself known and on the pundit circuit will extend your brand and lead to new opportunities as people start coming to you. Remember that producers are always looking to fill expert slots and conferences always need content, so by being bold and putting yourself forward you are actually helping them out.

If you do intend to speak publicly on a subject, then again it may be worth seeking media training beforehand. This might be voice training for radio or tactical training on dealing with difficult interviewers and on-the-spot questions. Journalism conferences such as News Rewired in the UK offer one-day training courses and unions; universities and colleges often have a list of shorter training programmes or distance learning. There are also a range of free online courses via MOOCs (Massive Open Online Courses) such as edX and Future Learn on topics such as data journalism and journalism for social change. Whatever you do, research the training provider first to ensure that they offer a quality service and are a well-established organisation with a good track record. Ask around in forums and networks to see what other freelances would recommend so you don't end up throwing your money away.

Protecting your brand

Once you have built up a brand over a number of years, it is important not to get complacent and to be proactive in maintaining it. Don't let old content languish on your website and make sure to update your portfolio regularly. If it looks like the last thing you published was five years ago, editors may think you are no longer working as a journalist. Keep your social media profiles active with current posts and only set up accounts on new platforms if you can keep on top of the postings. Some freelances employ virtual assistants to do this work for them to ensure all of their accounts have up-to-date cuttings and daily fresh content.

Attacks on your brand are also something to be aware of. This could be a blog, tweet or comment on a story which undermines you or your output. If the remarks breach the rules of the platform report them so they can be removed or blocked. If you have good SEO on your website and social media platforms, this will help to filter out negative content and push it further down in search engine rankings so you are able to set the narrative surrounding your brand.

People with the same name as you can also cause problems whether they work in journalism or not. It is important to protect your brand, so this may mean approaching people to ask if they would consider using an altered professional name or branding themselves more distinctly from yourself. If your brand is new then it is probably worth taking the initiative to adjust it to avoid confusion with someone with the same name. But if you are an established freelance journalist, then your brand is already fully developed and you should take measures to protect it. For example, one UK journalist had to challenge a 'high class escort girl' who shared her name, after she wrote an explicit piece for a magazine that the freelance journalist also wrote for. After tracking her down the journalist explained that she wrote about parenting and sharing a name with an escort girl who was trying to carve a niche in the media was potentially awkward and confusing. Eventually the girl agreed that it was not in her interests to pursue a media profile under the same name as a well-established journalist and changed her name.

Some journalists go a step further and trademark their brand name. In the UK, this is a simple process of applying to the Intellectual Property Office where they consider whether you have a unique claim to the name or not. Once you receive a trademark, it prevents anyone from using the name or similar names in media and publishing. Following advice from a marketing expert, motorcycling journalist Chris Wheal secured a trademark on his nickname and brand name Whealie, which has appeared in several publications and is his Twitter username.

Box 9.3 Case study: Daniel Bates

Working in America as a foreign correspondent, Daniel Bates covers general news stories for international titles, including the *Mail on Sunday*, *The Guardian*, The Daily Beast and middle eastern publication *The National*.

He admits that as a generalist who covers America, he struggles with branding at times, but he says it is still vital to look professional and promote yourself as a legitimate journalist.

"The most important thing is to have a website, it is your main public face. As a writer it is a way to introduce yourself to people and it allows you to show your cuttings. It also enables people to find you and says that you are a professional".

Business cards are also a useful branding tool for Daniel even in the world of digital contacts. They add an air of professionalism and complement a good website, he says.

"Mine are plain and simple and just say my name and have my phone number, email and website. For me it is best to have something bland with information on it rather than having something flashy. It is as inoffensive as possible because sometimes I am leaving a note and a card and it can be for something that is very sensitive or involves a bereavement".

Branding on social media is also important for Daniel who has an active Twitter profile and can be found on LinkedIn. But it comes with the warning that it can be a double-edged sword.

"Everything you put out there is your brand. I want to have a degree of impartiality about things so it's important for me to think before I post on there. I have also been hammered on Twitter for my stories in the past. You have to have a thick skin and it is always best not to engage if you are being attacked online. Overall though the benefits out way the drawbacks. People contact me regularly through Twitter".

Another way to develop your brand is to put yourself forward as an expert whether that is on a television or radio show, or at an event.

"It is something I am developing and I am setting up interviews with Fox News and CNN as a British specialist so I can talk about a Royal visit or the impact of Brexit. Doing discussion panels and talks also builds up your brand, or if you write a book, you become an expert on a topic. Entering awards is also good for your brand and there is a way to write stories to target awards".

But at the end of the day Daniel believes the best thing for branding is to have strong relationships with editors and be a reliable journalist.

"The brand is not just about how the public see you. My brand is for an editor and it is within the industry. The best thing I can do for my brand is to do a good job".

danielgbates.com
@danielgbates

Getting started

- Clean up your digital profile – be brutal!
- Write down your brand values, personality, mission, vision and positioning and use this as the starting point to shape Brand Me
- Brainstorm your areas of expertise and decide whether you wish to be a generalist or a specialist
- Search your name online to see how visible you are and who your potential competitors are
- Select a photograph or image to use across all of your branding

Notes

1 BBC News. 2019 "James Gunn: Disney rehires sacked Guardians of the Galaxy director" www.bbc.co.uk/news/entertainment-arts-47577507.
2 Love, D. 2014 "17 people who were fired for using Facebook" www.businessinsider.com/17-people-who-were-fired-for-using-facebook-2014-7?r=US&IR=T.

10
Setting up at home

OBJECTIVES

In this chapter you will learn:

- What equipment you will need to work from home
- How to create the right working space
- Techniques for managing your time
- How to stay motivated and avoid isolation
- Whether working on the move could be an option for you

Increasing numbers of us are working from home, at least some of the time. In the UK, official figures suggest more than 4 million people are home workers (or use home as their base while travelling to meet clients). There are several immediate and obvious advantages, including setting your own hours, working flexibly around other commitments and reducing time spent on the commute. For the freelance journalist, working from home can be both liberating and lonely (sometimes in the same week). This chapter will set out how to make a success of working from home as well as discussing what facilities or equipment you might need.

When planning to work from home there are several considerations you need to make, including having a dedicated space, a phone (or way to make calls), computer and desk, and an environment as free as possible from distractions. Although it may be tempting to sit cross legged on the sofa or in bed with a laptop on your knee, you may not be able to afford the physiotherapy bills when you have been working that way for months. Have you got a working computer, reliable internet access and a way to make phone calls without getting cut off? Are you at risk of constant interruptions from children, housemates or pets? Many of the decisions you make will be personal to you. One person's peaceful escape from a loud, open-plan office may drive the next person to tears of boredom.

The publications or outlets you end up working for will not care what your 'office' at home looks like as long as it means you can deliver the goods. The goal is to be organised enough in your set up – however that looks for you – to be able to meet those deadlines without being in an office with the facilities and oversight that brings. If you get the right balance, it could even mean working for a few highly productive hours before taking a break to go and do something else.

Equipment

Reliable access to a computer is of course a must, but for most freelances, this will not need to be an all singing, all dancing, top of the range piece of equipment. You will need access to the internet, word processing capability (Google docs will do the job if you need a free version) and a way to store and send files. Dropbox and other cloud-based tools can help you manage and share files from different locations as well as having a back-up should your computer die. Depending on the type of work you do, you may also need a way to edit audio and or video.

A way to make phone calls is, of course, also a must. But again, there is no need to break the bank with a huge phone bill. Use free minutes from mobile or landline phone providers but also experiment with free internet call services, such as WhatsApp, Skype or Zoom. The set up you opt for will depend on your internet reliability and mobile phone signal among other factors, but, if you are careful, this does not have to be an expensive part of your overheads. As long as commissioning editors and contacts can easily get in touch with you (or you with them), the decision should come down to what works best for your situation. And be aware that apps such as WhatsApp and Signal can be very useful if you are working with someone that you do not want people to trace, for example, an anonymous source. Both use end-to-end encryption to prevent data being read or modified by a third party. For keeping up to date with useful digital tools for journalists, the Poynter 'Try This! – Tools for Journalism', weekly newsletter is invaluable.

You may also need a way to record phone or face-to-face interviews. In addition to digital recording devices, there are online apps of varying quality to help with this, although some require complicated steps in the way the call is made. Most smart phones also have a function to record a conversation already built in. The decision on whether to invest in specific recording equipment will depend on the type of work you are doing. For example, recording a discussion for a podcast will require much higher quality sound than just recording a conversation so you can type up a transcript for a written piece. A print journalist with good shorthand may not need anything other than a pen and notebook.

For anyone working routinely at home, a desk or table with a comfortable supportive chair will make life a lot easier (and less painful). If you are sitting for a long period of time, an adjustable chair which supports good posture will be a sound investment. Screen height is also important for avoiding back and neck pain. As a general rule, the top of the screen should be level with your eyebrows. If you use a laptop computer and are sitting at a desk for a long time, a laptop stand and separate keyboard can help to get everything in the right position. Other than avoiding a work-based injury, having a dedicated desk or table will make sure you have everything to hand and prevent you having to get everything out and put it away every time you need to work. That is not to say that you should not enjoy the luxury of the odd time you really fancy working from bed, the kitchen table or the sofa.

In terms of online facilities, you will need an email address and professional social media as well as considering setting up a website to showcase your work. More detail on how to do that can be found in Chapter 9.

One of the most tedious and time-consuming aspects of journalism can be transcribing long interviews. There are apps that can do this for you to varying degrees of success, depending on factors such as accents and how technical the topic. There can also be big differences in what you can pay for the transcription; for example, Rev.com is $1 a minute, whereas Otter.ai offers 600 minutes of free transcription a month. Another option is to use Google voice typing to transcribe an audio file in to text, but to do this, you do have to play the audio file out loud for the speaker on your computer to pick it up. Some journalists say transcription apps have revolutionised their working life, while others are yet to be convinced.

Working environment

One of the first bits of advice that anyone gives to home workers is to get dressed – to treat working from home as if you were in the office. Whether this makes a huge amount of difference is debatable. Pyjamas are comfortable. Sitting at your kitchen table in a suit is not likely to, on its own, suddenly turn you into freelance dynamo. But there is an important message underneath the fashion advice, which is to take freelance work as seriously as you would any other job. What that means to the individual will vary. If you work better after getting dressed as if going into the office, then do that. If the whole joy of freelance work is that you get to dress down, do that instead. A couple of respondents to a journalism survey carried out by the Press Gazette even admitted to working naked.[1]

Other aspects to getting the right working balance for you include having a dedicated space free from distractions; finding your most effective working patterns; setting boundaries around domestic chores or for friends, housemates or family members who want to take advantage of your being at home; having the right facilities in place; and knowing when to take a break.

Box 10.1 Author's experience

When Emma first began to freelance, she lived in a small one-bedroom flat but set up a desk in the far corner of the living room in order to have a dedicated work space. At the time, she was spending much of her time doing freelance shifts in offices so this suited her needs well. After moving to a bigger house outside London, she set up her office in a spare room, which meant she could shut the door on work once done for the day and could work productively even if other people were around. She now has a purpose-built office in the cellar of her home, which is quiet and has everything she needs. Whatever space you have, Emma says, it is really important to carve out that place that is just for work and allows you to sit comfortably and concentrate. When it's all happening in the same place, it also helps to build as clear a divide as possible between your leisure time and work time.

Where possible, it is useful to have a dedicated area for work. If you are short on space, that might mean a desk in the corner of a living area or bedroom, but at least there is an element of stepping into a 'work zone' where everything you need is to hand and you can be productive. A spare room (if possible) can be very useful as it means you can shut the door on work once you are done for the day and avoid other tasks around the house that may stop you fully concentrating. A dedicated space also helps to delineate between work and leisure time. That does not stop you taking your laptop to work somewhere else should you get sick of staring at the same bit of wall. That flexibility is part of what makes freelance work attractive.

Avoiding distractions

It can sometimes be harder to focus when working from home given the number of potential distractions there are. This is the place where you also relax, watch TV and spend your free time. Setting the boundaries between the two will be vital if you intend to get anything done. Family members, housemates, children, partners and pets can also get in the way of concentration. And once the procrastination sets in, it can be hard to get back to it. Some freelances have found it useful to set up a system so that people around them know when they are working and need to be left alone. If you tend to work flexible hours, that might not be clear, so a note or other sign that you are 'at work' may be useful, especially if those around you feel you are available anytime because you work from home.

The most common source of distraction for freelance journalists working from home is highly likely to be social media. You are at your computer all ready to do lots of work and before you know it, hours have gone by while you disappeared down an internet rabbit hole. If this is a problem for you, have set times to check your social media accounts, set limits or make sure you complete a certain number of tasks on your list before letting yourself check in. This may depend on the work you are doing because social media could well be central to your working day in terms of sourcing ideas, case studies or keeping track of an issue or current news story. If your self-control needs help, there are a wide range of apps you can use to help 'lock you out' of both social media and your phone for self-imposed periods of time, including Offtime, Freedom and ForestApp. If working to a very tight deadline, you could even disable your email.

It can be very useful to take advantage of the fact you work from home to get on with those household chores but beware spending too much time keeping on top of other jobs that take you away from paid work or mean that you will end up working unintentionally late. Some freelance workers say they cannot start until everything is tidy and clean; others will be happy to shut the door on it and deal with it later or even opt to pay a cleaner to avoid it being a distraction. Whichever your approach, be mindful of not letting it take precedent over your freelance work, which could never happen if you were in the office.

Alternative locations

If you have not got space for a decent working area at home or you feel that being on your own is sapping your enthusiasm, there are plenty of other options you can explore, even if just to give yourself a new environment every once in a while.

Cafes with WiFi can be a useful way to get work done while still feeling part of the real world. As a change of scene, it can get you over a period of procrastination and some actively encourage freelance working with speedy internet connections and free refills. For some the lively buzz of working around other people can support concentration and productivity. However, the downside can be uncomfortable seating, lack of space and too much noise to have a phone conversation or focus on a project.

If you need somewhere quieter, try the local public library. This can be a great option for those who just need somewhere quiet to work outside the home but are not in a position to spend money on a co-working office space. Most libraries offer free WiFi and have desk space with power outlets for your laptop as well as useful information resources for those needing to do research. You also do not have to worry about overstaying your welcome as you might in a café where you have not bought a hot drink in a while. However, it may not be for you if you are looking for somewhere with more of a social buzz to get you motivated. It is also not that useful if you need to be making a lot of phone calls and will have to decamp from the quiet sections at regular intervals. Many universities or colleges also allow members of the public to use their library spaces (usually you will need to bring ID). Systems and rules vary between in-stitutions, so it would be best to research the options locally before turning up.

For those who need a more office-like set up and would prefer to work with others around, co-working spaces can be a relatively cheap (compared with renting a dedicated office space) and flexible option. These are usually large, often open-plan spaces divided into spots for freelancers or small business to rent at far more affordable rates than a standard office rental. Prices and type of contract can vary depending on the type of co-working space and facilities on offer.

Desk space and free WiFi come as standard but some also have meeting rooms, kitchens and more informal relaxed spaces for networking or chatting to col-leagues. If you want a more permanent, regular arrangement, some offer annual fees more akin to renting an office. Others offer drop in options with hourly or daily rates for those who may just want a different space to work in on a less regular basis or better facilities than they have at home.

As more of us choose to work for ourselves, co-working spaces are becoming more common and if you live in a city you are likely to have a fair bit of choice ranging from social enterprises offering an ethical way of renting desk space (with some even including yoga sessions as part of the fee) to more traditional office space with some admin support. Many will include networking events as part of their offering. If you find you need other people around to inspire you and keep the creative juices flowing, this could be well worth considering. Proponents say co-working spaces have boosted their productivity and enabled them to meet others working in similar industries who they would not other-wise have connected with.

Time management

When working for yourself, time management is key but even the most experienced freelances may not get this right all the time. In theory, you can be completely flexible around when you work – perhaps you are a night owl or work best at the crack of dawn – but if you are not available to some degree within standard working hours, there is a risk you lose out on work. You will also need to factor in getting hold of contacts and interviewees when they are available, which for most people is unlikely to be 3 am.

It is important to try to calculate how much work you are able to reasonably do and still meet deadlines so you do not take on too much and then fail to deliver. This is a fairly individual judgement that will depend on your other responsibilities. Unfortunately, it can be almost impossible to space things out evenly and a flurry of pitches sent when work appears to be scarce may result in a panic when editors all come back at once loving your ideas and wanting pieces to be turned around quickly. While there will be aspects of workload that are out of your control and at the whim of whomever is commissioning you, there are simple steps you can take to make sure you remain on top of things.

Whatever way you choose to manage your workload and time, you will need to be organised from the beginning to make sure you do not drop the ball. If you were working in an office, there would be processes to ensure things did not get missed or go missing. Freelancing should be approached in the same way. Save all your files in a way that you can easily find them when needed. Have a system to follow work from commission to submission and importantly to payment. While no one else is likely to see or know about your 'system', it will help you to come across as professional and reliable. Importantly, it will also prevent payments not being made because you forgot to chase or invoice (see Chapter 7).

Taking regular breaks can be really useful for keeping focused. This can be anything from stepping away from the computer to do something else for ten minutes, to a visit to the gym, meeting a friend for a coffee, popping to the shop or walking the dog. Build a plan for the day so you know how what tasks need to be done and what else you need to fit around that. It will be easier to get through the work you need to do knowing you have other things planned than feel that you are denying yourself any of the benefits of working for yourself.

Keeping track

You need to have a way to keep a record of all the pitches you have sent and where you have sent them (and when). It means you can take note of whether there was any interest and if it's been a while and you have not heard anything maybe consider pitching elsewhere. Without a record it may be difficult to remember everything you have suggested and for what outlet. It also gives you a place to record ideas that you may have when you are up to your eyeballs in deadlines and have not got time to do anything with (see Chapter 3).

As part of this system, you may also find it helpful to record any pertinent feedback, for example, if a magazine is not interested in a particular idea but they are looking for articles on a different topic. Or if you learn a good time to pitch to a certain publication – say on a Thursday morning before the afternoon's commissioning meeting – then make a note of it to help make future pitching more efficient. It also means if you have sat down to work but do not know where to start, you have a ready-made plan to get you going.

Box 10.2 Author's experience

Keeping track of ideas, pitches, commissions and deadlines is vital for managing your workload, says Lily. She has a colour-coded Google doc with all of her commissions, which includes details of the deadline, word count, client and payment for each story. Priority deadlines are highlighted in red and then turned green when they are submitted to the editor. This also has a dual purpose as an accounts spreadsheet. Story ideas are listed on a separate Google doc which she can add to as soon as an idea strikes her. Lily also keeps a good old-fashioned physical diary in which she loosely plans out a month ahead with flexibility to add additional work as and when it crops up. She then plans out the week ahead in detail so she knows exactly what she is working on each day. This includes breaks for exercise each day which she fits around work and childcare early in the morning, at lunchtime, or later in the evening.

Once you have a commission, it is definitely worthwhile recording what, when and how much. By keeping a simple spreadsheet or Word document outlining what work or shifts you have with deadlines, you are far less likely to miss a date for submitting a commission, or double book yourself (see Chapter 7). You do not need to be a wizard in Excel to do this. In one straightforward document you should be able to tell at one glance if you have the capacity for any more work or need to start hunting around for more ideas to send out.

Consider this scenario, one quiet week you send out multiple pitches and on the Friday three editors get in touch asking you for 1,000 words on each by the following Tuesday. If you have an easy to view record of your workload, you can take a quick look to check whether you will actually be able to deliver all of these in the timeframe. Of course, it is unlikely that any freelance would say no, but there may be discussions to be had around flexibility in deadlines. Better that, than say yes without thinking then realise when it is too late you have no chance of meeting the deadline.

The same goes for keeping track of payments owed. As soon as you have submitted work or done a shift, you need to invoice. And once you have sent an invoice, make a note of it and mark when it needs chasing. As explained in Chapter 7, outlets may have very different systems for invoicing and make you jump through several hoops. It can get very confusing and easy to miss late (or non-existent) payments.

Depending on your preference, keeping track of ideas, pitches, commissions and payments could all be done in one document or separately, and there are several examples in earlier chapters of this book. The important thing is that it becomes routine. And of course, having an up-to-date record of earnings will make things very much simpler when it comes to the tax return. This may seem like very boring admin (and it is), but without it, it is highly likely that deadlines will be missed or forgotten. And you run the risk of not getting paid because you forgot to chase.

Contacts

Part of being organised is to have a way to keep contact details. Most new journalists are unlikely to keep an actual book of contacts as was once expected of the profession, but equally just having names and numbers listed in your phone may not help when you are searching out someone to provide an expert view on a topic and you cannot remember their name. It can be useful to have some sort of spreadsheet, or perhaps a Google doc, of email and phone numbers where you can also make useful notes about their area of expertise or what you have spoken to them about in the past. Breaking this into categories can help you find contacts quickly. While time-consuming to set up in the first instance, this could spare valuable wasted time down the line.

Have a to-do list

One of the first jobs of the day should be to create a 'to-do' list of tasks that need to get done. This is especially important if you are juggling more than one piece of work. A freelance with regular work is unlikely to be working on one thing at a time. More realistically there will be multiple projects on the go. At the very least you should be pitching ideas and promoting yourself and your work at the same time as getting on with commissions in order to keep the work ticking over and avoid gaps when projects are finished. Setting time aside for all the jobs that need to get done in any given day will prevent things being forgotten or a panic late in the day when you realise that a vital task has not been done.

A daily task list, whether done electronically, in a diary or on a post-it note stuck to your computer, will also allow you to build space and flexibility in your day should you need it. Want to go to the gym or meet a friend for lunch? Have children or other family commitments which mean you only have so much time to work in? As a freelance, you have much more control over juggling all these aspects of your life, but in reality that only works if you plan your time to account for the fact you do not live a nine to five existence.

We all procrastinate, it is easily done and some days will always be more pro-ductive than others, but half the battle is turning the large mental list that may feel overwhelming in the abstract into something that is manageable and achievable. Be careful not to put too much on the list that will never get done as that is a sure-fire recipe for despondency. A good guide is around five tasks that absolutely have to get done that day. Also try and put a range of small and large tasks on there to break up the time and enable you to take on some simple admin when you are running out of steam.

Some freelances also find they are more productive if they try to finish one task before moving on to the next, rather than trying to do multiple bits of work simultaneously or be constantly breaking off to answer an email that has popped through. It may depend what the tasks are for that day and how much work you have on, but if you try this approach, it is a good idea to calculate how long each task might take so you avoid running out of time to finish something off.

Build in breaks

Taking regular breaks can help to keep the creative juices flowing as well as boosting productivity. Some people swear by the Pomodoro method, which breaks work down into 25-minute intervals. The idea is to set a timer (or use one of many apps) and work solely on one task until the time is up. After a break of a few minutes – perhaps a quick look at social media – you start the timer again. Once you have done four of these sessions, take a longer break, say, of 15–30 minutes before repeating the steps again. Freelance journalist Emma Higginbotham says the technique has dramatically improved her productivity. "I just break my time down into 25-minute chunks of fully-focused work, so no looking at social media or making tea or putting the laundry on, and do those 'fun' things in my three to five-minute breaks in between. It's amazing how quickly you get stuff done", she explains.

If this feels too rigid for you then having a short break after finishing a task may be a better solution. And if you are one of those people who struggle to stop and take a break once you get started on a project or work for the day but feel you are getting too bogged down in the daily grind, make sure you have a plan to leave your desk that you cannot break, such as a coffee with a friend or gym class.

Motivation

This chapter has already covered several aspects that will help you to stay motivated when working from home, in particular the advice around time management. But in addition to being organised and having a pleasant working environment, self-imposed deadlines and goals can also help to keep you on track. As an employee, it is likely you would receive an annual appraisal through which you would outline things you want to achieve and how you would get there, for example, through additional training, and there is no reason why you cannot do a similar exercise as a freelance.

Of course, this does not have to be a formal process once you are working for yourself, but it can be a useful way to keep focused. Is there a particular publication you would love to work for? Or a topic or issue you think needs more attention? There will be times when you are not sure what your next step will be or feel like the work has become too monotonous or comfortable. This is when you need to refer back to your goals to reinvigorate your work. It can be particularly helpful to have these goals in mind if you are going through a sparse patch work wise. There will be periods when things are a bit quieter or commissions are not getting picked up that can dent the intentions of even the most focused freelance.

There will be longer term goals you would like to achieve that might involve some training or learning a new skill, such as sound editing, but there are also smaller goals you can set to aid motivation. This could be setting a specific day aside every week to come up with a certain number of new pitches. Or finding a certain number of new potential publications or organisations to approach.

Another way to motivate yourself can be to give yourself small rewards for completing a task. 'Once I've done this, I can meet a friend, or watch that TV programme I saved.' Make sure you achieve some balance – an hour's work followed by five hours browsing the shops is not particularly productive, but, done on a smaller scale, these little rewards may encourage you to be efficient then take a break.

If you are really struggling with motivation, you are likely to find it helpful to reach out and speak to other freelances about how they manage to keep going when they are tempted to bunk off and ignore the deadlines piling up (or lack of commissions). Just knowing that others struggle with the exact same thing can really help to reset the unmotivated brain on its own, and at the same time you are likely to pick up some useful tips. This is where joining journalism networks can pay dividends in providing that support, wisdom and encouragement (see Chapter 5).

Working on the go

Technically it is possible to freelance from anywhere. That is why some journalists choose to work for themselves as a means to move to another country. Others might take the 'digital nomad' approach and freelance while moving from place to place. And this is not just an option for travel journalists. With a laptop and good enough WiFi, this could be a very tempting and viable option for anyone.

The downsides to this are that you may lose connection with regular gigs that you had when settled in one place and be warned if you tell editors that you are going travelling they may assume you are not available for work – a version of out of sight out of mind. One aspect to bear in mind is visa requirements as some countries can be strict about you doing any kind of work while on a travel visa. You will also need to consider that time zones may prove tricky when trying to contact editors or interviewees in other parts of the world to where you are.

For travel journalists, working on the go may seem a logical step, but this is not just an option to those working in that specialty. Some freelance journalists have managed to travel for months or even years at a time, visiting multiple countries, but doing the same work they were doing back at home. UK freelance journalist Jake Tucker did just this for a couple of years before a relationship and job offer put a stop to his nomadic lifestyle. His travels took him across Europe, hopping between cities but also to New York for a few months. "Freelancing is great for this because no one cares what hours you keep for features, and if you can offer a UK site freelance news cover at odd hours because you're in a different time zone (you'll need stable internet for this) they'll often take your hand off", he says.

Managing workflow can be very different to working from home, and being away you may not want to spend all day working anyway. Jake found the best system was to set aside time for each part of the working process, doing the writing part when there was no or poor internet connectivity and then researching and sending pitches when he was able to get connected again.

Other freelances have found that the ability to do the job from anywhere has proven invaluable when partners have found work in another city or country or even the other side of the world. Freelance journalist Emma Lunn says she lived in Sydney for two years and carried on freelancing for UK publications under work rights she had as part of her partner's visa. "The tricky thing was being in a different time zone to my contacts – lots of late-night phone calls on my part", she adds.

Box 10.3 Case study: Javaria Akbar

Working as a freelance was not on the cards for Javaria. But when she was made redundant at five-months pregnant she 'was thrown in at the deep end' and has never looked back.

After initially working as a content writer for some of the clients she had worked for before the company who employed her went bust, she soon also started pitching to online magazines.

She now has two children and has written for Buzzfeed, Vice, Refinery 29, The Pool, *The Daily Telegraph* and *The Guardian*. She has also collaborated on a book on motherhood, called *The Best, Most Awful Job*. Javaria mixes writing with her new venture teaching Pakistani cooking (she also originally trained as a confectioner).

"In the beginning, because I was so used to working nine to five, I just continued on with it and I was very conscious of sticking to that. I would get ready as I had done for work, get my laptop out and start", she explains.

"And because I was fearful of not having enough work, I took too much on and ended up working longer hours".

Javaria, who first studied history of science before doing a postgraduate journalism course in order to become a food writer, has now perfected her routine which these days also has to fit around the kids.

"Now I have to be very flexible. I have a proper work station, which is a desk that closes up, so whenever the kids are asleep or I have time, I open it up and get to work".

She has found she works best with a desk and now even has two screens at her PC, which she says has been really helpful.

"I can't do the working in bed thing, I can't even do cafés. I think that probably comes from having an office job first. I did continue with the same set up as I find it puts me in the zone".

Javaria, who is based in Chester, UK, has also found that although she can no longer work the steady nine to five that defined her start in free-lancing, she likes working in the evening when it's quiet and she can get a lot done. And to avoid feeling isolated she uses social media to connect with other freelances.

It is also vital to build relationships with the editors you are working for, she adds.

For those just starting out, she says getting a routine in place is key.

"It can be really easy to be distracted, by your phone for example. Or doing the laundry. I'm not one of those people who says don't ever do that because it's one of the benefits of working from home as long as you make sure the work gets done too".

javaria-akbar.com
@javaria_akbar

Getting started

- Work out how you can create a productive working space
- Research alternative working locations in your area
- Set up a document that allows you to keep track of your work
- Start a to-do list
- Try out a new time management technique when you feel like procrastinating

Note

1 Turvill, W. 2016 "Press Gazette survey finds freelance journalists are happier than staffers – but pay is falling" Press Gazette www.pressgazette.co.uk/press-gazette-survey-finds-freelance-journalists-are-happier-staffers-pay-falling/.

11

Supplementing your income

OBJECTIVES

In this chapter you will learn:

- The value of transferable skills
- What a portfolio career is and how to make it work for you
- How to find work outside of journalism
- The most popular ways to make an additional income
- How much you can expect to earn

In reality many freelance journalists supplement their income by taking on other types of work to develop a portfolio career. This may be to fill the gaps when they are having a dry patch or to ensure that they have a regular salary, perhaps with additional benefits such as pension contributions. For others, it is a way of keeping their work varied, as freelances can be restless in nature, and a means of making new contacts that open up journalism opportunities.

Side hustles can be a welcome break from news, a way to work more creatively or collaboratively, and in some instances can end up being quite lucrative. People's reasons for taking on non-journalistic work are varied and can be driven by personal, economic or normative goals. For instance, some freelance journalists are happy to work on a side project if it gives them the financial freedom to use the rest of their time to conduct socially driven journalism which may be undervalued and underpaid.

Whatever the motivation, there is a wealth of opportunity to earn money using transferable writing and communication skills. In this chapter we cover the most common income sources, which are public relations, copywriting, copyediting, blogging, ghost writing, podcasting, teaching, training and consultancy – but this is by no means an extensive list. Indeed, journalists moonlight in many weird, wonderful and totally unrelated ways, working as bricklayers, DJs, yoga instructors, drag queen comedy writers and landscape gardeners.

Knowing how to spot an opportunity is a key skill for acquiring work on the side. This might sprout from a conversation with a source or follow a particular story you have written or produced. The crucial part is making others aware that you are available for a variety of assignments and are happy to take on a new challenge. This may mean turning your hand to something different, but as a journalist you will already be equipped with excellent communication skills and the ability to research and understand new topics fast.

Part-time work or short-term projects can also be found via more traditional methods such as scouring social media posts, subscribing to job newsletters and keeping track of employment websites. There is also a growing number of gig economy platforms such as Fiverr, PeoplePerHour and Upwork where you can bid for projects that match your skills or upload a profile for companies to browse. And remember that just because you have not got experience in a particular area it does not mean that you lack the knowledge and skills to do a great job. For instance, if you are a freelance journalist specialising in health, then you may be the perfect candidate for a copywriting job for an international nutrition brand.

Portfolio careers

Part of the burgeoning gig economy, portfolio careers enable workers to pursue their various interests and manage a mix of part-time jobs and self-employed work. A career for life is no longer the expected norm, and a growing proportion of the labour market chooses to take on short-term engagements and temporary positions for a number of different organisations. A study by business software firm Intuit predicted that by 2020 40% of American workers would be independent contractors.[1]

This on-demand economy is driven by digital mobility which enables the workforce to decouple job and location, giving people the freedom to select short-term jobs from around the world. It goes beyond simply being self-employed or freelance, as the worker is employed in a variety of disciplines. This might be a journalist who spends 60% of their time writing commissioned articles for a range of publications on a freelance basis whilst working as an employed university lecturer for the remaining 40% of their working week. More complex portfolio careers can involve several part-time jobs alongside freelance work.

For instance, this might involve being contracted one day a week to work for a public relations firm, spending two days a week copywriting as an employee for a marketing agency and working on a self-employed basis as a reporter for a trade magazine for the final two days.

Juggling jobs

The main challenge of a portfolio career is the management of time, tasks and identity. It is more complex than a solo freelance journalism career because you may have contractual obligations to meet and less autonomy. Keeping everything separate can help you to switch between your different employee hats. Setting up a different email address for each line of work can enable you to compartmentalise assignments but also makes it less confusing for those contacting you. If you work part-time for an employer, use the company email account for all activities related to that job and on your signature include a sentence which explains which days you work for them. Then set up an independent email for freelance work and make this the one that people can easily find online.

Setting up a variety of social media profiles is more problematic as prospective employers/commissioners may only stumble across the irrelevant one, and you do not want to be doubling up the number of accounts you need to keep track of. Think about your branding (see Chapter 9) and whether you need to promote all of your careers on social media or just focus on one aspect of work. Similarly, it is important to have a website and you will need to make a decision over whether this concentrates on your journalism or expresses your whole portfolio. For example, Fiona Scott who works in Swindon, UK, as a journalist, public relations manager and media trainer brings her portfolio together under the brand Fiona Scott Media Consultancy and reflects all aspects of her work via her website and numerous social media profiles.

Choosing how to split your time is extremely important, and you may need to keep days separate so clients know which day you are available for their work. Alternatively, some people find it impossible to keep to a strict diary in this way and want to be available to everyone, all of the time. If you do take this approach, make sure you learn how to say no or push back deadlines to avoid making mistakes due to fatigue or juggling too many jobs at once.

When it comes to administration, expenses and bookkeeping, separating your income streams is strongly recommended because it will make managing your taxes much easier especially if you hand it over to an accountant who needs to make sense of it all and charges by the hour.

In the next section we look at the most common forms of supplementary income earned by freelance journalists.

Public relations

Often referred to by journalists as the dark side, public relations is the management of the public image of an organisation or person, and the maintenance of their reputation. It involves a considerable breadth of tasks; many of which are relatively easy for journalists to pick up. In practice, public relations is an umbrella term for any kind of internal or external communications, whether it be within a private, public or third sector organisation. The most important thing to remember is that you are working from the subjective viewpoint of the client rather than as a critical and objective journalist.

Assignments may involve writing press releases, putting together newsletters, developing campaigns, event management, social media marketing, video production, podcasting and other side hustles such as copywriting, editing and blogging. For example, it may be producing an internal newsletter for a start-up tech company on a monthly basis. Ideally you would want to estimate the number of hours involved and then agree a fixed monthly fee. Or you might be tasked with writing ad hoc press releases for a professional body and have a set fee for producing one and mailing it to relevant media contacts.

Freelances may be paid a retainer for a set amount of work each month, have a contract for a certain number of hours a week or agree a fee for a particular assignment based on an hourly or daily rate. Occasionally work will be based on a rate per word, but this is more unusual as it encourages quantity over quality. Work may come via an agency or directly from a client. Rates differ substantially depending on the size and budget of the commissioning organisation, so you should not expect to be paid the same rate from a local charity as from an international commercial brand. In America, the rates range from $20 an hour to $500, with the average sitting at around $125.[2] Meanwhile in the UK, fees range from £150 to £800 a day with an average of £400.[3]

Copywriting

Copywriting, also known as content writing, is probably the most common form of supplementary income for freelance journalists because it builds on their writing and storytelling skills. It involves writing content for a client to a particular brief, which is usually for the purpose of advertising a product or building brand awareness. Ultimately it is about informing a particular group and persuading them to take a particular action. The development of websites and social media is an integral part of digital marketing, which means there is a wealth of work for people who can write clearly and correctly. You don't necessarily have to be able to write persuasively or have immense creative flair as many clients are looking for accessible, informative content rather than something quick witted and hyperbolic. Companies, large and small, will often prefer to take a journalistic approach in the form of interviews, case studies and the presentation of facts to give their product legitimacy.

The work of a copywriter can involve research, interviewing, editing, proof-reading, managing projects, sourcing images, implementing marketing campaigns, measuring analytics and, of course, writing. This might be writing all of the web content for a small business launching a new website; conducting and writing up an interview with an expert for an international health brand to feature on a section of their website; writing a leaflet for a local charity; or writing advertorials for a trade cleaning magazine. As the examples illustrate, copywriting can be digital or print, but there is a growing market for writers who are savvy with search engine optimisation (SEO) and can create web-friendly copy.

Getting into copywriting can often happen by chance or luck, as people are recommended by friends and former colleagues, or journalists are approached by companies they have previously written stories about. Work might be via a client directly or through a marketing company and it is possible to spot call outs on social media and via job adverts. If you have a particular journalism niche such as women's motoring then this can help you build a brand (see Chapter 9) which can put you in a better position for related copywriting work. There are also websites such as Content Cloud and Contently where you can register for free, create a profile and post your resume outlining your specialisms. The platform will then match you against suitable projects which you can bid for. There is also an excellent up-to-date monster list of American and UK writing opportunities at Makealivingwriting.com and www.clippings.me/blog/freelance-writing-jobs/.

There is also no harm in pitching for this type of work, which often doesn't get advertised anywhere. It can lead to ongoing retainer arrangements and a regular, high paying income. You can approach companies speculatively much like you would when pitching a story to an editor. Freelance writer Anna Codrea-Rado recommends emailing a letter of interest to a content marketing company, agency or trade publication asking if they are interested in working with you. She describes it as a "halfway house between a pitch and a cover letter". Try to solve a problem for the client by offering your services rather than asking for work. You can send an email asking if the company works with freelance writers and say you would love to contribute if they are open to pitches. Describe your areas of specialism and key clients to date, and if relevant say you have some ideas that you think may be a great fit for their blog.

You can use the same type of email to inquire about editing copy, writing branded content or any other specialism you may have. "Find companies in your field of expertise, read their websites and come up with some ideas about how you could work with them. Find the right people to contact (anyone with 'content' or 'marketing' in their job title is usually a good place to start)", says Anna.

The pay for writing content can often be more lucrative than journalism, particularly if it is for a big brand or via a large marketing agency. Sometimes writers will be commissioned for one piece or work, or they will be brought on at a day rate for a particular project on a short-term contract. In the UK, the average day rate for copywriting is £300, but it can range from £150 for a small charity to £600 for an international corporation. It is also possible to earn around £250 for 800 words. If you are a specialist in your field, you may be able to charge $30 to $70 in America for copywriting. Similarly, in Australia copywriters can charge $50 to $240 per hour depending on their experience, and day rates range from $300 for a junior copywriter to $1,200 for a top-level writer.[4]

Box 11.1 Author's experience

Over the years Lily has been approached by numerous people and organisations following news and feature articles she has written. After a feature on sustainable transport she was approached by a local Sustrans group to produce the text for a cycling leaflet, run a community campaign and even take minutes at their monthly meetings. She gained copywriting work with Medela who make breastfeeding accessories after they read some of her health articles in *The Daily Telegraph*. She has even been asked to write email newsletters for a fashion brand that makes handbags from pineapple leather following a story on the cost of veganism in the *Metro*. This work has also extended to ghost writing blog posts for chief executives and co-writing an academic textbook in just five months.

Copy editing

If you know your practise from your practice, or are a dab hand at spotting an erroneous punctuation mark, then editing could be your side line calling card. Copy editors are concerned with the format and style of a piece of writing as well as the word count, spelling, punctuation and grammar. The role can involve spotting and correcting inconsistencies in house style, adjusting British to American spellings, ensuring accurate referencing and in text citations are used, proofreading, indexing and cutting articles down to size.

Editing is used in all forms of publishing, be it newspapers, magazines, books, pamphlets or digital content, and a sub section of this is sub editing. As a sub editor on a newspaper or magazine you would be expected to spot errors and legal issues as well as write headlines, jazz up copy and even layout pages using software such as In Design or a Content Management System. Freelance sub editors often work shifts at newspapers or are contracted for a certain number of hours a week and can expect to earn around £150 a day. For example, this could be working from home for a charity magazine editing all of the copy and writing all of the headlines. The copy could be sent to you as and when it is ready so you would have to negotiate a rate for the time you actually spend on the work. This could be an hourly rate of around £30 to £50, a day rate of around £350 or a rate per edition, which will depend on the time involved and number of stories or pages to edit.

Other forms of editing include proofreading documents, reports or books, re-writing academic works into plain English or leading marketing projects which involve commissioning copywriters. Rates for editing and proofreading vary depending on the publishing sector, what needs to be done with the text, how quickly it needs to be turned around, whether any specialist knowledge is re-quired on a subject and the experience of the editor. The price will ultimately be decided via a negotiation between both parties but guidance on minimum rates are set out by bodies such as the Society for Editor and Proofreaders in the UK and the Institute of Professional Editors Limited in Australia. For example, in the UK the recommended minimum hourly rate for proofreading is £25, rising to £33.50 if work involves substantial editing and rewriting. In Australia rates vary immensely from $30 an hour to more than $120.

Similar to copywriting, this line of work can rely on word of mouth or being approached due to your specialism but editing gigs are advertised online. If you feel confident in your editing abilities, then it is a useful string to add to your freelance bow and should form part of your online branding.

Blogging

The blogosphere contains 488 million blogs on Tumblr alone,[5] with hundreds of millions more hosted on platforms such as Blogger, WordPress, Joomla and Drupal. The market continues to grow as people worldwide share their hobbies, experiences and knowledge. There is also a burgeoning industry of vloggers and social influencers who post videos and photos on video-sharing websites such as YouTube and social media platforms, particularly Instagram. Celebrity vloggers are now worth millions of dollars and make their income from adverts and sponsorship deals. Swedish video game commentator PewDiePie, who has over 60 million subscribers, has a reported net worth of $20 million from his vlogs on YouTube.[6] But for the freelance journalist, blogging and vlogging is a means of making additional income rather than seeking international fame and fortune.

Blogging can be performed as an extension of public relations, and freelance journalists can find themselves writing blogs posts on a particular topic for a commercial or charitable organisation in return for a fee, which may be per post, word count or based on an hourly or day rate (see public relations and copywriting). It is also possible to earn money from running your own blog if you have knowledge or experience of a niche topic which can attract a large enough audience and you have plenty of time to develop your content. There are five key ways of making your blog financially viable.

The best-known way to earn money is fairly traditional and comes via display advertising from services such as Google Adsense. You earn income every time an advert is shown on your blog and additional funds when it is clicked on. Google uses internet search technology to ensure the adverts on your site are relevant to the content. So, if you write about vegan food recipes, then Google will serve adverts for vegan restaurants and products. The key to earning more money is the click through rates which are based on a Cost Per Click (CPC). You can earn from $0.01 to $1 per click and the amount of people that actually click on an advert is 1% on average. To drive more traffic to your site and increase your potential ad clicks, you need to find a niche and write content using lots of Search Engine Optimisation that Google can find. For example, there are lots of people blogging vegan recipes, but how many write about vegan pet food?

A variant on display advertising is affiliate marketing where you promote a product or a service and earn a commission for every sale that comes via your site. Money blogger Emma Drew earns more than £5,000 a month from this revenue stream and offers a free affiliate marketing masterclass. You can also raise funds via sponsored posts or promoted content where a company asks you to write about their products or services for a fee. According to a survey by The Bloglancer, bloggers charge anywhere from £10 to £150 per sponsored post, and those with up to 5,000 unique users charge similar amounts to those with almost 300,000. The highest paid sponsored bloggers in the UK tend to be food bloggers, followed by family bloggers, and then fashion, beauty and lifestyle.[7]

It is also possible to monetise your associated social media accounts using tools such as Buzzoole, SocialPubli and FameBit or to make money by selling related products and services. Many bloggers end up collating their posts to create an e-book, or offer blogging and social media training.

An extension of blogging is newsletters, and freelances often set these up with a free teaser version and an in-depth subscription version. Often, they will also be supported by crowdfunding and donations. If you have useful, informative, hyperlinked advice to give on a particular topic rather than giving it away for free on a blog, you could consider setting up a newsletter.

Ghost writing

Writing material for someone else who is the named author is known as ghost writing. This could be writing someone's memoir, producing a newspaper column for a celebrity or writing an opinion piece for an industry figure in a trade publication. This type of work is likely to evolve from contacts you build up a rapport with. It could be a celebrity who has enjoyed working with you on an editorial piece or a business executive you regularly interview for specialist pieces. High-profile business people are often asked to contribute features and opinion pieces to various publications, but they do not have the time or skills to sit and craft a piece. This is where a ghost writer will come in, and they are usually someone the person has worked with before or has been recommended to them. The ghost writer will call the subject to get an outline of their thoughts on a subject and gauge their 'voice' before writing the piece and running it by them. The ghost writer is usually paid directly by the person they are ghosting, and this can be around 40p per word.

Payment varies from the exploitative to the lucrative, so you should always consider how much time is involved before signing a contract or agreeing to an assignment. In the UK, ghost writers on newspapers tend to be paid the same for a ghosted piece as a bylined piece. The real money is to be made from ghost writing books which can be an hourly rate for a vanity project for someone wealthy, or a set fee that comes out of the subject's fee from the publisher, via their agent. On average an experienced book ghost writer can earn $20,000 to more than $50,000 in America if the client is a celebrity. However, a novice ghost writer will earn an average of $5,000 for a project that could take six months to complete. Established ghost writers can work for a huge range of clients, including ordinary people with extraordinary stories, billionaires, celebrities and politicians. British ghost writers can earn anywhere from £2,000 to £100,000 from private clients and publishers.

Podcasting

This increasingly popular platform is already home to 750,000 shows and can be a great place to explore a niche interest or bizarre hobby. The crowded marketplace means it can be difficult to gain a large audience and monetise a podcast, but it is possible. Journalists are setting up new podcasts every day to promote their brand and expertise but also earn a little money on the side.

The most straight forward way to make money, like with any media, is with advertising. This can be via a podcast media host such as Acast who source advertisers. Acast offers free hosting and distribution of your show, but there is a selection process and you have to have more than 10,000 downloads and the host takes a cut of the revenue. It is more labour intensive, but there is nothing to stop you from selling your own advertising and slotting them into your show – but you may have to produce the adverts as well. This could be a one-off payment but is more likely to be modelled on payment per 1,000 downloads, the more downloads the more advertising money you can generate. For example, if you get 3,000 downloads per episode, you'll get $54 for a 15-second pre-roll ad and $75 for a mid-roll slot with the cost per impression model popular in the US. This method is used with Serial and British crime podcast Untold Murder: The Daniel Morgan Murder Exposed.

Another alternative is getting a business to sponsor an episode or series for a set fee in return for advertisements or recommendations for their service/products before and during the podcast. Affiliate marketing meanwhile is similar to product placement and involves talking about something during the show. For the podcast Scummy Mummies it might be a baby gadget that they test out. This can also be based on number of downloads, so if your show is 'evergreen' in that it is timeless and it grows over time, old episodes will still be generating 'passive income' in the future. With all of these methods you can offer additional exposure by including advertiser/sponsor in additional social media, blogs and weekly newsletters.

Since most podcasts are available for free, you may want to consider asking for your community's contribution; this is a common tactic in America which has pledge drives to support public radio and associated podcasts such as This American Life. For your podcast you might ask for a donation or have a special edition with a suggested fee of £5, a method used by The Guilty Feminist podcast. Patreon is the crowdfunding platform for media organisations and is specifically designed to support creatives to ask their supporters – or patrons – for one-off or recurring contributions. Patrons are then offered some form of reward, based on the level of their support. On top of that, shows set Patreon goals where they commit to give something new to the listeners when they reach certain levels of support. For example, when the Cinematic Universe podcast, which looks at comic book movies, launched on Patreon in 2016, it had a number of milestone goals. At $50 (£40) a month in total contributions, it is committed to launching a website, featuring show notes and blog posts; at $100 (£79) a month, the team will record a fan commentary over a film of backers' choosing, while once it hits $350 (£277) a month one of the team will start a series of retro superhero video game reviews.

Charging for premium content such as longer episodes, extra interviews, newsletters and additional documents is one way to set up a subscription service by stealth. There are also some grants available for tackling topics such as diversity, global issues, or education and it is worth hunting around for these. And if your podcast starts to take off there are opportunities to sell merchandise, tour with a live show version or even turn the series into a book.

Teaching

This can be one of the most profitable ways to make ends meet particularly if you gain work at a university, but there may also be (less well paid) opportunities at further education colleges and on adult education courses. Universities use a lot of zero-hour employees to plug the gaps because student numbers fluctuate each year. If a course suddenly recruits an extra 20 students the existing staff will have limited capacity to teach them so the work is often subbed out. They also like to bring in guest speakers for one-off lectures or workshops to cover specific topics, so students can meet someone active in industry with up-to-date experience. Other potential work includes marking or one-to-one student supervision on a dissertation or project. The key to gaining a sustainable amount of teaching work is to get your foot in the door, be reliable and say yes to everything even if you only have a day to prepare. One lecture can soon snowball into three months of teaching, eight hours a week, and become a regular income source.

Much of this work is not advertised and instead relies on recommendations or proactive journalists contacting the institution outlining their experience and availability. The work is often at very short notice and based on an hourly rate, which includes preparation time. Rates in the UK can range from £30 to £60 an hour. Universities may insist that you join their pay roll, meaning you are taxed at source but in many cases this comes with the added benefit of pension contributions, maternity leave and paid sick leave.

If you feel you can command a lecture theatre of 100 students or work over the shoulder of 25 students in a computer lab, then it is worth mining your resume to highlight your relevant experience. Knowing the journalism industry inside out is not enough, but having experience training staff, presenting at conferences, or running news days for school children will demonstrate your ability to teach. These are the things that need to be at the top of your application followed by your journalism expertise. Universities are also interested in your academic achievements, so if you have an undergraduate or postgraduate degree then this is more relevant than any journalism qualifications. And if you are a rare gem with a PhD, even in a completely unrelated subject matter, then this is likely to put you to the top of the pile.

To get into teaching you first need to contact the course leader/programme leader/subject group leader at the institutions you are interested in. Email a resume specifying any relevant speaking or training experience, your areas of journalism expertise and academic qualifications. Suggest potential lecture topics or refer to their course modules to show you have an understanding of what they teach and how you can give added value to this. Once you are offered work, be prepared to be as flexible as possible and teach things a little out of your comfort zone, as the most important thing is getting that first session. Don't expect masses of work straight away, it may begin with a guest lecture, lead onto some dissertation supervision and then develop into teaching a seminar group before it becomes steady work.

If you feel teaching is not for you but you would like to be involved in journalism education, then it is worth exploring exam-marking opportunities for professional journalism bodies such as the National Council for the Training of Journalists in the UK. They pay a rate per script and expenses for attending training and examiner meetings. Although the work can be time-consuming, it can be conducted at home and you can earn around £150 a day.

Box 11.2 Author's experience

A couple of years into working as a freelance, Emma was offered some work on a short course at her old university teaching journalism skills to science students. This turned into a more regular gig when a Science Communication MSc was set up and she was also offered more hours teaching news writing to international students. As her experience (and contacts) in teaching grew, she was offered a position as an associate lecturer at Sheffield Hallam University, where she now contributes to multiple journalism modules. Emma has also been able to use her fairly unique qualifications in both science and journalism to provide an editing and proofreading service for scientific papers, reports, and grant proposals. She has also organised conference speakers, consulted on website redesign and re-written material for in-house publications. If someone offers you work outside your usual comfort zone, think of it as an opportunity to gain experience in something new, she advises.

Training and consultancy

This is similar to teaching but rather than educating young people, training and consultancy tend to be geared towards professionals and people already working in industry. The benefit of this is that your participants will be eager and engaged, and will be actively seeking to learn from your experience rather than students who may be more sporadic in their attendance and attention. You can usually set a fixed fee for this type of work which is negotiated with the contractor.

If you have specialist expertise, such as podcasting, then you might want to approach organisations that run journalism training programmes such as journalism.co.uk or Guardian Masterclasses in the UK and Australia, with a training plan to add to their schedule. Research the market first to find out which organisations offer training and see if there is a gap in their offering which you can fill. This might be a media outlet, training business or an educational institution. You will need to demonstrate that you have the knowledge and experience to deliver the particular topic and an understanding of how to structure training sessions and the types of learning materials and equipment you will use. You should also expect the organisation to take a cut of the training fees charged to participants. Your earnings will depend on your experience, the length of the workshop and how many participants are signed up, but a ball park figure would be £300 to £400 a day.

Many universities are looking for opportunities to run continuing professional development courses for businesses and employed individuals, so it is worth exploring options by contacting relevant course leaders and those charged with business development roles. For example, The University of Queensland in Australia runs science journalism training for working journalists in conjunction with Econnect Communication in Brisbane and the Australian Science Media Centre in Adelaide, which is part of a government strategy to improve science communication and engage the public.

Another option is to set up your own training programme if you can secure a venue and are confident that you can recruit enough paying participants. You may have overhead costs, but you won't have to share the fees with anyone. This might be working one-to-one or in small groups with journalists running pitching workshops, or giving feedback. Again, it is important to research what else is offered locally, how much it costs, if there is any demand for training, and where you can add value. There may also be grants available to help train and support community journalism start-ups, so make sure you explore these such as Nesta in the UK, Local News Lab in the US, and the European Journalism Centre.

Consultancy work tends to be more individualised and may be working with a business to come up with a specialised training programme to meet their employee needs such as media training or giving advice on their communication strategy. This type of work tends to evolve from contacts and can be harder to develop but higher paid due to it being tailored to the client. In this instance you are being paid directly by an organisation to train their own staff rather than putting on training on their behalf for the wider public. Commercial training in media skills is more profitable than technical skills training, and well-established trainers can name their price, earning up to £2,500 per day in the UK, whilst technology training in Photoshop, for example, would be priced at around £500 a day. Journalists can also earn good money sitting on specialist panels, for example, media events for pharmaceutical companies. For two hours you could earn £300 upwards.

Alternative revenue streams

Freelance journalists are particularly adept at turning their hand to anything and never saying no to a project because they don't know when their work might dry up. This can lead to diverse side incomes; some of which are related to the profession and others that are not.

The old adage that everyone has a book in them is especially relevant to freelance journalists who have specialist knowledge on niche topics and exclusive access to experts and case studies. Writing a book on money saving tips is not too far of a stretch for a personal finance journalist, and writing a text book on interviewing skills is arguably a walk in the park for people who do it every day. If you have an idea for a book then be aware that you have to put in a considerable amount of work before seeing a pay cheque. Publishers will expect to see a thorough proposal outlining why there is room in the market for the particular topic, a detailed outline of each chapter, explanation of the author's experience and sample chapters.

There are different types of publishers for fiction, textbooks, and academic texts but the royalty rates are pretty low all round. You may be lucky enough to secure an advance of a few hundred to a few thousand pounds, but this will be deducted from any royalties you earn, which are usually between 5% and 10% of sales. Publishers may only do a print run of 500 copies initially, so you will be earning less than minimum wage for the amount of time you put in. However, once you are more established or if you are able to co-write with an experienced author, you can expect to see thousands, if not tens of thousands, of copies published and potentially sold, significantly raising your royalty income.

Alternative writing gigs include scriptwriting for television and radio, transcribing, educational course writing, project evaluation and writers in residence, amongst endless others. The key is maximising your strengths and keeping a keen eye on short-term projects via freelance newsletters, recruitment websites and social media. If you are handy with HTML then think about offering your services building websites or if you have great video editing skills offer your services to small businesses in need of online content. You could even set up a side business selling classic motorcycle parts and renting out garages if you are a motoring journalist in the know.

Box 11.3 Case study: Marissa Carruthers

As a culture and travel writer based in Phnom Penh, Cambodia, Marissa Carruthers spends 75% of her time working as a freelance journalist.

She writes for a range of news, lifestyle and business-to-business publications in Cambodia, Hong Kong and Singapore including the *South China Morning Post*.

She previously worked part time as the editor of ASIALife after contributing freelance content to the website for several years.

Although she spends most of her time writing about the lifestyle and culture scene in Cambodia, Marissa has found copywriting a useful way to earn additional money.

"It is a nice way to get extra income. It is writing at least but it can be a bit boring and it doesn't challenge me. I would cry if I had to do it all the time but needs must and the money is a lot better".

"Freelances need to understand that there isn't anything wrong with doing copywriting. People can be disappointed that they can't make their whole income from being a journalist but it is really difficult with budgets being cut".

Marissa's copywriting work began when she was editing ASIALife and was approached by companies to write content.

"I was asked to rewrite content for a website, to rewrite a school brochure. I did web copy for condos and travel agents, blog posts for websites, and general promo literature. People came to me and I am really bad at saying no".

However, one of the challenges of switching between journalism and copywriting is the loss of autonomy, warns Marissa.

"When I did my first copywriting job I wasn't sure if I was going to get the tone and language right. I still find it difficult when a client doesn't like it or wants to change it and it doesn't make sense to me. But that's because I am using my journalist's brain. You have to accept that they are paying for it and you are writing for the client".

There are also benefits to copywriting as it enables you to access new networks and gain knowledge of different industries, says Marissa.

And despite viewing herself as a journalist first and foremost, Marissa has recently taken on a new freelance contract to write content 25 hours a week.

"It is a seven-month copywriting job with a tour operator rewriting all their literature and tours. I applied for the work because I could never make the same amount of money from freelance journalism in the same amount of time. I am worried about how it will impact on my freelance journalism but I couldn't turn it down, it was too nice an offer. But journalism will always be my number one love".

Marissabr.com/
@LittleMsChief

Getting started

- Identify your core strengths and list three of your key transferable skills
- Create a list of all the types of jobs/projects these skills would be valuable for
- Decide which alternative income streams appeal to you most and write a list in order of preference
- Find someone who is successful at the job at the top of your preference list and ask for advice on securing this kind of work
- Identify five recruitment websites, social media groups or profiles which post opportunities listed in the top three of your preference list

Notes

1 Intuit. 2019 "Intuit 2020 report: twenty trends that will shape the next decade" https://http-download.intuit.com/http.intuit/CMO/intuit/futureofsmallbusiness/intuit_2020_report.pdf.

2 Gentile, M. 2019 "The average hourly rates for public relations services" Chron https://work.chron.com/average-hourly-rates-public-relations-services-21859. html.

3 Freelance Fees Guide. 2019 "Photography/public relations" www.londonfreelance. org/feesguide/index.php?language=en&country=UK&section=Photogra phy&subsect=Public+relations.

4 Clever Copywriting School. 2019 "Recommended rates for Australian copywriters: the ultimate guide to copywriting pricing" www.clevercopywritingschool.com/ courses/recommended-rates/.

5 Statista. 2020 "Cumulative total of Tumblr blogs May 2011-January 2020" www. statista.com/statistics/256235/total-cumulative-number-of-tumblr-blogs/.

6 Leskin, P. 2019 "The career of PewDiePie, the controversial 30-year-old YouTuber who deleted his Twitter and will take a break from YouTube in 2020" www.businessinsider. com/pewdiepie-youtube-felix-kjellberg-life-career-controvery-2019-9?r=US&IR=T.

7 The Bloglancer. 2018 "How much do bloggers charge for sponsored posts?" https:// thebloglancer.co.uk/how-much-do-bloggers-charge-for-sponsored-posts/.

12

Conclusion

OBJECTIVES

In this chapter you will learn:

- What the future of freelancing looks like
- How we can work to improve freelance rights
- The importance of training student journalists in freelance skills
- Whether setting up your own media business is the answer
- Why positive change is needed and how to achieve it

Freelancing is becoming a more common career path for journalists. Some of that is because, as with other professions, journalists are making an active choice to work for themselves and enjoy the freedom and flexibility that brings. Portfolio careers, where people opt for variety over stability, are no longer a rarity or the preserve of a privileged few. A traditional nine-to-five job for life is far from the dream for most journalism students, at least in our experience. They are keen to try new and different things, starting from the time they are studying when many are already experimenting with creating websites, blogs and podcasts.

The authors are among those who made an active choice to freelance for a myriad of reasons, not least greater autonomy, job satisfaction, the opportunity to try new things and improved work-life balance. There has been much to learn along the way, and the aim of this book is both to make a positive case for freelancing and to guide new freelance journalists on how to make a success of it.

Yet it cannot be ignored that part of the reason for ever-increasing numbers of journalists taking the freelance route is not one of choice but necessity. A precarious job market, the cost of living in our major cities and an ever-changing media market have all contributed to making freelance working the only viable option for some. At the start of 2019, Buzzfeed announced it was laying off hundreds of staff, followed a month later by Vice cutting 250 jobs. In February that year, online women's magazine The Pool finally folded after months of speculation about its financial position. HuffPost had two rounds of lay-offs over the final year of the decade, and it is no secret that local media has been suffering from cuts for years. Often those who lose their jobs have no choice but to take up freelance working, at least as a stopgap.

Freelance rights

A report from the International Labour Organization examining employment in culture and media in 16 countries pointed out that the 30 million people across the world working in these sectors make a 'significant contribution to their respective countries' social and economic development.[1] Yet the combination of the creative nature of the work of professionals such as musicians, actors, dancers, journalists and screenwriters as well as technological advances has had an impact on working conditions, bargaining power and basic social protections. Practices such as unpaid internships and companies forcing workers onto freelance contracts as a way of avoiding rules on working conditions or to reduce tax bills are all having a pervasive and negative effect on media workers. For those who choose to freelance, they may well value the freedom and flexibility that brings, but to have those contracts imposed frequently results in lower income, job insecurity and a lack of protection and benefits legally required for employed staff.

The report particularly points to 'revealing' statistics on the journalism sector from countries such as the UK and Germany which suggest that freelancing, once an atypical situation, has become typical.[1] A survey by the UK National Council for the Training of Journalists in 2017 found that one in three of the freelance journalist respondents was on state benefits and a third also did work outside of journalism to supplement their income. Respondents also cited increasing trends towards late payment and reduced rates.[2]

It is clear that freelance workers are at the mercy of a major power imbalance. When The Pool went bust after four years, 24 members of staff were made redundant and it owed freelance writers many thousands of pounds, which they had little hope of recouping. This was a popular site and included articles from well-known and well-respected writers. How were those offered a decent word rate for columns and topical articles to know that their hard work would not be rewarded?

For those who worked in the office, perhaps the signs were there. But as a freelance, working from home, it may be far from obvious. For all intents and purposes, you have a client who likes your work and keeps commissioning you to do your job and you receive reassurances that the money is on its way. No one pays on time, it's normal right? When it finally emerged that many of those working for the company had not been paid in months, the organisation collapsed within weeks. For many freelance journalists, at least in the UK, this was a wake-up call regardless of whether you had worked for them or not. A reminder of how important it is not to let those invoices slide or to be fobbed off with excuses.

There were some important lessons to learn. First, that respecting a publication you work for or feeling 'lucky' somehow to be part of it is not enough. You have a right to be paid on time for every piece of work you are commissioned to do, and you need to put those rights front and centre. We should not be afraid to talk about money, know our true worth and value our skills. It is not an easy job; not everyone can write, report and put together packages, and it is not acceptable, morally, ethically or legally, to hire someone to carry out a service then not pay them once they have delivered that service.

The second lesson was how important it is to connect with other freelances. It may feel like you are an army of one, sat at home in your pyjamas coming up with idea after idea and hoping someone will accept your pitch. Yet the problems at The Pool first came to light because freelances started sharing their difficulties with getting paid. There is strength in numbers. Networks such as those offered by the National Union of Journalists or Society for Professional Journalists are invaluable as a source of wisdom, guidance and also for bolstering your confidence on knowing your rights. If you have a legal quandary or financial predicament, you can bet there is a freelance journalist who has gone through and learnt from the exact same circumstance. The authors cannot state strongly enough how vital such networks and contacts can be. Working for yourself can be an isolating experience, but it does not have to be. A Go-FundMe page set up after the closure of The Pool led to contributions from well over 1,000 people who wanted to clear the debts of those left high and dry. Community is important.

There have been high-profile admissions from large companies that their treatment of freelance journalists was simply not good enough. In 2016, Vice Media made a public announcement about steps it was taking to improve how it works with and pays freelances after a report in the *Columbia Journalism Review* (*CJR*) cited multiple examples of journalists not being paid at all, being paid late or having commissions cancelled.[3] HuffPost announced in 2018 it would pay for all written contributions after years of expecting writers to provide content in return for exposure. Another piece in *CJR* pointed out this was a welcome development but did not undo much damage that had been caused in driving down rates and undervaluing journalism.[4]

Many journalism unions and training organisations have started to realise they need to do better for their freelance members. The European Federation of Journalists is among the those pushing for positive change to organise and train freelances and facilitate collective bargaining.[5] The International Labour Organization report discussed above concluded that 'capacity-building for trade unions in the culture and media sectors is needed so that they can meet the challenges raised by non-standard forms of employment'.[1] This may include incorporating freelance workers within existing unions or setting up new organisations.

In addition, freelance journalists are starting to organise themselves to fight back. An open letter organised by freelance journalist Anna Codrea-Rado made three demands for pay reform: an end to payment on publication, respect for late payment fees and updating payment systems that lead to bottlenecks. Launched under the #fairpayforfreelancers campaign hashtag, the letter had more than 1,000 signatories at the time of writing this book.[6]

The letter reads:

> We are journalists calling upon our industry to pay its freelances fairer, better and faster. Freelances are an integral part of our media ecosystem. As staff teams across our industry shrink, it's increasingly falling to us to turn around well-reported, high-quality journalism. The reality for freelance journalists, however, is that in doing our work we routinely experience overdue invoices, find ourselves acting as de facto creditors and battle with bureaucratic red-tape when getting paid. Some report that the financial hardship they experience as a result leaves them with no option but to leave the profession.
>
> We want to work together towards a sustainable future for our industry. We believe this starts with media outlets paying freelances fairly and on time.

Box 12.1 Anna Codrea-Rado

Anna Codrea-Rado is a freelance business and culture journalist based in the UK. She also writes The Professional Freelancer newsletter and started the #FairPayForFreelancers campaign, calling on the media to improve its freelance payment practices. Here she gives her view on why freelances need greater protection from financial vulnerability.

There has never been an easier time to go freelance. Changing attitudes towards work culture, the rise in digital tools and the availability of affordable training resources have opened up a new career path for journalists. Self-employment has democratised the historically elite media industry, making it possible for more diverse voices to join its ranks. The pay mechanisms, however, continue to keep it a closed shop. When faced with long payment lags on work that's been completed, it becomes increasingly difficult to stay freelance without independent financial wealth. Freelancing was supposed to swing the door open for diversity; instead, it revolved.

Money is the root of all freelancing evil. The National Council for the Training of Journalists found that freelance journalist's biggest concerns are all to do with finances: irregularity of income, lack of security and lack of ability to save worry freelances the most. According to the Association of the Independent Professionals and the Self-Employed, the average freelance spends 20 days a year chasing payments and 43% have not been paid for their work at all at some point in their freelance career. And in journalism, there is an insidious payment quirk that makes it even harder to be self-employed: payment on publication (POP).

Media bodies including the National Union of Journalists, the British Association of Journalists and the Frontline Club have all criticised this practice of only processing an invoice after a piece has run because it leaves freelances financially vulnerable. Not only does it make budgeting a challenge, in cases where a publication folds before payment has been processed, the freelance journalist can be left out of pocket.

To address the power imbalance in freelance journalism and in order for self-employed journalists to be able to carry out their work as reporters free from financial worry, we need to see the end of POP. While the issue is endemic, it's not insurmountable. It behoves every freelance to know their rights and to enforce them in the face of bad practice. The Late Payment of Commercial Debt Act protects the rights of freelances to payment and entitles them to a late payment fee if a company fails to pay on time.

The biggest investment a journalist can make in their self-employed career is learning about the business of freelancing. As dull as shopping around for good bookkeeping software might sound, it could be the difference between staying in the black and being forced out of the industry. A number of organisations, from unions and trade bodies to charities and grassroots organisations, offer free or affordable financial training sessions. And where the rules aren't good enough, freelance journalists should support the organisations, bodies and individuals fighting for change.

In France, freelance journalists published their own letter calling for better treatment from media organisations. Some journalists have started to publish the rates they have been paid from well-known media organisations to try to make the process more transparent. On social media, individuals are pushing back, calling out bad practice including expecting journalists to work for free and encouraging others to stand up for their rights. Freelance journalists need to be aware of these efforts, and the authors would strongly advocate, where possible join in.

Setting up a business

This book has focused on working for others as a freelance rather than setting up your own product. But there are now more opportunities than ever to dive into entrepreneurial journalism and set up your own digital media business to supplement or replace your freelance income. One small step might be to set up a newsletter offering advice, tips and links on a topic of your choosing. The popular model is to provide a free version alongside a paid-for subscription service with bonus material. Or you might ask for small donations via sites such as ko-fi.com where people can support your work for the price of a cup of tea or coffee.

If you do decide to take the next step and launch a digital media start-up, be aware that this is an entirely different beast to working as a self-employed freelance. You will need expertise in market research, analytics, coding, audience engagement, revenue streams, app development, legal structures, employment law and more. But don't let that put you off. There are more options than ever and more tools at your disposal, the hardest thing is developing your own path. Digital native media enterprises may well be the journalism of the future, or at least a substantial market share, as can be seen via the growth of BuzzFeed, HuffPost, The Tortoise, ProPublica and The Ferret. Be inspired by these start-ups and identify a specialism you can develop niche content around to fill a gap in the market.

However, be forewarned – setting up an online media enterprise is only partly about great content. Equally important is the business model and how you are going to sustain and grow your passion project into a viable income. Income is usually derived from a mixture of native advertising, sponsored content, pre-roll video adverts, crowdfunding, membership, paywalls, subscription, micropayments, grants, training and even merchandise. You may be lucky enough to win the support of a philanthropist who will donate annually to your business in order for you to remain advertisement free and produce high quality investigative journalism. It is most likely, however, that your revenue streams will involve a mixture of approaches, and these may develop over time. The most crucial factor is to have a strong business model before you launch and to place adequate time and resources into accounting for this.

There are countless online platforms to help support entrepreneurial start-ups, so make sure you research tools like Patreon, Indiegogo, Blendle, Kickstarter, Crowdfunder and Unbound. There is also a wealth of books and resources online, so start mining through relevant information on Tow Knight Centre, Reuters Institute and the Nieman Lab. And get yourself a copy of *Entrepreneurial Journalism.*[7]

Box 12.2 Case study: Robyn Vinter

Robyn Vinter is the founder of journalism start-up The Overtake based in the north of England.

The online news site covers social affairs outside of London and was launched by Robyn after she moved back to Leeds in 2017.

She had previously worked for a business news website in London before being made redundant.

"The company had 10 people working there and I saw that potentially there was money there to support good journalism if you did it right".

Robyn freelanced in London for a while before moving back home to Leeds with her boyfriend.

"I had been thinking about doing The Overtake for quite a few years. When we moved back to Leeds I had to do it because there were no other freelance opportunities in Leeds".

Robyn found someone to develop a dedicated website and gave them a share of the business in return.

Using £5,000 of her savings to set up the website and pay freelances, Robyn found the site took off quicker than expected.

"In the beginning it was just me writing and commissioning freelances. Then a lot of students started contacting me wanting to do work experience. Before I knew it I had a team of people who were voluntary at first and then I started to pay them".

Some days the website would receive 100,000 unique users especially through stories listed on smart phone app Upday.

But Robyn says they measured their success by impact rather than statistics.

"We try not to focus too much on traffic as otherwise we get into click bait. Our key performance indicators change. But really we want our stories to be changing people's minds and resulting in action from government".

She also admits the site went in a different direction to her initial intention but she was happy to adapt along the way.

"I planned for it to be irreverent and light hearted but not click bait but it ended up being a lot more worthy".

The website has now been running for over two years and was nominated for the Paul Foot Award for Investigative Journalism in 2019 and the Georgina Henry Award for Digital Innovation in 2018.

It is now funded via Patreon and some sponsored content, but Robyn has struggled to manage all of the commercial and editorial aspects of the business. At one point she hired two sales staff, but they did not manage to bring in enough funds.

"We couldn't compete with Facebook which has highly targeted adverts".

The whole process has been a huge learning experience for Robyn, and her key piece of advice is to secure the commercial side before launching a digital publisher.

"From way before I launched, I needed a business partner. I can do marketing, content, and the website but I needed someone to focus on the revenue. I did a business accelerator programme and I was persuaded that finding a business partner wasn't the right thing to do when actually it was. I really regret listening to that advice and it is the only definite mistake I made. My advice to others would be to trust your own instincts and only take advice when you can see that it makes sense".

theovertake.com

The future of freelance training

If freelance working continues to grow in the field of journalism, as the authors predict, then it is essential that students are equipped with appropriate expertise during their training. Currently journalism and media students on undergraduate and postgraduate university courses in Europe only receive minimal education on freelancing or entrepreneurial skills. Research of 25 universities across the UK, The Netherlands, Poland, Norway, Denmark, and Austria found that 76% of lecturers wished to teach more freelance journalism content, and over two thirds of students were undertaking paid or unpaid freelance work whilst studying.[8] The results were even more stark in the UK where only a third of journalism lecturers taught any freelance skills despite 90% of students wishing to have this content on their curriculum.[9]

Where freelance skills were being taught, these tended to focus on forward facing skills such as pitching, networking and branding. Less frequently taught were back office skills including book keeping, rights, payment rates and supplementary income streams. There is a desire for teaching on the practical side of the job rather than simply on story creation and writing skills which we hope this book has been able to provide. Students and graduates want to understand the machination of being self-employed, getting paid and paying tax. They want to feel confident negotiating fees, adding late payments penalties to invoices, and winning kill fees. They also have a right to know about juggling multiple deadlines, whether they need insurance, should join a union and what risk assessments they will have to make.

So, there is a wider question here about how we prepare our future freelance journalists. Students are taught how to write news and features, the mechanics of media law and shorthand and how to operate as journalists. But there is a hidden world of labour exploitation, poor rates, and delayed payments which we are not preparing our students to deal with or challenge.

The authors advocate a far greater emphasis on freelance tutoring at both undergraduate and postgraduate level in order to reflect changes in industry and the cultural and market shifts away from institution-based employment. Freelancing is no longer just a way for journalists to resist salaried labour in pursuit of autonomy; instead, it has transformed into a strategy for media firms to intensify exploitation of freelance writers' labour power.[10] Self-employed journalists face growing challenges in the remote workplace with unfair fees, benefits, rights and most commonly – payment on publication policies – creating a minefield for the novice freelance.

Future freelances need to be equipped not only with networking and pitching skills but also the confidence and knowledge to protect their rights and receive fair treatment and payment. There is now an urgency for journalism educators to fill this gap in knowledge and provide students with the necessary tools and wisdom to thrive – and change – the freelance workplace.

This knowledge and empowerment requires colleges and universities to take a close look at their curriculum and make a concerted effort to do more than simply encourage students via informal advice. Freelance journalism should be profoundly integrated into existing modules with more than just a light touch approach, particularly feature writing, magazine publishing and student projects. Another, perhaps more effective, approach is to create dedicated freelance journalism modules and make a judgment on whether this should be mandatory given the current labour climate. Within this there could be scope to develop partnerships with publications where students get paid to publish work.

A call to action

It is only through training, education and campaigning that freelance journalists can improve their working conditions and help prepare the way for the next generation. As a freelance journalist you are an extremely valuable asset to educational institutions. You manage your own time and autonomy, meaning you are able to speak to students without gaining the permission of your editor. Seize this opportunity to approach managers and tutors on journalism courses and stress to them the importance of equipping their students with freelancing skills. Offer your services to run a workshop on negotiating rates or a lecture on successfully working from home, rather than the obvious pitching and networking talk. Think about what you wish you had known about freelancing when you were a student and offer it as the subject of an interactive seminar.

Freelances can be notoriously protective and secretive about their contacts, the way in which they secure work and the rates they are paid. With this book, the authors aimed to lift the lid on freelance trade secrets in the hope that sharing experiences will affect positive change for everyone. But now it is over to you. It is only by meeting and questioning freelance journalists that students will begin to gain a better understanding of how to navigate this clandestine world. It's time to open the vaults.

Notes

1 Gruber, M. 2019 "Challenges and opportunities for decent work in the culture and media sectors" International Labour Office, Geneva www.ilo.org/wcmsp5/groups/public/---ed_dialogue/---sector/documents/publication/wcms_661953.pdf.

2 Spilsbury, M. 2016 "Exploring freelance journalism: report for the National Council for the Training of Journalists" NCTJ www.nctj.com/downloadlibrary/EXPLORING%20FREELANCE%20JOURNALISM%20FINAL.pdf.

3 Schwartz, Y. 2016 "Vice shows how not to treat freelancers" *Columbia Journalism Review* www.cjr.org/the_feature/vice_freelancers.php.

4 Hays, M. 2018 "So now HuffPost decides to pay writers. Its effect on the industry still lingers" *Columbia Journalism Review* www.cjr.org/analysis/so-now-huffpost-decides-to-pay-writers-its-effect-on-the-industry-still-lingers.php.

5 European Federation of Journalists. Freelance Policy https://europeanjournalists. org/policy/freelance/.

6 #FairPayForFreelancers. Open letter. https://docs.google.com/document/d/1BvCJ bsaLVlNkgCPCqiyBxnqHtFincmCyvIOvRiw5LOo/edit.

7 Briggs, M. 2012 *Entrepreneurial Journalism: How to Build What's Next for News.* London: Sage.

8 Canter, L. and Wilkinson, E. 2019 "Risk and reward: are we preparing students for the contemporary paradoxes of freelance journalism?" Conference proceedings 5th World Journalism Education Congress. Paris, France.

9 Canter, L. and Wilkinson, E. 2018 "Why teaching freelance journalism matters" Conference proceedings AJE Summer Conference. Canterbury, UK.

10 Cohen, N. 2016 *Writers' Rights: Freelance Journalism in a Digital Age.* Montreal: Queen's University Press.

Resource list

Acast podcast platform: www.acast.com/en.

Accountable Journalism global codes of ethics: https://accountablejournalism.org/ethics-codes.

Association of British Science Writers: www.absw.org.uk/.

Association of Independent Professionals and the Self Employed: www.ipse.co.uk/.

Australian Associated Press medianet directory: www.medianet.com.au/.

Australian union Media, Entertainment and Arts Alliance: www.meaa.org/.

Authors' Licensing and Collecting Society: www.alcs.co.uk/.

BBC commissioning rounds: www.bbc.co.uk/programmes/articles/174PXpF8VbfSH0mNNthb44p/current-commissioning-opportunities.

British Journalism Awards: www.awards.pressgazette.co.uk/about-british-journalism-awards/.

British Society for Magazine Editors awards: www.bsme.com/awards.

Business card companies: www.vistaprint.co.uk/, www.moo.com, www.solopress.com/.

Byline Festival: www.bylinefestival.com/.

Channel 4 commissioning rounds: www.channel4.com/commissioning.

Chartered Institute of Journalists: https://cioj.org/.

Cision Jobs: www.cisionjobs.co.uk/.

Committee to Protect Journalists: https://cpj.org/.

Copy Writing School: www.clevercopywritingschool.com.

Copywriting gigs: www.thecontentcloud.net/, https://contently.com/.

Crowdfunding platforms: www.patreon.com/, www.indiegogo.com/, https://launch.blendle.com/, www.kickstarter.com/, www.crowdfunder.co.uk/, https://unbound.com/.

Customised email signature: https://app.zippysig.com/login, https://signature-maker.net/, www.wisestamp.com/.

Deadline Club: http://deadlineclub.org/.

European Federation of Journalists: https://europeanjournalists.org.

European Investigative Collaborations: https://eic.network/.

European Journalism Grants: www.journalismfund.eu/.

European Press Prize: www.europeanpressprize.com/.

Evernote: https://evernote.com.

Example business terms: http://tim-dawson.com/?page_id=1045.

Freedom of information: https://ico.org.uk, www.foia.gov.

Free online courses: www.edx.org/, www.futurelearn.com/.

Freelance rates: www.londonfreelance.org/feesguide, www.journoresources.org.uk/freelance-rates/, https://contently.net/rates-database/rates/.

GDPR guidance: www.journalism.co.uk/news/what-does-gdpr-mean-for-journalists-/s2/a721821/.

Global Investigative Journalism Network: https://gijn.org/.

Gorkana jobs: www.gorkana.com/journalist-services/cision-jobs/.

Guardian Freelance Charter: www.theguardian.com/info/guardian-news-media-freelance-charter.

Hostwriter: https://hostwriter.org/.

HMRC, working for yourself: www.gov.uk/working-for-yourself.

Influencer marketing tools: https://buzzoole.com/, https://socialpubli.com/, https://famebit.com/.

Information Commissioner's Office GDPR guidance for journalists: https://ico.org.uk/for-organisations/guide-to-data-protection/guide-to-the-general-data-protection-regulation-gdpr/exemptions/.

Information Commissioner's Office journalism guide on Data Protection Act 1988: https://ico.org.uk/media/for-organisations/documents/1552/data-protection-and-journalism-media-guidance.pdf.

Institute of Professional Editors Limited in Australia: http://iped-editors.org/.

International Consortium of Investigative Journalists: www.icij.org/.

International Federation of Journalists Global Charter of Ethics for Journalists: www.ifj.org/who/rules-and-policy/global-charter-of-ethics-for-journalists.html.

International Federation of Journalists International Press Card: www.ifj.org/press-card.html.

International Journalism Festival: www.journalismfestival.com/.

International payments: www.paypal.com/uk/, https://transferwise.com/, www.xe.com/moneytransfer/, www. moneygram.com, www.westernunion.com/gb/en/home.html.

IPSO Editors' Code of Practice: www.ipso.co.uk/editors-code-of-practice/.

Journalism innovation centres: www.nesta.org.uk/, https://localnewslab.org/, www.ejc.net/, www.journalism.cuny.edu/centers/tow-knight-center-entrepreneurial-journalism/, www.niemanlab.org/, https://reutersinstitute.politics.ox.ac.uk/.

Journalism news and training: www.journalism.co.uk/.

Journalism portfolio services: www.journoportfolio.com/, www.clippings.me/, https://pressfolios.com/, https://muckrack.com/journalists.

Journalisted: http://journo-lists.com/.

Journalists' Charity: http://journalistscharity.org.uk/.

JournoLink: https://journolink.com.

Journo Resources death knock guidance: www.journoresources.org.uk/death-knocks-how-tackle-reporter-journalism/.

Journo Resources: www.journoresources.org.uk/.

Judith Neilson Institute for Journalism and Ideas: https://jninstitute.org/.

Late payment calculators: https://europa.eu/youreurope/business/finance-funding/making-receiving-payments/late-payment/index_en.htm, www.londonfreelance.org/interest.html.

Media Entertainment and Arts Alliance code of ethics: www.meaa.org/meaa-media/code-of-ethics/.

MediaBeans media jobs: https://mediabeans.io/.

Mediabistro US media jobs: www.mediabistro.com/.

Mediargh media job and paid internships: www.mediargh.com/.

Medical Journalists Association: www.mjauk.org/.

Melbourne Writers' Festival: https://mwf.com.au/.

Mongabay Special Reporting Initiative: https://mongabay.org/programs/special-reporting-initiatives/.

Muck Rack: https://muckrack.com/journalists.

National Council for the Training of Journalists: www.nctj.com/.

National Union of Journalists: www.nuj.org.uk/home/.

National Union of Journalists Code of Conduct: www.nuj.org.uk/about/nuj-code/.

National Union of Journalists stress guidance: www.nuj.org.uk/documents/nuj-stress-factsheet/.

Ofcom Broadcasting Code: www.ofcom.org.uk/tv-radio-and-on-demand/broadcast-codes/broadcast-code.

Out of Eden multimedia project: www.nationalgeographic.org/projects/out-of-eden-walk/.

Pacific Media Workers Guild: http://mediaworkers.org/.

Podcast Insights: www.podcastinsights.com/.

Poynter Institute: www.poynter.org/.

Professional Publishers Association awards: https://ppaawards.co.uk/.

Pulitzer Prizes: www.pulitzer.org/.

Radio Festival: www.radioacademy.org/radio-festival/.

Reporters Without Borders World Press Freedom Index: https://rsf.org/en/ranking.

Response Source: www.responsesource.com.

Rory Peck Trust: https://rorypecktrust.org/.

Royal Television Society: https://rts.org.uk/.

Royalty free images: https://unsplash.com/, https://pixabay.com/.

Royalty free sounds: http://freesounds.org/, www.zapsplat.com/.

Sian Meades-Williams Freelance Writing Jobs newsletter: https://mailchi.mp/69d207801f23/freelancewritingjobs.

Signal: https://signal.org.

Skype: www.skype.com/en/.

Society for Editors and Proofreaders in the UK: www.sfep.org.uk/.

Society of Professional Journalists: www.spj.org/.

Sonia Weiser newsletter: https://soniaweiser.wordpress.com/opportunities-of-the-week-newsletter/.

Sports Journalists Association: www.sportsjournalists.co.uk/.

Style Guides (available online): www.bbc.co.uk/academy/en/collections/news-style-guide, www.theguardian.com/guardian-observer-style-guide-a, www.buzzfeed.com/emmyf/buzzfeed-style-guide.

Suicide Reporting Toolkit: www.suicidereportingtoolkit.com/.

Susan Grossman career and writing coach: https://susangrossman.co.uk/.

Sydney Writers' Festival: www.swf.org.au/.

Time management apps: https://freedom.to, https://offtime.app/index.php, www.forestapp.cc.

The European Journalism Centre: https://ejc.net/.

The International Association of Women in Radio and Television: http://iawrt.org/.

The Media Society: www.themediasociety.com/.

The News Guild: www.guildfreelancers.org/.

The Professional Freelancer newsletter: www.annacodrearado.com/newsletter.

The Walkley Foundation: www.walkleys.com/.

Transcription apps: www.rev.com, https://otter.ai.

TravMedia: https://travmedia.com/.

Trello: https://trello.com.

Try This – Tools for Journalism: www.poynter.org/try-newsletter/.

Tweetdeck: https://tweetdeck.twitter.com/.

UK Press Card Authority: www.ukpresscardauthority.co.uk/.

USA freelance guide: www.makealivingwriting.com/.

Whatsapp: www.whatsapp.com.

Worldwide Freelance Writer: www.worldwidefreelance.com/.

Zoom: https://zoom.us.

Index